Evaluating
Instructional
Programs

Bruce Wayne Tuckman

Dean, College of Education
The Florida State University

Evaluating
Instructional
Programs

SECOND EDITION

ALLYN AND BACON, INC.

Boston   London   Sydney   Toronto

Library of Congress Cataloging in Publication Data

Tuckman, Bruce W., 1938–
  Evaluating instructional programs.

  Bibliography: p.
  Includes index.
  1. Educational surveys. I. Title.
LB2823.T93 1985   379.1′54   84-16873
ISBN 0-205-08356-0

Printed in the United States of America.

10 9 8 7 6 5 4 3 2 1 90 89 88 87 86 85

*To My Parents
Jack and Sophie Tuckman*

Contents

Preface   xiii

PART I
BACKGROUND AND CONCEPTS   1

Chapter 1   **An Overview of Instructional Program Evaluation   3**

Introduction   3

Outcomes and Their Measurement   4

Input/Process Specification and Evaluation   7

Design and Comparison   7

Conclusion   8

The Approach of This Book   10

Chapter 2 **Defining the Quality of Instructional Programs** **13**

The Measurable Dimensions of Education *13*

Overall Perspective *25*

Chapter 3 **Program Components: Outcomes, Inputs, Process** **27**

Outcomes *27*

Achievement as the Typical Outcome *27*

Other Important Outcomes *28*

Specifying Outcomes by Category *29*

Input vs. Process *34*

Differentiating Between Inputs *34*

Instructional Programs Effects *34*

Teacher Effects *36*

Student Effects *36*

Subject-Matter Effects *38*

Environmental Effects *38*

Determining Process or Level of Implementation *40*

Chapter 4 **Different Kinds of Evaluation Design** **41**

Design Considerations *41*

Units and Levels *43*

Evaluation Designs *43*

Conclusion *55*

PART II
MEASUREMENT AND DETERMINATION 57

Chapter 5 **Specifying and Auditing Outcomes** **59**

Specific Knowledge and Comprehension *59*

General Knowledge and Comprehension *61*

Thinking and Problem Solving 63

Attitudes and Values 65

Learning-Related Behavior 66

Specifying and Measuring Outcomes 68

Auditing and Evaluating Program Outcomes 69

Conclusion 80

Chapter 6 **Surveying the Inputs and Processes from the Classroom 81**

Instructional Materials 84

Instructional Activities 84

Instructional Organization 87

Subject Matter 88

Teaching Style 89

Environment 91

Student Factors 91

Conclusion 94

Chapter 7 **Assessing the Type of Teaching 97**

The Dimensions of Teaching 97

Measuring the Dimensions of Teaching 99

Observational Measures of Teaching 103

Student Rating Scales 105

Some Suggestions 107

Chapter 8 **Evaluating the Quality of Criterion-Referenced Tests 109**

Appropriateness 110

Validity 114

Reliability 119

Interpretability 123

Usability 127

Conclusion 128

PART III
CARRYING OUT THE EVALUATION   129

Chapter 9   Operational Guidelines for Doing Formative Evaluation   131

Preparing Objectives and Test Items   133

Collecting Data   145

Determining and Interpreting Results   149

Decision Making   151

Chapter 10   Operational Guidelines for Doing Summative Evaluation   153

Goals and Objectives   155

Measurement of the Program Objectives   158

Evaluation   161

Identifying a Comparison Group   161

Data Collection and Analysis   165

Decision Making   166

An Illustration   167

Chapter 11   Operational Guidelines for Doing Ex Post Facto Evaluation   171

Analyzing Prior Achievement   172

Making Normative Comparisons   176

Decision Making   184

The Program Evaluator's Checklist   185

Chapter 12   Qualitative/Case Study Evaluation   189

Characteristics of Qualitative Evaluation   189

Specifying the Questions to Be Answered   190

Data Sources   192

Conducting the Evaluation   196

"Analyzing" the Data and Preparing the Report   198

Chapter 13   **Issues and Advice   203**

Current Issues in Program Evaluation   203

Using Evaluation Data to Influence Decision Making   205

Evaluation Pitfalls and How to Avoid Them   208

References   216

Appendix A: **Case Studies   221**

Case Study 1:   Formative Evaluation   223

Project: Open Classroom—Formative Evaluation Report
by B. W. Tuckman

Case Study 2:   Summative Evaluation   247

Evaluating an Individualized Science Program
for Community College Students by
B. W. Tuckman and M. A. Waheed

Case Study 3:   Ex Post Facto Evaluation   257

An Evaluation of Individually Guided Education in
a School District by B. W. Tuckman and A. P. S. Montare

Case Study 4:   Qualitative Evaluation   271

Evaluation of the Instructional Program
for Preparing Counselors at Alpha College

Appendix B: **Glossary   279**

Index   287

Preface

When the first edition of this book appeared, we had entered (as I said in my original preface) "an era of accountability," characterized by concern on the part of taxpayers as well as public officials with the effectiveness of public education. Not only has this era of accountability remained with us through the intervening years but its economic realities and the consequent pressures imposed on the schools have worsened. School districts have increasingly been called upon either to justify existing programs or to choose those ongoing programs that they will eliminate in order to meet tightening budgets. In this context, the importance of the evaluator's role in the general scheme of decision making has continued, and even increased.

This book was originally written to provide the evaluator with the information and techniques to carry out instructional program evaluations in the schools. The emphasis in the original version on being both *practical* and *understandable* has been carried over to this new edition in order to make it as useful as its predecessor. I have tried to avoid the theoretical and technical pitfalls that, unfortunately, typify too many of the books in this area.

The success of the first edition in providing evaluators with workable guidelines in an important area of need is attested to by the appearance of this new edition. New and innovative approaches to evaluation, all of which had been developed and tested on the "firing line," were welcomed and used by evaluators to provide data for decision making. These included the specification of multiple outcomes and auditing forms for assessing their presence, techniques for surveying the degree to which program inputs were actually being implemented in the classroom, designs and techniques for using the backlog of achievement test data to evaluate instructional outcomes and procedures for evaluating district-built tests. Highly detailed, operational guidelines for doing three kinds of evaluation—formative, summative and ex post facto—along with sample or case studies illustrating each were also features that contributed to the impact of the book's first edition.

Now there is the second edition, containing all of the features of the first, with some new ones added. Because evaluators are more often than ever called upon to perform qualitative or case study evaluations, that is, evaluation based primarily on visitation and observation, there is an entirely new chapter devoted to this timely topic. The new chapter helps evaluators specify the questions they want the evaluation to answer, identify data sources for answering these questions, conduct the evaluation (that is, collect the data), and use the data to answer the questions. This chapter shows the evaluator how to make a site visit report or set of observations into a systematic and defensible undertaking.

Another new chapter is devoted to assessing the type of teaching, a variable that accounts for much of the effect of instruction. As in the rest of the book, forms, guidelines, and suggestions are offered for assessing teaching.

This edition includes two new case studies that are informational not only as illustrations but because of their content as well. Both of these case studies enable the book's coverage to extend to collegiate programs of instruction and illustrate methods for dealing with limited sample sizes, on the one hand, and qualitative evaluation using the visiting team approach, on the other.

And, of course, the text has been updated to reflect the current state of the art of instructional program evaluation. That current state of the art is no longer a frill that schools and school districts may or may not become involved in. As budgets become tighter, the informational demands of decision making become more stringent. Programs that do not meet their goals can no longer be afforded; they must be modified or abandoned. The only way we can tell that they are not meeting their goals is by evaluation.

Today, administrators, educational researchers, curriculum specialists, and even teachers must all be evaluators. When it comes to the evaluation of instructional programs, all professional personnel have a "need to know." Evaluation can no longer be an esoteric collection of jargon, statistics, and techniques known only to a specialized few. Everyone involved and everyone who has something at stake must know how evaluations are done. So the purpose of this book, in this edition as in the previous one, is to provide that knowledge in terms clear and practical enough so that everyone can understand what evaluation is all about.

Bruce W. Tuckman

Evaluating Instructional Programs

PART I

Background and Concepts

CHAPTER 1

An Overview of Instructional Program Evaluation

Introduction

The purpose of evaluating an instructional program is *to provide the means for determining whether the program is meeting its goals;* that is, *whether the measured outcomes for a given set of instructional inputs match the intended or prespecified outcomes.* The sole purpose of evaluating an instructional program is to determine how "on-target" it is by comparing achieved outcomes with intended ones.

However, instructional program evaluation ordinarily takes place (or should take place) within the context of planning. Such planning includes: (1) a set of procedures to solicit and include broad-ranging inputs to the goal-setting process that precedes program evaluation; (2) an input/process evaluation to assess the level of implementation of the instructional program; and (3) a set of procedures to adjust and reassign resource inputs based on the findings of the evaluations. Hence, instructional program evaluation should be seen as a step in the larger context of planning. In this context, evaluation is preceded by goal setting and establishing priorities based on community interests and succeeded by examining how the current program is operating. Evaluation may lead to a subsequent reallocation of resources utilizing a decision-making activity often called "master planning." Instructional program evaluation itself will be discussed here as a circumscribed and delimited process aimed at acquiring information about program outcomes and input use that can be compared to desired target levels.

The three elemental components of instructional program evaluation are: (1) a set of outcomes about which levels of attainment are of interest—called *objectives;* (2) a set of standards or *criteria of attainment* on these objectives—called target levels of attainment; and (3) a set of measuring devices or *tests* that will reveal actual levels of attainment on the chosen objectives.

Evaluating instructional programs also includes two more elements. The first is a specification of what will be evaluated (*input*) and an assurance that such input is operating as intended (*process*). If inputs are missing or not operating as intended, then their effects cannot be fairly evaluated. The second element is a procedure for establishing some *certainty* that the outcome can validly be said to have been caused by the inputs and to enable the evaluation result to have some *generality.* This procedure is an evaluation *design.*

Not all evaluations contain this design element. In building a program and attempting to improve its strictly internal function, concerns of certainty and generality are premature. It is enough to know how closely a set of outcomes matches a desired level. Such an approach is a *formative evaluation: Given a specified set of inputs operating as intended and a set of outcome objectives, a formative evaluation determines the extent to which measured results on the objectives match intended results.* Alternatively, using all five components yields a *summative evaluation: Given a specified set of inputs operating as intended and a set of outcome objectives, a summative evaluation determines the extent to which measured results on the objectives match or exceed results from alternative input systems; this determination should be done with both adequate certainty and generality.* We simply add the design component and the idea of comparison to formative evaluation to make it summative evaluation. If we take the definition of summative evaluation and compare the alternatives on an after-the-fact basis, sacrificing some certainty and generality, we have ex post facto evaluation, the third basic type to be discussed in this book.

Outcomes and Their Measurement

A component that is common to all three types of evaluation is intended outcomes (called *objectives*) and their measurement.

A school district cannot evaluate instructional programs accurately unless it develops a statement of its instructional program objectives. A district can accomplish this in two ways. The first is to begin with the district's goal statements, based on the needs assessment process, and then to spin off statements of objectives from each goal. These objectives then can be mapped onto its instructional program to be sure they are consistent with existing inputs or to produce an immediate alteration of existing inputs.

The second, more practical way is to have teachers prepare instructional objectives by discipline and grade level that then can be mapped back on to goals to form instructional program objectives. This process is shown in Figure 1.1.

We are now focusing on the preparation of *instructional objectives,* that is, statements of *intended learner outcomes,* as viewed within schools. Lists of such statements should meet two immediate criteria—completeness and acceptability. *Completeness* means that objectives match instructional events—nothing taught has been left out and nothing has been included that is not taught. *Acceptability* means that the objectives represent what teachers at a particular grade or block of grade levels are trying to accomplish as understood and accepted by themselves, administrators, and parents, and teachers at adjacent grade levels or blocks of grade levels.

To establish a complete and acceptable list of instructional objectives, in-

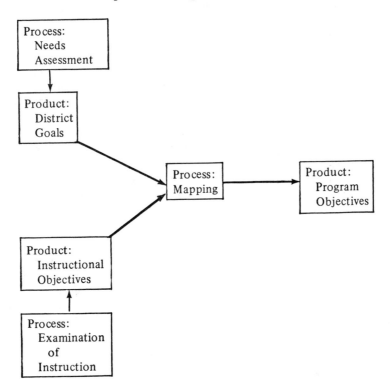

FIGURE 1.1 *Preparing Instructional Program Objectives*

dividuals and teams must write and react to them. For this, they need time and resources, usually in the form of professional assistance. Preparing objectives is best done by teachers with the direct involvement of administrators. Like anything else in education, evaluation costs money. Teachers must either be freed from some classroom responsibility or be paid for their time after school. Resource people and material also should be provided.

After the objectives have been written, they can be discussed and refined in an effort to attain completeness and acceptability. Then the objectives can be mapped onto district goals to be sure that instructional objectives can be considered program objectives.

So, the first major step requires a major commitment by the district and results in a set of objectives. (Since instruction in many disciplines is fairly basic, districts would do well to collaborate in or share this process. Regional or statewide objective banks would simplify this step considerably.)

In preparing their objectives, district committees should not restrict themselves to just the "lower" cognitive processes. Objectives dealing with "higher" cognition (thinking and problem solving) as well as with the affective domain (attitudes, values and learning-related behavior) also should be included.

The second major step common to all three forms of evaluation is to develop or select tests to measure objectives. Published tests now come with lists of objectives, and publishers can report outcomes on each individual objective (as can some state assessment programs). By comparing the objectives measured by a published achievement test battery to those of the district, a good match may be found and the test development process shortened. Such a fit is especially likely in basic skills (communication and computation), in which commercial testing is very advanced, but unfortunately much less likely in higher cognitive and affective areas. A district using a broad set of objectives probably will not be able to find acceptable published test measures of all of them. Unfortunately, the gaps in published test coverage represent the most difficult measurement areas, which thus are left to the district.

The following strategies are recommended to districts. (1) Use available tests where possible; consult test compendia and publishers' catalogues for more information. (2) Have teachers or teams of teachers prepare test items, but provide consultation and resource material to aid in this difficult task.* (3) Move to establish local, regional, and statewide test-item banks to provide necessary test items and customized tests for evaluation purposes. Using existing computer hardware and software will be very helpful. (4) Try to measure all objectives at least once a year, but do not be concerned about measuring each student on each objective since this is not necessary for purposes of program evaluation.

---

* See *Measuring Educational Outcomes—Fundamentals of Testing,* Bruce W. Tuckman (Harcourt Brace Jovanovich, 1975) for more information.

Input/Process Specification and Evaluation

Most of the difficult work of evaluating an instructional program is complete when you have objectives and tests to measure them. Now, you just give the tests to students and see how well they do, and you then will have completed an instructional program evaluation.

Unfortunately, program evaluation is not quite that simple. It helps, for example, to know what you are evaluating; that is, what the components of the program are (inputs), and to what extent they are being carried out as intended (process). If you want to use the evaluation results for master planning, you will need to know what you are doing so you can consider improvements or alternatives. It helps to list the components of the program and their costs. Materials, environments, content, and teachers are the areas in which delineation can take place. There also should be a checklist or observation form to report on the use of inputs to be sure that they are being used as intended. If, for example, you are running an open classroom program, you would want to know whether environmental arrangements and teacher behaviors conform to the configuration and model set forth in your program specifications. Observational instruments for this purpose can either be homemade or taken from the literature. They can be used by supervisors or by persons employed expressly for this purpose. It makes little sense to evaluate programs until you know that they are operating as they are supposed to. If there are no program specifications to govern the instructional process, then this step can be eliminated or circumvented, although some program input information invariably can be used, such as results from the ongoing practice of teacher evaluation.

Design and Comparison

We now come to the problem of standards or criteria of performance. No simple rules can be stated for establishing standards; in fact, on some objectives it is not reasonable to attempt to evolve absolute standards on anything other than the very arbitrary basis of 80 percent success on test items that measure those objectives. Relative standards on published tests of basic skills can be put forth, taking a form such as performance at grade level or no lower than one grade level below one's age group. Typical performance standards for formative evaluation, therefore, take the form of 80 percent success on an objective as measured by a criterion-referenced test and/or average performance at grade level on an objective as measured by a norm-referenced test.*

Simple comparison to a criterion is the most elementary form of evaluation *design;* it offers neither much certainty that the program is responsible for

---

* Criterion-referenced tests report raw percent passing results per item and per objective; norm-referenced tests report performance relative to members of the same age group.

the outcome nor much generality in extending the results beyond the specific group and situation tested. More suitable designs provide a basis for comparison between outcomes that takes us beyond formative evaluation to summative evaluation.

Summative evaluation involves creating comparisons by which alternative educational avenues are contrasted to see which one produces the higher level of desired outcomes. By comparing alternative means to the same end, namely, mastery of objectives, effectiveness can be determined without recourse to arbitrary standards. Unless there is a particular reason for a given set of standards, it is wiser to make judgments in terms of the comparative (e.g., "better") than in terms of the simple evaluative (e.g., "good"). When we do not know what to expect, it often is unreasonable to be expected to know what to demand. We must depend on arbitrary standards of success until we have built up a backlog of data. Looking at outcomes retrospectively over time is called the ex post facto (or "after-the-fact") evaluation. This type of evaluation also may involve projecting comparison data through the use of norm groups.

How might the design question be put into operation? On an immediate level, a district may make comparisons with neighboring "like" districts or may implement alternative programs within its own borders in an effort to provide a systematic basis for comparison. If neither summative approach is possible, then a district can choose the ex post facto route. It can begin to collect performance data on district objectives on a regular basis, altering the program as deemed necessary on the basis of formative evaluation (that is, on a pretest-posttest basis or by comparing results with chosen criteria). After a series of such examinations, that is, after three to five years of such testing, examining the kinds of change tendencies apparent over time will show whether the trend is toward improvement. Changes that lead to improvement should be kept; changes that offer no positive result should be discarded. The overall sequence of events is shown in Figure 1.2.

Conclusion

Schooling is a dynamic process; fairly dramatic shifts in emphasis become apparent from decade to decade. In such a context, evaluation, too, must be both viewed and operationalized as a dynamic activity. Objectives must be reviewed and updated periodically, as must the tests and other procedures that measure them. Criteria must be reexamined and reevaluated over time as more data are accumulated. Long-term evaluations will help provide perspective, but such reviews cannot be expected to span periods much longer than five years if they are to be timely and meaningful in a current context. Districts should routinely adopt tentative performance criteria for large-scale programs and should conduct formative evaluations on a yearly basis. More specialized programs should be pilot tested on a more limited basis so that their outcomes can be

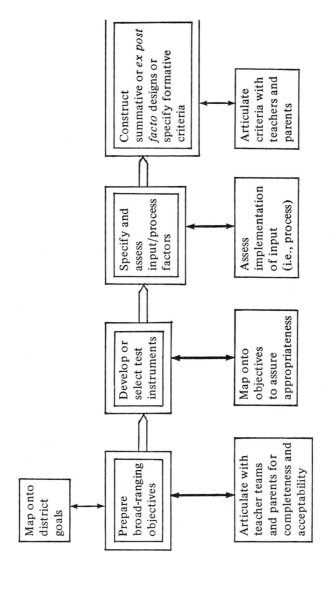

FIGURE 1.2 *Evaluation Steps*

contrasted with those of alternative approaches on a one-to-three-year cycle. Data should be accumulated longitudinally on a district-wide basis to permit ex post facto examinations of patterns of change on a five-year basis. Thus, districts can take profitable advantage of all three designs, given a set of objectives and the means to measure their mastery, to determine the "thoroughness" of their educational program.

Finally, input specification and process measurement must undergo continual refinement and utilization—moving more and more into the realm of explicit costs, both financial and human. Until we can delineate the costs of our programs, we will not be able to comment on their "efficiency." Until we know the extent or level at which intended instructional programs are being implemented, we will not be able to make decisions based on our evaluation results. Programs that do not achieve their outcomes may need improved implementation; they should not necessarily be dropped as deficient in their basic conception.

The Approach of This Book

This book gives evaluators the information they need to conduct or supervise instructional program evaluations in a school. These instructional program evaluations will fall into three categories, as described below.

Formative Evaluation

In the formative approach to evaluation, results are fed back into the system in order to improve its function and quality. Hence, the purpose of the evaluation is not to *judge* but to *improve* or *enhance* program operations. Such evaluations primarily serve an internal function and are based on comparing program outcomes with program goals.

Summative Evaluation

This is the evaluation for demonstration and documentation purposes. Alternative ways to achieve program goals usually are compared on some systematic basis across a variety of outcomes in an effort to choose among them (to select or reinforce use of the most effective).

Ex Post Facto Evaluation

This is the study over blocks of time of students and programs. It attempts to reconstruct the past by examining past outcomes in order to determine whether programs are producing desired results. Data must be produced continually in order to make such a longitudinal approach possible.

Evaluation Steps

All three types of evaluations require the same four steps.

1. *Specify the outcomes and their measurement.* In this first step, you decide what you are trying to achieve and how to determine whether you have achieved it. This step includes considering what outcomes to include (chapter 3), specifying and auditing these outcomes (chapter 5), and evaluating the quality of your tests (chapter 8).
2. *Specifying and evaluating inputs and process.* You also must be able to state the elements that constitute the program in order to understand what you are evaluating; you must be able to assure yourself that these inputs are actually operating and at a suitable level of implementation. This step includes considering what inputs to specify (chapter 3) and surveying the operation of these inputs in the form of process (chapter 6).
3. *Constructing a design.* After understanding the principles behind how we can make valid and generalizable evaluation conclusions, it is possible to construct various formative, summative, and ex post facto evaluation designs (only at this point do the three evaluation approaches begin to diverge). These designs are described in chapter 4.
4. *Carrying out the evaluation.* Instruments often must be developed, and once developed (or otherwise obtained) they must be administered, analyzed, interpreted, and reported. Standards must be set and designs implemented. Operational guidelines for carrying out the three types of evaluation are provided in chapters 9, 10, and 11.

The Program Evaluator's Checklist

The conclusion of chapter 11 (Figure 11.6) contains a series of questions that evaluators should ask themselves in completing an instructional program evaluation in order to be sure to cover all elements. This Program Evaluator's Checklist is presented toward the end of the book rather than here at the beginning because it integrates or synthesizes all that the book covers and largely depends on concepts and vocabulary presented throughout the book. However, the reader is encouraged to turn to the checklist and read it over now, not to fully understand its meaning and significance, but rather to use it as a "road map" to follow in reading through the book. Thereafter, it will be helpful to refer to the checklist after completing each chapter.

Qualitative/Case Study Evaluation

The three types of evaluation described above are all quantitative in that they are based on the collection of numerical data. However, evaluations are also conducted that are based on judgmental data which result from observations, interviews and the perusal of program documents. Such qualitative or case study evaluations are covered in chapter 12, which includes information on specifying questions; qualitative data sources; and analyzing, interpreting, and reporting qualitative results.

Case Studies

Actual evaluations provide useful models for doing evaluation. Appendix A presents four case studies that vary in several important ways. Each case study illustrates a different approach to instructional program evaluation as previously discussed in the text. The first study illustrates formative evaluation; the second, summative evaluation; the third ex post facto evaluation; and the fourth, qualitative/case study evaluation. Readers are urged to examine each case study carefully.

CHAPTER 2

Defining the Quality of Instructional Programs

The Measurable Dimensions of Education

It is convenient to separate the educational variables we are interested in measuring into *input, process,* and *output.* This division is particularly convenient when we are interested in describing or evaluating the performance effects of programs, schools, or school districts as opposed to the performance effects of individual students. *Measurable educational inputs* can be considered as the givens of an educational system—such things as school budget, facilities, community needs, and the characteristics that students and teachers bring into the school system. *Measurable educational processes* can be considered as the performance characteristics of the system itself—the teaching behaviors of teachers and administering behavior of administrators. Process variables like school climate and teacher style represent the effect of inputs, that is, they vary primarily as a function of the quality and quantity of school inputs. Finally, we have *measurable educational outputs* (or outcomes), which are of greatest concern in measuring the quality of instructional programs. These are learner behaviors and performances—attitudes, achievements, and the like. When taken together, they reflect on the inputs and processes of the school. These relationships are shown in Figure 2.1.

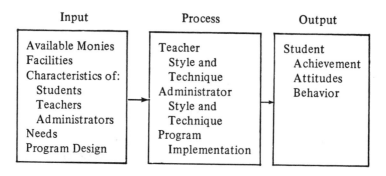

Input	Process	Output

Available Monies
Facilities
Characteristics of:
  Students
  Teachers
  Administrators
Needs
Program Design
	Teacher
	  Style and
	  Technique
	Administrator
	  Style and
	  Technique
	Program
	  Implementation
		Student
		  Achievement
		  Attitudes
		  Behavior

FIGURE 2.1 *Examples of Input, Process, and Output*

It is possible to measure school inputs, processes, and outputs using various types of measuring instruments. To measure input, we have to measure the static qualities of the schools, or what they look like at 8:00 A.M. on Monday as the students and staff pour into the buildings. What are the capabilities of the teachers, their needs, and expectations? How experienced is the superintendent? How well equipped are the schools? How does the community feel about education? What programs are available in the schools for the students? What is the size of the school budget? What is the size of the educational tax base? As you look out at the people entering on Monday, you see the raw material for that week's worth of education. Needless to say, what you start with the next week will not be identical. It will reflect the effects of the education process during the week.

What goes on in the school is process. How teachers handle disciplinary problems, the amount of individual attention students receive, the extent to which kits and other learning devices are used, the extent to which teachers are given suitable and constructive supervision, the use of math workbooks, the taking of nature walks—these are all manifestations of educational process.

The chief focus of educational measurement is on output. The outputs of education are reflected in its clients, the students. The purpose of specific educational experiences or processes is to develop and improve student growth. The "product" of education is a student who has acquired skills, knowledge, attitudes, and behaviors that enable him or her to be a satisfied and contributing member of society. We are interested in measuring the collective acquisition of these skills, knowledge, attitudes, and behaviors across students as a way of determining the quality of the educational experience and the extent to which it meets student needs. That is the topic of this book.

We are also, of course, interested in measuring the individual acquisition of these skills, knowledges, attitudes, and behaviors as a way of determining the growth and progress of each student in order to evaluate, facilitate, and attest to that growth and progress. This is another measurement matter and is not central to this book.

	Individual	Group
Input	* How well trained is teacher X? * What is administrator Y's attitudes toward pupil control? * How bright is Johnny?	* What is the average amount of training of teachers in the system? * What do the administrators believe is the best way to control students? * How bright are the first graders in the school?
Process	* Does teacher X use individually designed workbooks? * Does administrator Y have an open-door policy? * Are students in teacher Z's class permitted to choose their own tasks?	* How many teachers use individually designed workbooks? * What is the policy of the administrative staff? * In how many clases may students select their own tasks?
Output	* What aspects of reading give Jane the most trouble? * How does Emil feel about the rights of women? * How well-mannered is Bobbie toward adults in the school?	* How well can the second graders in the district read? * How do children in the school feel about women's rights? * How well-behaved are our students?

FIGURE 2.2 *Potentially Measurable Dimensions of the Schools*

Thus, for purposes of measuring education, we can distinguish between individual effects and group effects on school input, process, and output, as shown in Figure 2.2. Group effects are the sum of individual effects and thus represent tendencies.

Measuring Educational Output

The instructional evaluation program should focus on measuring educational output, both individual and group, because output measures indicate the quality with which education has been accomplished. Let us examine what the testing component of the instructional evaluation effort should look like if it is going to qualify as the indicator of educational or instructional quality.

We must measure the attainment of a district's educational goals by its clients, the students. Instead of restricting ourselves to conventional school subject goals, let us consider a broad set of education goals, such as those offered by Phi Delta Kappa, a national professional education organization. These goals and subgoals appear in Figure 2.3. Note that the goals cover a vari-

EDUCATIONAL GOALS

(*These are not in any order of importance*)

LEARN HOW TO BE A GOOD CITIZEN

    A. Develop an awareness of civic rights and responsibilities.

    B. Develop attitudes for productive citizenship in a democracy.

    C. Develop an attitude of respect for personal and public property.

    D. Develop an understanding of the obligations and responsibilities of citizenship.

LEARN HOW TO RESPECT AND GET ALONG WITH PEOPLE WHO THINK, DRESS, AND ACT DIFFERENTLY

    A. Develop an appreciation for and an understanding of other people and other cultures.

    B. Develop an understanding of political, economic, and social patterns of the rest of the world.

    C. Develop awareness of the interdependence of races, creeds, nations, and culture.

    D. Develop an awareness of the processes of group relationships.

LEARN ABOUT AND TRY TO UNDERSTAND THE CHANGES THAT TAKE PLACE IN THE WORLD

    A. Develop ability to adjust to the changing demands of society.

    B. Develop an awareness and the ability to adjust to a changing world and its problems.

    C. Develop understanding of the past, identify with the present, and the ability to meet the future.

DEVELOP SKILLS IN READING, WRITING, SPEAKING AND LISTENING

    A. Develop ability to communicate ideas and feelings effectively.

    B. Develop skills in oral and written English.

FIGURE 2.3 *List of Educational Goals taken from* Phi Delta Kappan. *Reprinted by permission of* Phi Delta Kappan, *Bloomington, Indiana.*

UNDERSTAND AND PRACTICE DEMOCRATIC IDEAS AND IDEALS

A. Develop loyalty to American democratic ideals.
B. Develop patriotism and loyalty to ideas of democracy.
C. Develop knowledge and appreciation of the rights and privileges in our democracy.
D. Develop an understanding of our American heritage.

LEARN HOW TO EXAMINE AND USE INFORMATION

A. Develop the ability to examine constructively and creatively.
B. Develop ability to use scientific methods.
C. Develop reasoning abilities.
D. Develop skills to think and proceed logically.

UNDERSTAND AND PRACTICE THE SKILLS OF FAMILY LIVING

A. Develop understanding and appreciation of the principles of living in the family group.
B. Develop attitudes leading to acceptance of responsibilities as family members.
C. Develop an awareness of future family responsibilities and achievement of skills in preparing to accept them.

LEARN TO RESPECT AND GET ALONG WITH PEOPLE WITH WHOM WE WORK AND LIVE

A. Develop appreciation and respect for the worth and dignity of individuals.
B. Develop respect for individual worth and understanding of minority opinions and acceptance of majority decisions.
C. Develop a cooperative attitude toward living and working with others.

DEVELOP SKILLS TO ENTER A SPECIFIC FIELD OF WORK

A. Develop abilities and skills needed for immediate employment.
B. Develop an awareness of opportunities and requirements related to a specific field of work.
C. Develop an appreciation of good workmanship.

LEARN HOW TO BE A GOOD MANAGER OF MONEY, PROPERTY, AND RESOURCES

A. Develop an understanding of economic principles and responsibilities.
B. Develop ability and understanding in personal buying, selling, and investment.

C. Develop skills in management of natural and human resources and man's environment.

DEVELOP A DESIRE FOR LEARNING NOW AND IN THE FUTURE

A. Develop intellectual curiosity and eagerness for lifelong learning.
B. Develop a positive attitude toward learning.
C. Develop a positive attitude toward continuing independent education.

LEARN HOW TO USE LEISURE TIME

A. Develop ability to use leisure time productively.
B. Develop a positive attitude toward participation in a range of leisure time activities—physical, intellectual, and creative.
C. Develop appreciation and interests which will lead to wise and enjoyable use of leisure time.

PRACTICE AND UNDERSTAND THE IDEAS OF HEALTH AND SAFETY

A. Establish an effective individual physical fitness program.
B. Develop an understanding of good physical health and well being.
C. Establish sound personal health habits and information.
D. Develop a concern for public health and safety.

APPRECIATE CULTURE AND BEAUTY IN THE WORLD

A. Develop abilities for effective expression of ideas and cultural appreciation (fine arts).
B. Cultivate appreciation for beauty in various forms.
C. Develop creative self-expression through various media (art, music, writing, etc.).
D. Develop special talents in music, art, literature, and foreign lanlanguages.

GAIN INFORMATION NEEDED TO MAKE JOB SELECTIONS

A. Promote self-understanding and self-direction in relation to student's occupational interests.
B. Develop the ability to use information and counseling services related to the selection of a job.
C. Develop a knowledge of specific information about a particular vocation.

DEVELOP PRIDE IN WORK AND A FEELING OF SELF-WORTH

A. Develop a feeling of student pride in his achievement and progress.

B. Develop self-understanding and self-awareness.

C. Develop the student's feeling of positive self-worth, security, and self-assurance.

DEVELOP GOOD CHARACTER AND SELF-RESPECT

A. Develop moral responsibility and a sound ethical and moral behavior.

B. Develop the student's capacity to discipline himself to work, study, and play constructively.

C. Develop a moral and ethical sense of values, goals, and processes of free society.

D. Develop standards of personal character and ideas.

GAIN A GENERAL EDUCATION

A. Develop background and skills in the use of numbers, natural sciences, mathematics, and social sciences.

B. Develop a fund of information and concepts.

C. Develop special interests and abilities.

ety of learning areas, all of which are an important part of growing up but not all of which are covered in the schools. After a school adopts such a list of goals for student output it should then establish procedures for measuring these goals.

Educational output usually is measured by means of educational achievement tests, at least regarding the acquisition of skills and knowledge. Measuring outputs in attitude and behavior areas requires attitudinal and behavioral instruments. Even though it often has been emphasized that reading and math are the most critical areas of school responsibility, it is important to acknowledge the many areas of development at which schooling is and should be aimed. The *Phi Delta Kappan* list represents an attempt at a broad and comprehensive list of such goals that can describe a thorough education. Regardless of the quality of educational experience, if students are not developing to some degree in each area, then the value of those experiences must be suspect.

Ideally, each school district should generate its own list of goals (working cooperatively with teachers, parents, and students) and should be prepared to measure the group attainment of those goals as the major purpose of the group school testing program. To build such a testing program, existing achievement and attitude scales can be combined and probably streamlined by eliminating undesired content areas. The major advantage of using standardized instruments is to make possible comparisons across districts; their major disadvantage is the difficulty in expecting a single instrument to fit a variety of districts. High schools in New York state have been guided by a series of subject-matter examinations called State Regents Examinations, which are used to measure and specify levels of performance in each subject as a prerequisite for academic credit. Although these tests are part of the *individual* testing program, their use as *group* measures for judging school district outputs would represent a type of basis for evaluating the quality of a district's educational program.

Educational output measures can be used effectively to measure educational effects primarily because: (1) these outputs represent the product of the educational system; and (2) we have developed some facility for measuring educational outputs. Even though it is difficult to be sure that one way of doing something is better than another, we can have much more confidence in specifying that higher reading performance is better than low reading performance, for example.

In other words, it is easier to attach positive values to outcomes than to processes. Goals represent outcomes that are valued. Educators may not be able to agree on the best way to teach children to read, but they can agree that improving their reading skills is a goal of education. Thus, educational outputs are appropriate for measuring and evaluating educational effects because people are more likely to agree on desirable effects than they are to agree on ways of attaining them (that is, on processes).

A second reason for focusing on outputs as measures of educational program quality is that we are more adept at measuring output than we are at measuring process. Implementing an evaluation scheme requires suitable technology, particularly in terms of measurement. We are much more adept at measuring how students perform than how systems perform.

Also, we are an output-oriented society with a tendency to value our processes only if we also value their products. In the final analysis, we judge things (and people) by how well they "work." If we define output broadly enough to include more than acquiring traditional skills and knowledge, but include a wider range of knowledge and attitudes and behavior as well, we will have a "product-oriented" approach that should be sensitive enough to embrace the humanistic aspects of schooling as well as the more mechanical ones. People who criticize such an approach as being insensitive to human variability must note that it does leave total variability in the question of how the goals will be achieved as well as allowing districts latitude in defining their own goals. As a minimum essential for evaluating educational quality,* then, *each district should specify its own output goals and measure their attainment using a battery of measuring instruments.*

Measuring and evaluating predetermined educational outputs have long

---

* Although the term *effectiveness* is often used to label the extent to which educational inputs yield improvements in educational outputs, the preferred term here is *quality*. Using the label *quality* will avoid confusion with the term *efficiency,* to be introduced later.

been a part of the strategy of instructional program evaluation, particularly when the programs are intended to be exemplary and are financed by state and federal funds. If, as recommended, school districts are to evaluate their total offering as if it represented an exemplary program, then the mechanics of program evaluation can be applied to evaluating goals on a district-wide basis. Figure 2.4 provides a statement of issues and resource requirements that school districts should consider as part of an effort to implement district-wide output evaluation. To the extent that local funds and talent are not sufficient to accomplish output evaluation, it becomes state government's role to assist. The type of assistance that may be needed probably will be: (1) technical aid in needs assessment (determining the goals for the district); and (2) measuring

---

OUTPUT EVALUATION REQUIRES
Testing Information

Resources

1. Testing expert(s) on staff	a. Teacher in-service training
2. Consultants	b. Test selection
3. Reference sources and libraries **TO DO**	c. Design and interpretation of test programs
4. Catalogs and test publishers	d. Design of evaluations

Types of Tests

1. Teacher-built	a. Classroom-wide
2. Research tests	b. School-wide
3. Commercial tests and test programs **THAT ARE**	c. Grade-level or Department-wide
4. Tests that come with curriculum	d. District-wide

Questions to Answer

1. How is testing accomplished (i.e., what types of tests are used: what specific test instruments are used)?
2. What resources are available and how are they used?
3. What problems exist vis-a-vis the testing program?
4. How do testing procedures used fit the five test criteria? (See chapter 8.)

FIGURE 2.4 *Implementing Output Evaluation*

output with respect to each goal. Local teachers and administrative staff should be used insofar as possible for these tasks, but additional technical information in the form of consultants, in-service training, and resource centers also should be available.

Let us consider one more issue with regard to the use of district-wide output evaluation as the basis for evaluating the quality of instructional programs. That issue is how output performance levels are to be evaluated. Put another way, the issue is: shall there be levels of acceptable performance, and, if so, how shall they be determined? Obviously, it is hard to say exactly what the scores on any particular test mean. Interpreting test scores is difficult without absolute criteria. We cannot apply quality control if we do not know: (1) exactly what constitutes quality; and (2) how well our tests measure it. An individual classroom teacher may be able to prespecify exactly what she wants students to do and at what performance level, but it is much more difficult to do that on a district-wide basis.

The matter may be most equitably resolved by setting no arbitrary external standards for performance since such standards would be difficult to authenticate, but turning instead to significant growth or improvement as the criterion for judging the quality of the educational process, particularly in contrast to growth resulting from alternative educational processes. If a student completes the eighth grade with a certain reading comprehension capability, and high schools are committed to improving this ability, then significant gains from high school entry (input) to high school exit (output) would constitute evidence of instructional program quality. Such a procedure recognizes that educational output levels will be affected by educational input levels. Students who start out higher probably will end higher, even if the school makes little contribution.

Thus, it is recommended that the *criterion of quality be significant* improvement and not ultimate or final output level.* Comparing the test performance of students at different grade levels determines improvement. Needless to say, comparing students to others of like background and experience (comparing all eighth graders in the same district) rather than comparing all students in all districts to the same criterion level considers differences in potential, since potential also affects the input level at which the students enter the analysis (scores in the eighth grade). Hence, the mystery of absolute criteria is avoided in favor of self-improvement as a yardstick.

Moreover, even with self-improvement as the measure, the goal of this approach is to continue to try procedures that will increase improvement levels. Thus, an evaluation program is not seen as a contest to determine how good a program is or which program is better, but to provide both a gauge of success

---

* Significance can be based on statistical significance, that is, on gains of sufficient size and stability to exceed the chance expectation and reach the 95 percent level of likelihood of being real differences. This approach is described in more operational forms in chapter 9.

that one can then attempt to exceed as well as suggestions for program improvement. Evaluation should be seen primarily as having informational value, hence pointing to areas in which improvement is desirable, as well as suggesting ways of achieving improvement.

Measuring Educational Input

The matter of measuring input now is put into perspective by this discussion of output. To a great extent, educational input measures and educational output measures are the same. The only difference is that input measurement occurs at the start of a sequence and output measurement at the conclusion. If quality is based on the degree of gain from input to output, then input measurement is an essential part of determining quality.

Let us consider one further aspect of input, other than the level of performance of students at the beginning of a sequence, which must be taken into account in evaluating measurable gains. Some districts have students who begin, say, high school, with higher performance levels; however, this advantage is counterbalanced by adjusting output performance in terms of input performance, as suggested above. In addition, though, some districts spend more money on education than others, which may give them an advantage. To counteract this advantage, this formulation is suggested:*

$$\frac{\text{Educational Efficiency}}{} = \frac{\text{Educational Quality}}{\text{Per-Pupil Expenditure}}$$

or

$$\frac{\text{Educational Efficiency}}{} = \frac{\text{Group Output Performance–Group Input Performance}}{\text{Per-Pupil Expenditure}}$$

If we adjust learning gains to reflect the average number of dollars they cost the district, we are using this second input measure to help determine how much educational quality a district is getting for its dollars, hence its efficiency. This formulation should not be used to encourage educational miserliness, but it may help districts decide about their best allocation of money.

Measuring Educational Process

Information about educational process is helpful *not* for determining the quality or efficiency of an educational program but for helping a district, internally, to improve its quality through its level of program implementation.

An example will help illustrate this point. Suppose a principal works hard with his teachers in using varying teaching styles, but little improvement is

---

* This is a conceptual formulation, that is, an idea, rather than an operational formulation, that is, a ready-to-use formula. It could form the basis for subsequent development of usable formulae.

shown in student performance. Presumably, to improve student performance, the principal would do better to use the teacher in-service time on other topics or to observe to see whether teachers are changing their styles. As evaluators, we are primarily interested in the quality of the program and the cost; thus, we would not be concerned about what the principal did as long as quality did not go down or cost up. Suppose the principal decides to purchase more educational devices and equipment and install them in the classrooms. The result of these "improvements" in input depends first on whether these materials are used (that is, whether input is converted to process or level of program implementation) and, second, on whether these materials, when used, cause students to learn more. Our interest (as evaluators) in process is not in whether one process is inherently better than another but in: (1) whether and to what degree the process occurs; and (2) whether it improves learning—contributes to quality or output.

If educators can improve the processes of teaching, of classroom and school management, of school climates, of teacher morale, and so on, then the result should be to increase the gains in student learning, or to reduce the costs of these gains, or both. Educators should be motivated to measure and improve educational processes for just these reasons. If we were to attempt to standardize these processes or to use them as a direct measure of the quality of education, we would remove from professional educators their most important options. Thus, all accountability formulations should deal with process in terms of level or degree of implementation, leaving its choice to the discretion of the local district. However, schools are encouraged to measure process in order to: (1) determine whether and to what extent intended processes are being carried out (as a basis for improving their effect); and (2) begin to discover which processes increase the likelihood of maximizing gains per unit cost. Process thus remains an entirely internal part of the machinery of education. It is the area in which innovation, ingenuity, and commitment can be applied (and the level of implementation, while measured, used for improving internal conditions), whereas outputs relative to inputs provide the basis for evaluating demonstrable instructional effects. Measuring group outcomes can contribute greatly to effective education. Even though group results on tests do not contribute to individual learning as directly as individual results do, group results make it possible to determine the effects of specific instructional practices relative to desired goals and thereby to point out areas of improvement. Adding process measures often makes it possible to pinpoint areas in which improvement is needed and to suggest the types of improvements that might be tried.

To implement a system of instructional program evaluation, a district must *first specify its educational goals.* This process can be short-circuited, if desired, by adopting a list of goals such as those shown in Figure 2.3. The opportunity to set goals, however, is important and should not be short-circuited simply as a matter of administrative convenience.

Step two is to *measure the attainment of these goals among students* at some specific time in order to constitute the pretest or baseline. To accomplish this measurement, suitable test batteries must be developed or existing batteries amended, combined, or used together.

The third step is to *administer one or more tests to all students* at some time between the middle and end of the school year to serve as the posttest. Because evaluating program quality is based on group data, as opposed to individual data, it is not necessary that every student be measured on every goal. A sampling procedure can be used to insure adequate representativeness of subsamples. (Techniques for testing will be discussed throughout the chapters of this book.)

Step four is to *compare the performance on each goal for students at the different grade levels.* This comparison should determine whether growth or improvement occurs during the school years, and, if so, to what extent. This approach is discussed in chapter 11.

Step five is to *ascertain the per-pupil expenditure and divide all gains by it to arrive at the degree of gain per unit cost.* For a greater refinement of this procedure, you could determine the amount of money that the district was spending on the attainment of each goal (which is, unfortunately, difficult to calculate) and then compare the gains on each goal with the money being spent on that goal.

The sixth step is to bring in input and process information. *A district should make a chart indicating all the curriculum or programmatic activities in each goal area.* Presumably, in areas of small programmatic effort, gains should be slight or nonexistent, whereas in the areas with greatest effort, gains should be great. Any attempt at this point to link educational experiences or inputs and processes with gains (gains being the difference between test performance outcomes and starting points) would help the district evaluate specific instructional programs and events.

By examining measurable gains in student performance in many goal areas and relating these gains to costs, other inputs, or processes, districts can determine both the quality and efficiency of their instructional programs. By relating gains to the specific programs being offered, districts can pinpoint areas that are not working and can target resources on this basis to overcome their deficiencies. This basic evaluation or decision-making model is developed in more operational terms in the final section of this book.

Overall Perspective

A school testing and evaluation program as applied to group data provides a school district with the opportunity to determine: (1) the quality of its instructional efforts; (2) the efficiency of these efforts; and (3) the areas and kinds of improvements needed—all without the excessive application of value judgments. The measure of quality is the *difference* between student *output* or out-come performance on a variety of educational goals (selected by the district) and student *input* or baseline performance on these same measures. These differences or *gains* on its goals are determined by each district by comparing students within different programs with themselves over time or with students in alternative programs. The magnitude of the gains on each goal constitutes a measure of the quality of the program that the district is employing to accomplish its goals. The addition of *per-pupil expenses,* partitioned if possible into the *amount of money spent per goal,* provides the basis for calculating *efficiency* when gains in each goal area divided by costs. To determine money spent per goal, it probably will be necessary to ask teachers to report the amount of time they devote to each goal area and then to partition the per-pupil costs accordingly.

Measures of input and process do not contribute directly to determining either educational quality or efficiency. However, since the purpose of determining quality and efficiency is to improve local education, process measurement can be brought to bear. Input refers to the resources that teachers are given, and process refers to how these resources are used for instruction. If teachers are spending time (and hence the district is spending money) in a goal area (input) but the resulting performance gain (output minus input) is small in that area, it will be necessary to examine closely and measure (at least in a rough way) the process being used to achieve that goal (the type of instruction, instructional climate, and instructional quality), with an eye toward improving it. Additional monies then might be sought to implement process improvements in low-gain areas.

This kind of a system is noncompetitive; a district need only focus on self-improvement relative to its own goals. Moreover, not using process measures as criteria of either quality or efficiency avoids the excessive reliance on value judgments that the specification and evaluation of instructional process requires.

Finally, the use of both input and output in determining quality allows for an adjustment in terms of students' initial performance levels, while the consideration of costs per goal allows for an adjustment in terms of relative program emphasis. For example, less important goals may produce smaller gains but also involve lower educational costs since less time is spent on them. Considering all the variables in the formulation relative to one's own district, the accountability emphasis can be used as a positive force for self-improvement rather than as a basis for cutthroat competition and sniping.

CHAPTER 3

Program Components: Outcomes, Inputs, Process

Outcomes

The function of an instructional program evaluation is to demonstrate the outcomes that a program causes students to achieve or to achieve better than its alternatives in addition to any outcomes that the program cannot achieve as well. It is then the province of those-who-provide or those-who-experience or those-who-finance the program to decide whether its outcomes are a sufficient basis for continuing it. It must be emphasized, however, that all programs, even those considered alternatives to one another, cannot be expected to yield the same outcomes. One should be able to predict the kinds of outcomes that a program will maximize (if done optimally) by examining its goals and procedures. The job of the person responsible for the evaluation is not to decide which outcomes are the most important but to demonstrate which outcomes, if any, are maximized.

Achievement as the Typical Outcome

The typical practice is to rely on standardized achievement data as the basic criteria for evaluation. When an "experimental" program fails to produce greater gains in standardized achievement than the "conventional" or "traditional" program, people inevitably conclude that the experimental program therefore is not worth the extra trouble. This attitude may reflect a tendency by educators, parents, and, all too often, evaluators to rely on a limited number of outcome measures, which often are restricted to the standardized achievement variety.

This reliance is defended on the grounds that: (1) we get these data anyway (standardized achievement testing is a part of the regimen of most school districts); (2) other things cannot be measured as easily or as well (how do you measure a liking for school or creativity, for example?); (3) producing achievement of the standardized achievement-test variety is the important aspect of education; all the other outcomes, such as creativity, attitudes, and self-discipline, are frills.

Other Important Outcomes

Since different kinds of instructional interventions and programs should result in different outcomes, evaluators' questions about outcomes should be twofold: (1) What outcomes should you be measuring when you evaluate an instructional program or other form of intervention? and (2) How do you measure these outcomes? We can hypothesize that, when successful, programs yield different outcomes specific to those programs. We can also hypothesize that different students will maximize performance on different outcomes because of their characteristic ways of relating to their environments. This suggests that evaluators consider a range of outcomes that may accurately reflect the results of the treatment being evaluated. Three trends appear in many evaluations:* (1) the input side is described in detail, often with respect to some instructional model; (2) the outcome side often is restricted to achievement measurement alone; (3) little concern is given to differences between students other than to try to control for them.

Since achievement measurement has evolved alongside the basic classroom group-oriented instructional procedure—which we tend to label "conventional" or "traditional"—it is reasonable to expect that the conventional instructional approach will maximize achievement. If this expectation is correct, then using achievement as a sole evaluation criterion would favor the conventional, or tried-and-true, approach to instruction. Such evaluation would have to be considered shortsighted and even potentially biased in its limitations.

The position recommended in this chapter (and elaborated in chapter 5)

---

* It must be emphasized that most educational evaluations are unpublished. Published instructional research does not fall into this threefold pattern to the same degree as do evaluation studies.

is that evaluation studies should include a range of outcome measures specifically chosen to sample outcomes that are different both in degree and in kind.

Empirical Support

Gagné (1971, 1973) has distinguished five domains for classifying learning processes: (1) verbal information; (2) intellectual skills; (3) cognitive strategies; (4) motor skills; and (5) attitudes. These categories also can be used for classifying outcomes. They suggest a range of areas in which measuring program effects might be undertaken. Glaser (1972, p. 12) also suggests measurement outside the "narrow band of traditional academic outcomes," with the inclusion of "measures of process and style, or cognitive and noncognitive development, and of performance in more natural settings." He also wants to include individual difference measures of cognitive process within instructional research. Lohnes (1973), who argues for including intellectual development as an important outcome of many (possibly all) instructional treatments, cites arguments for including differentiated outcomes. Tyler (1951) said quite succinctly:

> Any learning situation has multiple outcomes. While the child is acquiring information, knowledges, and skills, there is also taking place concomitant learnings in attitudes, appreciations, and interests. This view indicates a shift from a narrow conception of subject-matter outcomes to a broader conception of growth and development of individuals. (p. 48)

And finally, Cronbach (1971, p. 460) states: "Consequently, an ideally suitable battery for evaluation purposes will include separate measures of all outcomes the users of the information consider important."

Specifying Outcomes by Category

Five categories or classes of outcomes, like those suggested above, are shown in Figure 3.1. They are: (1) specific knowledge and comprehension (or specific achievement); (2) general knowledge and comprehension (or general achievement); (3) thinking and problem solving; (4) attitudes and values; and (5) learning-related behavior. Figure 3.1 lists some possible outcomes in each category in order to make these categories clearer in meaning. (No attempt has been made to be exhaustive.)

One or more variable in each category should be included in every instructional program evaluation to determine the various effects of different educational interventions. *The specific outcomes chosen for measurement should be based, insofar as possible, on the objectives of each treatment being compared.* That is, program effects should be measured in terms of more than just specific knowledge and comprehension goals and should thus include objectives in all

A. SPECIFIC KNOWLEDGE AND COMPREHENSION
(SPEC ACHIEV)

Subject-matter achievement (e.g., knowledge and understanding of math, science, language arts, social studies, machine operation, etc., based on specific curriculum content and specific objectives of program).

B. GENERAL KNOWLEDGE AND COMPREHENSION
(GEN ACHIEV)

intelligence
aptitudes
general abilities
reading ability
reasoning ability
knowledge of culture

C. THINKING AND PROBLEM-SOLVING (HIGH COG)

(these characteristics do not typically have names and may not be measured in typical test situations)
analysis
synthesis
evaluation
decision-making

D. ATTITUDES AND VALUES (AFF)

attitudes toward school
attitudes toward self
attitudes toward internal-external control
vocational maturity
interests
prejudice
tolerance of ambiguity
value priority

E. LEARNING-RELATED BEHAVIOR (BEH)

attendance
time devoted to learning or problem-solving
self-discipline
initiative

FIGURE 3.1 *Categories of Differentiated Outcomes and Examples Within Each*

cooperativeness

performance (in an actual or simulated setting; not paper-and-pencil)

five areas. (It may be necessary first to get program designers to generate objectives in all five areas; otherwise, some areas will continue to be typically overlooked.)

Some Examples

It would be useful now to describe a few of the many published evaluations that distinguish between results on a single criterion as compared to those that employed a variety of outcomes. Thompson (1980) completed a comparative evaluation of two methods for teaching the first college calculus course, individual mastery and traditional lecture plus discussion. (No detail will be given regarding these inputs, since our primary concern here is with his multiple outcomes in contrast to the single, more traditional outcome.) He measured eight outcome variables: (1) traditional calculus achievement as measured by Form A of the calculus subtest of the Cooperative Mathematics Tests published by Educational Testing Service; (2) a 63-item, departmental achievement examination containing equation solving, problem solving, and graphing; (3) achievement in Calculus 2 and Calculus 3, the two next courses in the sequence; (4) mathematics reading comprehension, a measure of the ability to answer questions about the content of an unfamiliar passage of text on complex numbers; (5) grades in courses taken concurrently with the first calculus course, as a measure of facilitation by the program being evaluated; (6) outside study time as reported by students; (7) propensity for further math-related study as judged by the student; (8) student-reported satisfaction with instruction.

The first variable fits into the SPEC ACHIEV (see Figure 3.1) category and can be considered the kind of achievement measure that typically suffices as the "single criterion." Beyond this, however, the outcomes were differentiated to include one of GEN ACHIEV, that being number 4, mathematics reading comprehension; one of HIGH COG, that being number 2, the departmental calculus test; two of AFF, those being numbers 7 and 8, math propensity and satisfaction; and two of BEH, number 5, concurrent grades, and number 6, study time. It is hard to classify number 3, achievement in subsequent calculus courses. This is a measure of achievement but is not entirely specific to the program being evaluated. It is somewhere between SPEC ACHIEV and GEN ACHIEV.

Thompson's findings, unfortunately, were not nearly as differentiated as his outcome measures. He concluded that the superiority claimed for the mastery system in many reports was not supported by his results. However, given the breadth and completeness of his array of outcome measures, had there been any important differences, he would have uncovered them.

Let us consider two more illustrative studies so that a pattern may become detectable between the use of a single criterion and the use of multiple outcomes. Tuckman and Orefice (1973) compared four different teaching procedures varying in relative degree of student-initiation and teacher-initiation, with students being further classified as either abstract or concrete in personality orientation. Measured outcomes included, in addition to achievement of accounting objectives (SPEC ACHIEV, the single criterion), two differentiated outcomes: student time spent in the instructional process (BEH) and attitudes toward the form of instruction received (AFF). No differences between treatments or personalities or within their interaction were found on the single criterion (SPECIFIC ACHIEVEMENT). Differences between treatments were found on both of the differentiated outcomes. The most striking findings in this study were the interactions between treatment and personality on both differentiated outcomes.*

Tuckman and Orefice found no differences on the single criterion (SPEC ACHIEV variable) but did find differences on each of two differentiated outcomes (AFF and BEH measures). Moreover, the differentiated outcomes were sensitive not only to treatment differences but also to personality differences in combination with treatments (what Cronbach and Gleser [1965] call aptitude-treatment interactions and Hunt [1971] calls matching models).

The missing differentiated outcome in the study cited above seemed to be a HIGH COG measure, and so another study was done (Elliott and Tuckman 1977). The second study compared two instructional treatments: individualized versus conventional, on the single criterion-achievement on accounting objectives (SPEC ACHIEV) plus the following differentiated outcomes; student instructional time (BEH), student attitudes toward school (AFF), and a problem-solving measure that included measures of knowledge (SPEC ACHIEV), search initiative, time spent and solution length (BEHs), and adequacy of problem solutions (HIGH COG).

On the single criterion measure (SPEC ACHIEV), the measure that usually is used alone, again no treatment differences were found. In addition, no differences were found on the attitude (AFF) measure. Differences in time to complete instruction (the BEH measure) were found.

Let us look at the principal differentiated outcome, the multifaceted

---

* Abstract students (as described on p. 37) disliked the lecture-programmed textbook most among the four treatments, whereas concrete students preferred this approach; exactly the reverse was true for the programmed textbook without lecture approach: abstract students preferred it and concrete students disliked it. Consistent with their preference patterns, concrete students registered their dislike for the programmed approach alone by spending noticeably less time on it than on any other approach.

problem-solving measure, a take-home problem not covered in either treatment. The problem was unfamiliar in its specifics but within the range of subject matter, and it contained some unfamiliar terms. Students were asked to: (1) provide definitions for the unfamiliar terms (SPEC ACHIEV); (2) write as many solutions as they could for the problem (HIGH COG); and (3) keep track of and report time spent working on the problem (BEH). They were told to use whatever resources they chose to help them solve the problem, but that they must: (4) report the resources used (BEH). Finally, (5) the problem-solution length was examined (BEH).

You can probably anticipate the results. On the SPEC ACHIEV measure (a "single criterion" type), no treatment differences were found. On the differentiated outcome—problem solutions (HIGH COG) as judged by professionals in the field (with adequate scoring reliability demonstrated)—clear differences between students in the two instructional treatments were found in favor of the individualized approach. Higher scores on each behavior measure also were obtained by students in the individualized treatment.

So far we have reported on discovery and individualized instruction compared to more conventional approaches. The general finding is that no differences exist between approaches on the typical single criterion (specific cognitive achievement) but differences do favor one approach over the other on differentiated outcomes in the area of higher cognitive processes.

Let us examine one more illustrative evaluation. Tuckman and Waheed (1981; Case Study 2—see Appendix A) compared self-paced, individualized instruction to traditional, whole-class instruction in basic science at the community college level. In addition to obtaining results on subject-matter achievement using a short-answer test (a measure of SPEC ACHIEV), the authors also utilized two attitude measures, one a measure of attitudes toward science (AFF), the second a measure of satisfaction with instruction (AFF). Significant differences in favor of self-paced, individualized instruction were found not only in specific subject-matter achievement but in attitudes toward science as well. No differences were found in satisfaction.

In most of the illustrative evaluation studies cited, no differences between treatments were found on the single (specific achievement) criterion, which would have led observers to conclude that the treatments compared were equally effective. However, *in all instances,* including differentiated or multiple-outcome measures in affective and higher cognitive areas, the studies clearly yielded differences between treatments, suggesting that one treatment was more effective than the other. Had the differentiated outcomes not been included, these differences would not have been detected.

Innovative evaluators currently are measuring other differentiated outcomes that go beyond the single (specific achievement) criterion, including: student alienation (in modular-scheduled and conventional middle schools); attitudes about internal-external (fate) control (as a result of a high school political education program); teacher ratings of student behavior (in a junior high prevocational program for problem students); tolerance of ambiguity (in a high school senior-year alternative program as contrasted to a conventional program); life skills—health, money management, and family life self-reported behaviors (among Puerto Rican and non–Puerto Rican students); reasoning ability (among students in a school-district-wide program using instruction based on behavioral objectives); and ability to complete an unfamiliar experiment (among students having access on a self-initiated basis or those not having this access to single-concept filmstrips). In each instance, in addition to the outcomes mentioned, other outcomes are chosen in an attempt to cover all five categories of the model and to go beyond the single criterion, which is usually included in each evaluation study.

Input Versus Process

Input refers to materials or experiences that the program developer or designer intends to operate in the classroom, the characteristics of the teachers who are charged with implementing them, and the characteristics of the students who will be exposed to them. *Process* refers to the level of implementation of these materials and experiences; that is, how they are employed by the teacher to teach students. In considering what these materials, experiences, or characteristics are or might be, we will treat them as inputs. When we consider the level of implementation of these inputs, we will be examining process.

Differentiating Between Inputs

The effectiveness of instruction is likely to be a function of: (1) *instructional program effects;* (2) *teacher effects;* (3) *student effects;* (4) *subject-matter effects;* and (5) *environment (or milieu) effects.* Typical educational evaluations include only one of these categories of variables as input and ignore the others. Instructional program evaluations should include a variable from at least a second of these categories and perhaps a third in order better to account for variation in outcomes. The degree to which these variables operate, while originally introduced as inputs, may be considered processes because they occur as the result of inputs and in turn influence the resulting outcomes. In order to know what they are evaluating, evaluators must examine the implementation of these inputs. The subsequent discussion will serve to elaborate on and illustrate these points. (The model is illustrated in Figure 3.2.)

Instructional Program Effects

Evaluations of instructional program effects are fairly common. However, the findings of those that result in no difference often go unreported. Some studies

I. Instructional Effects: Method of delivery of instruction

e.g., lecture, discussion, ITV, CAI, programmed text

II. Teacher Effects:

A. Behavior or style of teacher
e.g., directive-nondirective, high questioning-low questioning

B. Expectation or philosophy of teacher
e.g., humanistic-custodial, open-mindedness, close-mindedness

III. Student Effects: Characteristics of students

e.g., personality, attitudes/expectations, I.Q./ability/aptitude, prior knowledge, sex, grade level, background

IV. Subject-Matter Effects: Nature of course content

e.g., mathematics, biology, reading, art

V. Environmental Effects:

A. Classroom organizational arrangement
e.g., structured-unstructured, open-closed

B. Classroom physical arrangements
e.g., arrangement of desks, open space, interest centers

FIGURE 3.2   *A Model of Differentiated Inputs*

suggest that single-input evaluations, such as those that attempt to portray instructional TV as a better teacher than a live lecturer, or computer assistance as more salutory than programmed instruction, may fail to find substantial differences because such instructional procedures vary in effectiveness for different students or different situations or may differ in their level of implementation (Edwards et al. 1975). Evaluating instructional programs as an input may be most viable only if student variables also are considered. (This topic will be discussed in more detail under student effects.)

On the other hand, evaluations with primary interest in examining the effects of student characteristics on learning and achievement would do well also to consider instructional program effects. Domino (1968) has shown that student achievement motivation styles in and of themselves do not predict differential achievement but they do predict differential achievement in classrooms using different instructional programs.

The name of the instructional program or the label by which it is commonly referred to is not a sufficient description of it. The program must be described in terms of its intended operational characteristics. Then, in conducting the evaluation, the extent to which these intended characteristics are actually carried out can be determined (see chapter 6). On this basis, outcome results can be converted into potential program improvements. Instructional program evaluations must be considered not as evaluations of the quality of the *intended* program but as evaluations of the program as *implemented.*

Teacher Effects

Evaluations that have set out to examine instructional program or instructional materials effects occasionally have discovered that teacher effects accounted to a greater degree for the outcome. The famous "first-grade studies" (Bond and Dykstra 1967), which contrasted different procedures for teaching reading, yielded the finding that teacher differences were greater than differences in reading programs themselves.

However, Veldman and Brophy (1974) report that variation in student achievement is more completely explained by a *combination* of student effects (based on pretest scores) and teacher effects, and that the contribution of the teacher is "both statistically and practically significant."

Teacher effects depend on the style that the teacher employs, which manifests itself in how the teacher deals with issues of control, structure, and interpersonal relations in managing instruction and classroom dynamics. These effects will be influenced by the teacher's age, years of teaching experience, prior training, philosophy, and attitudes. Many of these characteristics can be determined in advance. The effects themselves, as operationalized, must be determined by observing the teacher in the classroom and seeing how he or she manages both the instructional and interpersonal aspects of teaching. How these determinations can be made is described in chapters 6 and 7.

Student Effects

The simultaneous consideration of student effects and each of the other types of effects described has been called for with strong emphasis. Cronbach (1975) offers the Aptitude × Treatment Interaction (ATI) approach as a way of including student effects (see also Cronbach and Snow 1977).* Hunt (1975) has been a modern pioneer in the person-environment interaction approach. His findings indicate that the effects of different environments are different for

---

* This approach considers the outcomes of instruction, typically posttest scores, to be a simultaneous function of: (1) what students bring with them to the situation (such as pretest scores, intelligence, learning styles); and (2) the nature of the instructional treatment or approach.

different students. Two evaluative studies will illustrate this point in more detail.

Domino (1971) had instructors teach a psychology course in two ways: first, in a "conforming" way through lectures, with emphasis on factual knowledge, classroom attendance, and textbook assignments; second, in an "independent" way with emphasis on ideas and active participation. (His treatments seem to be a combination of most of the other types of effects enumerated in this chapter.) To include student effects, students were classified as either high in Achievement-via-Conformance or high in Achievement-via-Independence, as measured by the *California Psychological Inventory* (Gough 1957). Assigning students to conditions was made so as to equalize other potential student effects.

Domino obtained significant interactions on five of his seven dependent variables (multiple-choice achievement test results, factual knowledge ratings of essay results, student evaluations of teacher, student evaluations of the course, and course grade). On each variable, outcomes in the courses taught in a conforming way were higher for students high in achievement-via-conformance, whereas outcomes in the courses taught in an independent way were higher for students high in achievement-via-independence. Thus, while Domino did *not* find that one style of teaching was better than the other for all students, he did find that each type was better for those students having a learning style similar to that teaching style.

The second illustrative evaluation study (Tuckman and Orefice 1973) compared four instructional procedures for teaching a unit on junior college accounting: self-instruction via tapes and booklets, programmed instruction within a classroom setting, programmed instructions and lectures in a classroom, and traditional lecture-discussion instruction. Students were classified as either abstract or concrete in terms of how they indicated they normally dealt with problems of control, ambiguity, and interpersonal conflict. Abstract students were found primarily to prefer self-study and to prefer least the lecture-programmed instruction combination; concrete students least preferred programmed instruction by itself and spent substantially less time on it than on the other procedures. Neither instructional program nor student personality alone or in combination affected achievement; they affected only attitudes and time spent. Note, however, that in this study the duration of the treatment was considerably less than in the Domino study.

Both evaluation studies convincingly convert a no-difference finding—considering the instructional program effect alone—into a significant finding by including a measure of student characteristics that allows treatment effects and student effects to be considered simultaneously.

Because of the potential strength of student effects on the outcomes of an evaluation, they cannot be disregarded. They must be either controlled for or systematically varied in order to assess their effect. In either event, the students' characteristics—including prior achievement or prior knowledge in the instructional program area, academic ability, and attitudes or learning style—should be measured and included in the evaluation design. The age or grade level of students also should be considered, since motivation effects, especially among young children, can be profound in and of themselves.

Subject-Matter Effects

What is effective for teaching one subject matter is not necessarily effective for teaching all subject matters. Few studies, however, contrast effects across subject matters to discover this interaction. Smith (1968), for example, found that instructional TV was more effective for teaching general botany at the college level than it was for teaching finite mathematics. There is considerable room for work on this type of effect in combination with other effects.

Recent work on learning in elementary school (Stallings 1976) has shown that whereas small-group instruction was more effective in teaching reading, large-group instruction was more effective in teaching mathematics. Thus, it could not be concluded that one type of grouping was superior to the other, without considering what was being taught.

Of course, there are many subdivisions within the general category of subject matter. Language arts, for example, can include something as factual and specific as grammar and something as general and abstract as literature. Perhaps a more important distinction than mere content is the distinction between teaching *facts* and teaching *concepts*.

Then, too, there is the question of the kinds of materials used in conveying subject matter to students. Materials can vary from print to visual to approaches using technology or kits and simulations. These kinds of inputs must be considered in terms of what is being evaluated as well as in terms of how the materials are used.

Environmental Effects

The climate of the classroom is an important component in the achievement formula. Evaluators and developers alike have a tendency to label and examine global concepts such as "open classroom" rather than attempting to distinguish between instructional program effects, teacher effects, and environmental effects. Hence, it is difficult to separate these effects in the literature.

Ward and Barcher (1975) had teachers complete a self-report instrument called the *Dimensions of Schooling* (Traub et al. 1972) describing the nature of the learning environment they engender (including physical environment, materials and activities, teacher role, structure for decision making). On the basis of their responses, teachers were classified as either "open" or "traditional."

Students were classified as either "high IQ" or "low IQ." They found that among low-IQ groups, students performed equally across traditional and open classrooms in both reading and creativity. However, among high-IQ groups, traditional teaching produced higher scores in both reading and figural creativity than did open teaching. The combination of environment and student effects, therefore, produced unique results, beyond those yielded by either effect alone.

Some instructional approaches specify the characteristics that the classroom environment should take; others do not. When evaluating programs that specify classroom environment, such as open classroom, a detailed description of the desired environment should be given. (See Case Study 1, Appendix A, for an example of this.) This description constitutes the environment or milieu input system. Whether this described input system is converted into process— that is, whether the requirements are implemented as specified—must be determined within the evaluation. Again, the purpose of the evaluation is not just to determine whether the input system is effective but to discover ways of making the input system achieve its potential. Even though the next chapter presents evaluation designs, one design will be offered here. This unique design allows the evaluator to consider three input variables simultaneously in order to determine both their separate and combined effects. When this is the purpose, the design shown in Figure 3.3 should be used.

To the extent possible, the following input suggestions should be followed:

1. Study at least two and possibly three sources of influences simultaneously
2. Manipulate as many of the sources of influences as possible, rather than allowing them to operate under their own control
3. The sources of influence not studied should at least be controlled

	Instructional Program 1		Instructional Program 2	
	Teacher Type A	*Teacher* Type B	*Teacher* Type A	*Teacher* Type B
Student Type X				
Student Type Y				

FIGURE 3.3 *A Sample Design for Evaluating Three Input Systems at the Same Time*

4. The level of implementation—that is, the degree to which each input system is operating as intended—should be carefully examined in the evaluation; this is the process of the instructional approach.

Determining Process or Level of Implementation

Another reasonable supposition is that *the "treatment" group will not differ in outcome from the "control" or "comparison" group unless the former represents a different set of inputs from the latter.* (Moreover, it is not likely that a program will achieve its intended outcomes unless its planned inputs are satisfactorily implemented.) To categorize a group of classrooms as "open," for example, on an a priori basis because a school system has so categorized them, and then to compare them to a group of classrooms categorized as "traditional" on the basis that they have been excluded from the first group leaves much room for variability in "openness" among both groups. Suppose that about one-third of each group were in fact functioning more like the other group than like their own. This variability probably would obscure any real differences in outcome between the two approaches in question. It also would block the so-called "open" approach from achieving its objectives.

To eliminate or minimize this problem, evaluators are encouraged to determine the level of implementation of the approaches. That is, they should observe and measure the *process* operating in both sets of classrooms in order to be assured that there is a real operational distinction between treatments before comparing possible overlapping instances and thereby obtaining "no differences." Lewin, Lippitt, and White (1939), in their classic evaluation of leadership styles, observed and recorded leader behaviors to assure themselves that democratic, autocratic, and laissez-faire leaders were behaving according to the "rule book" that described the three climates.

The fact that a school district has designated a group of classrooms as fitting a new approach and another group as not fitting it does not necessarily mean that critical inputs as implemented will differ sufficiently between the two sets to insure an adequate comparison of real treatment and no-treatment effects.

Since categories of input rarely operate alone, we must build more complex evaluations that take inputs in combination in order to begin to account for variations in the outcomes examined. Moreover, we must take steps to be certain that processes carried out in classrooms in fact fit the labels and specifications that have been set for them. We must consider the many kinds and categories of input that are likely to affect student outcomes and deal with as many as possible. This means that input systems must be described in sufficient detail so that their level of implementation can be determined.

CHAPTER 4

Different Kinds of Evaluation Design

Design Considerations

The purpose of evaluation is to determine how closely an outcome fits or approximates a desired goal state. Because it is so difficult to prespecify desired levels of goal states, evaluations such as the summative and ex post facto ones are accomplished on a relative basis. These summative and ex post facto evaluations proceed by answering the question: Does the program being evaluated accomplish its purposes better than alternative ways to achieve the same end? To implement this approach to instructional program evaluation, the model shown in Figure 4.1 can be applied.

An attempt should be made to maximize both the certainty and generality of the results. *Certainty* is the degree to which you can be sure that learner outcomes have indeed been caused by program inputs. It is important because its absence will lead to faulty or invalid conclusions. *Generality* is the degree to which the results of your evaluation will hold on other occasions. It is important because you want to make decisions on the basis of the evaluation and have them apply to subsequent tryouts of the program in the same and other locations.

How to Maximize the Degree to Which Results Have:

In terms of the:	*Certainty*	*Generality*
Program experiences studied	Use a control or comparison group	Minimize student's awareness of experimentation and evaluation (keep conditions as normal as possible)
Students studied	Establish initial equivalence between groups compared on pretest	Select students who are a representative sample of population
Teachers involved	Have comparable teachers teach treatment and comparison groups	Select teachers who are representative of teaching staff

FIGURE 4.1   *Rules to Follow in Designing a Valid Evaluation*

In order to maximize certainty, outcomes from the instructional program to be evaluated should be compared to outcomes (on the same measures) from alternative programs. (This is true in summative and ex post facto evaluation but not in formative evaluation, which attempts only to get the program on target, not to demonstrate its relative superiority or inferiority to alternatives.) This requirement is to assure that *the desired outcomes would not be as likely to have occurred anyway,* even in the absence of special instructional experiences being evaluated. As will be seen later in this chapter, various alternatives may be chosen for comparison purposes in order to satisfy this requirement.

Certainty also depends on students and teachers in both the target program and comparison program being equivalent. This second requirement is to assure that *differences found between target and comparison programs were truly a function of programs and not of students (or teachers) participating in the two programs.* If students in the two programs were not equivalent initially, outcome differences might result from these initial differences. Later in the chapter, procedures for equating target and alternative groups will be described.

In order to maximize *generality,* students (and teachers) participating in both program and comparison groups should be of like background to the total student (and teacher) population of the district. Descriptive characteristics can be compared for the sample (students and teachers in the evaluation) and the population (those not in the evaluation) to insure equivalence. In addition, the fact that a program is "experimental" or that an evaluation is in progress should not be advertised; awareness of the evaluation may alter the outcomes of study. Subsequent program offerings will not be subject to these influences and will yield different outcomes if the evaluative outcome has been unduly influenced by students' or teachers' reaction to the "experiment." This rule must govern the mechanics of carrying out both the program itself and your evaluation of it.*

Units and Levels

For analysis purposes, the *unit* is the *student*. Even though program evaluation does not focus on students, the results of individual students constitute the raw material of analysis, what is analyzed. Interpretive interest, however, focuses not on the unit of analysis but on the *level of comparison*. The level of comparison refers to what is being compared to what. Various levels of comparison are recommended for consideration, depending on the evaluation design being used. These levels of comparison are:

1. *Classroom:* Classrooms receiving the target program can be compared to classrooms not receiving the program; since the classroom is the typical level of delivering the education programs, it can serve well as a level of comparison.
2. *Grade level:* When a program spans an entire grade level, the grade level can be the level of comparison; moreover, developmental trends can be detected by comparing across grade levels.
3. *Class:* Students who enter school at the same time constitute a class (the class of 1975, for example). The year of entry makes a convenient class designation. When some classes experience a program and others do not, an obvious basis for comparison exists. (A class also can be identified by year of testing.)
4. *Building.* School buildings using a particular program can be compared to buildings not using that program.
5. *District:* A district using a program can be compared to one or more districts not using that program.

Evaluation Designs

Ex Post Facto Evaluation

Again, it must be emphasized that evaluation designs are used in both summative and ex post facto evaluation. That is, designs are used to assure certainty and generality among evaluations undertaken to compare alternatives. Forma-

---

* For a more complete discussion of certainty (internal validity) and generality (external validity), see Tuckman, B. W., *Conducting educational research,* 2d ed., New York: Harcourt Brace Jovanovich, 1978; and Campbell, D. T., and Stanley, J. C., *Experimental and quasi-experimental designs,* Chicago: Rand-McNally, 1963.

tive evaluation (discussed in chapter 9) is done to put outcomes on target, whereas summative evaluation (chapter 10) and ex post facto evaluation (chapter 11) seek to demonstrate the quality of given programs in contrast to alternative ones.

Three evaluation designs will be presented. Each succeeding design has a higher degree of certainty than the preceding one(s), but each succeeding design requires more resources to carry out. Each design assumes that both outcomes (and their measurement) and inputs have already been specified. (The practical application of these designs is shown in chapter 11 and in Case Study 3, Appendix A.)

Longitudinal Design. The term "longitudinal" refers to following or examining changes over time. If a change in performance occurs, if it persists over time, and if its occurrence coincides with the introduction of the program to be evaluated, then there is a degree of certainty that the program is responsible for the change. If the change is a positive one, then the program must receive a positive evaluation. Hence, one approach to evaluation is to follow the progress of a class of students from grade to grade to see if their performance improves beyond that normally expected from maturation.

It is important to remember that student performance will improve from grade to grade as students progress. The appearance of more than normal gains coinciding with the advent of the program indicates program success. Of course, one cannot exactly project the size of the gains to expect, although certain testing companies will provide this information in conjunction with their reports of standardized achievement test scores.

A simple longitudinal design is diagrammed in Figure 4.2.

Scores on any of the output measures described earlier can be examined by using a longitudinal design. Its strength is its simplicity. Its weaknesses are: (1) the difficulty in distinguishing program gains from maturational gains, since this design is carried out along years and during this time students are improv-

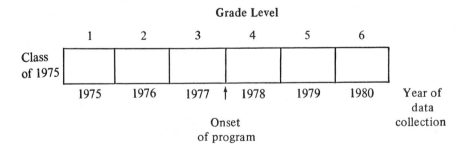

FIGURE 4.2 The Longitudinal Design (as applied for illustration to students who entered first grade in 1975.)

ing through maturation; and (2) the difficulty in determining whether a specific program is responsible for gains if that program did not begin near the middle of the testing sequence (it would be hard to tell if the outcomes might not have happened anyway even if the new program had not been introduced). We can look back at data (this is ex post facto), but unless our data extend back beyond the beginning of a "new" program, we have little hope of establishing certainty in our evaluation. Pre-program data are helpful for comparison purposes, that is, to establish a baseline.

If the evaluation extends over a short period (such as a single school year) during which time the program has been operative, the short "longitudinal" design becomes a formative evaluation. It lacks certainty because we cannot be sure that the program being evaluated is responsible for the outcomes. Even though gains may be obtained from pretest to posttest, without a comparison group we have little way of assuring ourselves that the program caused the change in outcome. It might have happened anyway. The longitudinal design yields results that can be attributed to the program through the preceding and succeeding years of pretesting and posttesting. (However, formative evaluation results can be used to help put a program on target or to keep it there.)

Cross-Sectional Design. Often it is inconvenient to make observations over time and difficult to separate maturation gains for program gains. These difficulties can be overcome by looking retrospectively at a number of classes at the same grade level. Rather than holding class constant and varying grade level, as in the longitudinal design, the cross-sectional design holds grade level constant and varies the class. This can be done by reconstructing the past (ex post facto) and requires that *data are available on classes before the installation of the program.* This design is shown in Figure 4.3.

The cross-sectional design also has some weaknesses. Its main weakness is the difficulty of separating program gains from gains based on other inputs, since a lot is happening in a district. Also, it must be assumed in using this de-

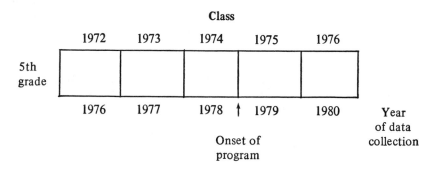

FIGURE 4.3 *The Cross-Sectional Design (illustrated at the fifth-grade level)*

sign that students in each class were equivalent. This assumption can be tested by comparing earlier test scores or by comparing mental ability test scores.* In this way, you can increase certainty by determining whether students studied in the program are equivalent to students they are compared to (see Figure 4.1).

Let us consider a specific instance of the cross-sectional evaluation design. A district and a state have been using a particular statewide achievement test for the past six years. Six years ago, the district also introduced computer-assisted instruction in mathematics for remediation at the fifth-grade level. The district now compares its results in math achievement on the statewide test for fifth grades across the past six years. (Each year a different class of students experiences fifth grade.) It compares itself to statewide results as well. The results of this example are graphically shown in Figure 4.4. They show a dramatic and progressive decrease in below-average performance and a similar increase in above-average performance by classes following the onset of the program being evaluated. Given the relative equivalence of classes statewide, as shown in the figure, the program seems to have had quite a positive effect on achievement in mathematics. The cross-sectional approach allows us to identify this improvement without having to separate maturationally induced gains from gains caused by the program. It is, therefore, a relatively simple yet potent procedure for ex post facto evaluation.

Combined Longitudinal–Cross-Sectional Design. The longitudinal and cross-sectional designs can be combined to yield a more comprehensive design that extends over both grades and classes and hence more accurately fits the pattern of program implementation in a school district. This design represents the most complete ex post facto analysis of system outcomes. It is diagrammed in Figure 4.5. An alternative way to lay out the same design is shown in Figure 4.6.

This design appears to be quite complex. It can be simplified by looking at the gains made by each class over grade levels and comparing them to one another from before the onset of the program to after the onset of the program. It also is possible, but less accurate, to pool the results across classes from before program onset and compare it to the pooled results after program onset. Comparing gain scores (longitudinal effects) of the different classes (cross-sectional effects) has the advantage of controlling for the different threats to certainty shown in Figure 4.1. Using gain scores controls for initial student differences, and comparing classes allow a comparison of pre-program effects to post-program effects. Thus, the combined design overcomes the weaknesses of each design used separately. However, it requires a considerable backlog of data both before and after program onset.

---

* A sophisticated approach is to use an analysis of covariance with earlier achievement test or mental ability test scores as the covariates.

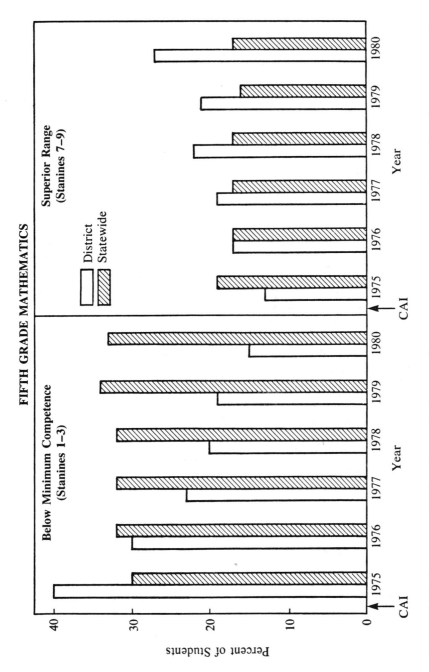

FIGURE 4.4 *Percentages of fifth graders in the district and statewide scoring in the bottom three and top three stanines on the statewide mathematics test from 1975 to 1980 (computer-assisted instruction was introduced in 1975).*

47

	1972	1973	1974	1975	**Class** 1976	1977	1978	1979	1980
1					1976	1977	1978	1979	1980
2				1976	1977	1978	1979	1980	
3			1976	1977	1978	1979	1980		
4		1976	1977	1978	1979	1980			
5	1976*	1977	1978	1979	1980				

Grade Level (rows 1–5)

Program onset ↑

* Dates in cells indicate the year in which data were collected.

FIGURE 4.5 *The Longitudinal–Cross–Sectional Design*

Applying variations of this design is illustrated in detail in Case Study 3 in Appendix A. This application is done retrospectively in cases in which the same achievement test has been administered over a five-year period. Improvement across grade levels (the longitudinal effect) is expected based on maturation at the rate of about one grade equivalent year per year of school. Improvement across testing years should occur after the program has been instituted. The analysis also will show whether the program is differentially effective at different grade levels, suggesting strengths and weakness inherent in the program, its implementation, or the school district.

	Grade Level 1	2	3	4	5
1972					1976
1973				1976	1977
1974			1976	1977	1978
1975		1976	1977	1978	1979
1976	1976	1977	1978	1979	1980
1977	1977	1978	1979	1980	
1978	1978	1979	1980		
1979	1979	1980			
1980	1980*				

Class (rows 1972–1980)

Program onset →

* Dates in cells indicate the year in which data were collected.

FIGURE 4.6 *Another View of the Longitudinal–Cross–Sectional Design*

This evaluation model maximizes the ex post facto approach. It is especially useful to school administrators because it allows for a full rather than a partial implementation of the program and uses data on hand. However, school administrators are cautioned to be sure that the classes (i.e., entering classes across the program years) are of approximately equivalent mental ability in order to avoid introducing a bias. This point is illustrated in Case Study 3.

Summative Evaluation

The preceding designs have been ex post facto in nature. That is, they are done after the fact without any systematic attempt to withhold the program from any students in order to determine its effect. Such ex post facto evaluations are *more convenient* to complete and require *less control* and *less planning*. However, they provide *less certainty* than the summative approaches described in this section.

Designs. Summative approaches use the design shown in Figure 4.7.

In the basic summative design, one group receives the program while a second group receives some alternative program, usually what everyone would have received if the program to be evaluated had not been available. Students can be assigned to one of the two groups on a random basis (which is the preferred way to do it); however, existing registration and assignment procedures as well as timing often preclude this possibility. In this case, the program is given to *intact groups,* such as existing classrooms, buildings, or districts, and is withheld from other intact groups. (Choosing the intact groups randomly does not constitute true random assignment. True randomness requires individual random assignment.)

The use of a comparison group or groups is a control to assure that outcomes attained following the program are indeed a function of the program

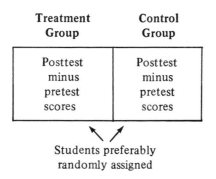

FIGURE 4.7 *Summative Evaluation Design*

and not of other events. In other words, the summative design uses so-called *treatment* and *control* groups to maximize *certainty* of the conclusion that the program makes a difference (as shown in the upper left-hand cell of Figure 4.1). Moreover, classrooms are selected to be representative of the schools and districts in which they occur in order to maximize the *generality* of the conclusion that the program makes a difference.

Student Assignment Bias. In the summative design in Figure 4.7, evaluation is accomplished by contrasting the treatment and control groups as shown. The evaluator is encouraged to employ assignment of *students* to conditions; when it is possible to assign students, it should be done randomly. This design also can be used with assignment of groups to conditions—a difference from assignment of students since we cannot be sure how students become assigned to classes in the first place (they may represent homogeneous ability groups, for example). The distinction between random assignment of students and assignment of intact groups affects the extent to which we can be *certain* that the students rather than the programs we have studied are not producing the differences. Bias in assignment affects certainty, as shown in Figure 4.1.

To examine the certainty that differences are due to programs and not to students, we must either: (1) randomly assign *students* to groups, thereby distributing all student differences relatively equally across groups; or (2) pretest students in our intact groups on outcome measures and compare their results to ascertain their initial equivalence. Other individual difference measures can and should be used as well. These relevant *control variables* are: (1) prior knowledge of what is to be taught (measured by a pretest or final exam given before instruction); (2) mental ability, measured by a mental ability or aptitude test; (3) prior academic achievement, measured by academic class standing, cumulative grade-point average, or by prior achievement test scores; (4) socio-economic status, measured by parents' income level, education, job status, or some combination of the three; (5) sex; and (6) age. Through the use of some of these measures, equivalence of groups should be determined.*

These general points apply to all summative designs. Three specific applications of the summative approach will be described below. In each case, the assumption will be made that the school district is not in a position to assign individual students to treatment and control groups but must rely on intact group comparisons—as is usually the case.

Between Classrooms. The summative design with the greatest potential certainty is done by making comparisons between classrooms in the same schools. This design is shown in Figure 4.8.

---

* Where equivalence is not found between treatment and control groups on a particular measure, it can be used as a covariate in an analysis of covariance to equalize groups statistically.

Students in classrooms who receive new programs	Students in classrooms who receive old programs

FIGURE 4.8 *Comparisons Between Classrooms*

The use of this design involves the following steps:

1. Identify classrooms in the school that will participate in the evaluation. Try to do this before the new program is introduced to these groups so that classrooms at the same grade level can be randomly assigned to the new or old program.
2. Administer a pretest to assure that students in classrooms in the two conditions are equally knowledgeable (or ignorant) in the content area of the program *prior* to their involvement in it. Obtain measures of mental ability and academic achievement as well, usually available from school records. Be sure that boys and girls are about equally represented in classrooms. (Dealing with pairs of classrooms at the same grade level will control for student age. Excluding or pairing homogeneously grouped classrooms should control for most individuals' differences.)*
3. After classrooms in the "experimental group" have experienced the program for a period of time that is expected to allow the realization of its outcomes (usually for approximately one school year), posttesting is done on the program objectives—extending insofar as possible across the outcome areas delineated in chapter 3.
4. Comparison between groups on outcome measures should be done statistically. Simple two-group comparisons can be done by t-test. More complex comparison procedures such as analysis of variance should be used when comparisons are to be made simultaneously across classrooms and grade levels.

Between Schools. The advantage of restricting comparisons to within schools is to eliminate the additional variability of the ways different schools

---

* Pairing here refers to pairing of classrooms and not to pairing of individual students.

operate and the different characteristics of the students and communities they serve. However, the decisions for program implementation are not made by the evaluator and usually fail to consider the needs and requirements of evaluation. In school districts, programs often are installed in all the same grade-level classrooms of a school building, thereby eliminating the possibility for establishing experimental and control classrooms in the same building. And since comparisons must be made at the same grade level to control for obvious maturation effects, control groups must be sought outside of the building in which the program has been implemented. The basic design for this comparison is shown in Figure 4.9.

The steps in using the between-school comparison are the same as in using the between-classroom comparison, with a greater emphasis on establishing equivalence of both the general program quality and student background in the schools being compared. In other words, in addition to establishing or demonstrating the equivalence of treatment and control students, the same must be done for treatment and control schools.

An illustration of this design would be to use three elementary schools in the same district. Two of the schools receive the treatment and the third is designated a control school. In such a comparison, we must be concerned about unique qualities of the treatment schools that are not present in the control school and that predispose the former to be a more likely medium for outcome attainment than the latter. Examining the original basis for the decision as to which school will receive the treatment is the best way to get some perspective on this issue. Making the school decision on a random basis is, of course, the most valid basis from the evaluation point of view, although perhaps the least valid from the political standpoint. (The socioeconomic status of the communities from which each school receives its students also can be compared.)

(The parallel in the between-classroom approach would be to have as-

Students in classrooms in buildings who receive new programs	Students in classrooms in buildings who receive old programs

FIGURE 4.9   Comparison Between Schools

Students in classroom in buildings in districts who receive new programs	Students in classroom in buildings in districts who receive old programs

FIGURE 4.10   *Comparison Between Districts*

signed the treatment to teacher volunteers or to preselected teachers who are more likely to succeed than other teachers. Any comparison between these classrooms and others obviously will reflect strong teacher differences over and above the program differences that are being evaluated. *From the evaluator's point of view, volunteerism is a source of bias and should be avoided.* Insofar as possible, the decision of which students, which classrooms, and which buildings are to receive the program should be made on a random basis.)*

Between Districts. When a program is implemented on a district-wide basis, summative evaluation is possible only by making comparisons between districts. (In these cases, the ex post facto approaches described in the first half of this chapter are a more convenient means of evaluation.) Because it is difficult to equate districts either in terms of student characteristics or program characteristics, this approach often imposes necessary limitations on certainty.

The basic design of this approach is shown in Figure 4.10. It is methodologically similar to the preceding summative designs, with an increased emphasis on establishing equivalence.

In implementing this approach, follow the same steps as previously outlined but focus on districts rather than buildings in the same district or classrooms in the same building. It will not be easy to get other districts to cooperate and serve as comparisons. Many districts will feel they have nothing to gain and everything to lose by serving in this capacity.

Identify districts that: (1) are of approximately the same size in student population at the grade levels in question; (2) spend approximately the same amount of money on each student (a control for program differences); and (3)

---

* Schools should be compared to establish equivalency in terms of such variables as their size, average years of teaching experience of their teachers, average mental ability or achievement levels of their students, and socioeconomic status of the communities they serve.

	Design	Strengths	Weaknesses
Ex Post Facto	*Longitudinal*	Controls for student differences since students are compared to selves. Easy to implement.	Fails to control for maturation (hard to judge what to expect). Hard to determine whether program is responsible for outcomes.
	Cross-sectional	Controls for maturation. Somewhat hard to distinguish program effects but less hard than with longitudinal.	Fails to control for student differences (since different classes are compared).
	Longitudinal Cross-sectional	Controls for both maturation and student differences. Greatest certainty of ex post facto designs.	Highly complicated. Requires extensive data. Difficult to analyze results.
Summative	*Between classrooms*	Has greatest potential certainty due to greatest potential control of non-program variables.	Has least generality. Often cannot be used because all classes experience treatment. Often involves volunteer teachers.
	Between schools	Allows for generality across schools. Provides high certainty if schools are equivalent.	May be difficult to enlist cooperation of "control school." Often involves volunteer teachers.
	Between districts	Allows for generality across districts. Provides high certainty if districts are equivalent.	Difficult to identify equivalent districts and to enlist their cooperation. Difficult to eliminate effects of other programs since districts are different.

FIGURE 4.11   *Summary of the Strengths and Weaknesses of the Various Designs*

have students of similar mental ability and academic attainments (a control for students' differences). Finding similar districts and soliciting their cooperation are both problematical.

Chapter 10 discusses summative designs from a more operational perspective.

Conclusion

This chapter has presented procedures for carrying out an instructional program evaluation. These procedures are called *designs* because they specify the comparisons to be made. Two basic approaches, ex post facto and summative, have been described (formative evaluation does not use comparisons other than with program objectives and will be covered in detail in chapter 9). Ex post facto evaluation designs are more convenient but yield less certainty than summative approaches. Since program implementation decisions often are made without evaluation in mind, an administrator or evaluator may have little choice in choosing a design. Administrators are encouraged to consider the requirements of instructional program evaluation before implementing the program so that better evaluation designs can be built in from the start. Doing this will enhance the ultimate value and credibility of the evaluation of a program.

A summary of the strengths and weaknesses of the various designs appears in Figure 4.11.

PART II

Measurement
and
Determination

CHAPTER 5

Specifying and Auditing Outcomes

Specific Knowledge and Comprehension

Description

Specific knowledge and comprehension (or achievement) is the major, and often all too exclusive, component of the school testing program. As pointed out in chapter 3, the school testing program must extend beyond this single area. Nevertheless, the measurement of specific achievement is still the backbone of school testing and can be better used in instructional program evaluation, as this book will illustrate.

Specific knowledge and comprehension refer to achievement testing, both the standardized, published achievement testing brought in from the outside and the combined teacher-built testing undertaken as part of normal course requirements. Thus, they refer to measurement of factual-oriented information generally acquired in basic subject-matter areas including and emphasizing the basic skills of reading and mathematics but also extending to language arts, science, and social studies. Such tests place a premium on recall.

Characteristics

The most important description of tests of specific knowledge and comprehension is that they are built around a given set of objectives. These objectives, set by the test writers, reflect what they feel a student should know and represent a guide to the content of the items. Tests that clearly represent or fit a set of objectives are called "appropriate" (Tuckman 1975). A test will be suitable for your purposes if it is appropriate for the set of objectives that *you want to measure*. Thus, a test can be appropriate for one use and not for another.

As mentioned in chapter 3, tests of specific knowledge and comprehension seem more appropriate for measuring the results of conventional instruction than for measuring the results of an unconventional approach, such as open classroom. To increase the appropriateness of measurement, other tests may be added. It is important to determine the appropriateness of a test for your purposes (that is, its fit to your objectives) before using it for instructional program evaluation.

Tests of specific achievement can be interpreted on either a *norm-referenced* or *criterion-referenced* basis. In norm referencing, a relative procedure, individual results are compared to group results, and outcomes are reported in terms of one's relative standing in the group. On a difficult test, low scores can still give one a high relative standing whereas an easier test demands higher scores for the same standing. In criterion referencing, an absolute procedure, individual results are reported in terms of number or percent of items or objectives answered correctly. On a more difficult test, individual performances decline; on an easier one, they go up. Norm-referenced test interpretation compensates for the ease or difficulty of a test, but it does not supply information on how much a student has learned, as criterion-referenced test interpretation does.

Uses

Norm-referenced tests are useful for *summative evaluation,* particularly because they have the standards of comparison built in. They also are helpful for *public information* value, that is, for informing parents about the outcomes of the instructional program. (This is, of course, above and beyond the use of these tests for individual reporting. Here we are talking about reporting of average results for classes, grade levels, schools, or the whole district.) Both summative evaluation and public information values are based on the high *credibility* of these published tests, in contrast to teacher-built tests. Published tests have high reliabilities and are not subject to local influence or bias.

Criterion-referenced testing, which lacks the built-in standard of comparison but instead has a direct instructional referent, is more useful for *formative evaluation* (as a group or district function) in addition to the individual functions of *diagnosis and prescription* and *monitoring student progress.* Criterion-referenced tests can be: (1) purchased from testing companies (this means either prescriptive tests or just criterion-referenced scoring of standardized achievement tests); (2) built from items obtained from item banks or exchanges (such as the Instructional Objectives Exchange at UCLA); or (3) constructed by teachers based on home-grown objectives.

Recommendations

1. Norm-referenced testing results should be used on a group or average basis for summative or ex post facto program evaluation by following these rules:
   a. Continue to use the same standardized achievement test battery over a five-year period to provide a basis for longitudinal analysis.
   b. Contrast the standardized achievement test objectives with district objectives to make sure they are compatible—if they are not, now is the time to switch tests.
   c. Examine trends in average scores over time and between grade levels simultaneously to see what kinds of changes are occurring. (This model is described in more detail in chapter 4, on designs, and chapter 11, on ex post facto evaluation, and is illustrated in Case Study 3, Appendix A.)
2. Use criterion-referenced testing for formative evaluation, with teachers writing the items if:
   a. Teachers are trained and assisted in item writing and articulate between one another, grade levels, and schools.
   b. Teachers and principals are willing to institute program changes based on the results, since that is what formative evaluation is all about (this approach is illustrated in chapter 9).
3. Use criterion-referenced testing for monitoring student progress only if your test objectives are ratified by teachers, indicating that the objectives represent what teachers are trying to teach.
4. Use criterion-referenced testing for individual diagnosis and prescription only if you have within your system instructional options to prescribe; if your instructional program is lockstep, do not bother to test for individual needs since you are not in a position to cater to them.

General Knowledge and Comprehension

Description

This category of measure refers to intelligence, mental ability, and aptitude tests. These tests differ from specific achievement tests by their generality. Specific achievement tests are linked to specific learning objectives and specific educational experiences, whereas tests of general knowledge and comprehension are much less situation-specific and refer to general verbal and mathematical ability. These two categories of tests use similar items and measure in similar areas; again, however, the difference is in terms of the link to specific school experiences.

Characteristics

Mental ability test scores of the verbal type begin to show stability at the fourth-grade level (whereas nonverbal scores stabilize at about seventh grade [Hopkins and Bracht 1975]). Moreover, these scores tend to correlate reasonably highly with success in school and hence can be thought of as predicting school success. Rather than eliminating such tests as biased, it would be reasonable to consider their use as predictive measures and diagnostic tools for further instruction.

Uses

Mental ability tests are not as useful for measuring outcomes in instructional program evaluation because of their relative stability and lack of clear connectedness to specifics of the educational program. However, they do provide a stable input or individual difference measure, which can be helpful in interpreting other outcome differences. Where specific achievement test score differences occur, for example, an examination of corresponding mental ability scores can help you tell whether these achievement differences are a function of program effects or of individual student effects. If these differences are based on what abilities the students "bring with them" to school, then program changes cannot be expected to ameliorate them easily. Such a stable individual difference measure is a *control* measure or *covariate*.

Recommendations

A general mental ability test should be included at about three points in the program (fifth grade, eighth grade, and eleventh grade), if testing is done in the fall, to reflect the results of fourth, seventh, and tenth grades.* A mental ability test coordinated to the standardized or specific achievement test program is recommended. The testing emphasis, at least in the early grades, should be on verbal ability. The value of this testing for instructional program evaluation as an individual difference measure has been discussed in the preceding chapter.

---

* Even though scores on these tests are relatively stable, certain aspects of what these tests measure do tend to develop and change as the result of schooling and maturation. Changes that do occur usually can be most readily detected at these growth points.

Its value is not as a specific educational program outcome measure but as a measure of developing student capability, which, because of its early stability, allows you to separate program effects from student effects (over which the district has little effect after the early grades). However, it also can be looked on as an outcome measure, albeit a somewhat stable one (see particularly Case Study 3, Appendix A).

Thinking and Problem Solving

Description

Measures of thinking and problem solving pose a *problem* for which the student is called on to provide a *solution.* In other words, rather than simply having to select or provide the right answer, the student must generate a solution to a problem, such as how to traverse an island, where to locate a city, or how to make a mechanical limb.

Problem-solving and thinking measures have two additional features. First, they require *transfer of prior learning* rather than recall of it. Students must do more than remember what they have learned; they must do something with it (application, analysis, synthesis, or evaluation, to use Bloom's 1956 terms). Hence, these measures deal to some degree with the *unfamiliar* in contrast to the familiar. When students can solve a problem using their memories, they will. *Problem-solving tasks must make solution by recall impossible.* Essay questions that test recall are not problem-solving measures.

Secondly, problem-solving measures include and emphasize the *means* or *process* used to obtain a solution itself. Not only is the answer important; how it was obtained and the logic behind it also are important. Consequently, we are not talking about typical short-answer tests. We are talking about something more akin to essay tests but perhaps more structured. At any rate, given the current state of the art, such measures must be home grown.

Characteristics

Such problem-solving measures differ markedly from standardized tests of special achievement in terms of administration and emphasis. They should not occur within severe time restrictions as regular classroom tests normally do. The "take-home exam" is a better model. The absence of time pressure eliminates reliance on recall and enhances the possibility of problem solving. In fact, rather than punishing the use of time, in problem solving time use should be rewarded as an indication of motivation and initiative.

Another restriction that must be eliminated is the requirement that resources not be used. The "open-book exam," on the other hand, rewards and reinforces the selective use of resource material in the service of problem solving, thus breaking the reliance on recall.

Overall, when taking a problem-solving test, students should not be told when, where, and how to proceed but should be rewarded for making these decisions on their own. Time spent, resources used, and initiative taken for problem completion, plus the quality of process (means) and product (solution), should constitute the performance evaluation criteria.

Uses

Most teachers tend to agree that teaching students thinking and problem solving is one of their most significant objectives. Moreover, thinking and problem-solving objectives (often called "higher cognitive") usually are found among any set of program objectives. Nevertheless, thinking and problem solving are rarely, if ever, measured in any instructional program evaluation. Perhaps this occurs because thinking and problem-solving measures generally are not commercially available and home-grown varieties lack outside credibility. However, such measures will have to be developed or refined if higher cognitive objectives are to remain in the curriculum.

As discussed in chapter 3, thinking and problem-solving measures have been linked to unconventional instruction. They clearly supplement the specific knowledge and comprehension measures in providing a more complete picture of program outcomes.

Recommendations

Since teachers must be relied on to construct thinking and problem-solving measures, and since these measures must possess adequate reliability and validity for program evaluation purposes, it is necessary to provide teachers with some in-service assistance in the construction of these measures. Most teachers have not had much training in test construction, and good thinking and problem-solving tests are not easy to construct. This training also should include problems of scoring, since these tests are difficult to score reliably. Specific scoring rules and standards must be constructed in order to objectify scoring to the greatest degree possible.

Thinking and problem solving represent a complex area, and performance requirements extend to the limit of our knowledge of cognitive functioning. Constructing measures and interpreting results would be enhanced by an understanding of major models of cognition, such as that provided by Bloom's (1956) taxonomy or Piaget's stages (Piaget 1952). In-service training in these areas or appropriate college coursework would be helpful.

Attitudes and Values

Description

We now shift from the *cognitive* domain to the *affective* domain. Measures in this area deal with how students *feel* about such things as themselves, school, and various topical areas (such as drugs, mathematics, a particular class, people of other backgrounds). As legitimate concerns of the educational program, attitudes and values require measurement if the program is to be evaluated. Evaluation of general school satisfaction or of particular outcomes of affective education requires affective measurement.

Attitudes and values refer to people's subjective orientation toward (that is, liking or disliking of) different people, objects, or events. These feelings can be measured by scales that provide attitude or value statements related to some topic that students are asked to indicate their *acceptance* or *rejection* of. Since feelings are a subjective state, our primary access to them is through the subjective responses of people.

Characteristics

Three major points about the measurement of affective outcomes must be made. First, such tests are *scored in conformance with prevailing social norms.* There are no right or wrong answers to attitude items; to score them, however, one response must be predesignated as the most acceptable one. (Actually, responses usually are scaled from most to least acceptable.) This predesignation is based on what the attitude scale explicitly measures, with the more socially acceptable pole considered the positive. Hence, the "right" answers in an attitudes toward school measure, for example, would express positive attitudes toward school.

Second, by virtue of their subjectivity and emphasis on social norms, *responses on attitude tests are subject to distortion.* Whether consciously or unconsciously, students sometimes make the socially desirable response to show themselves or perceive themselves in the most positive light. Such social desirability bias unavoidably reduces the validity of such tests.

Third, *attitude measurement often touches socially sensitive areas and may provoke public reaction.* Parents often endorse affective goals without truly realizing their nature. The consequences of their endorsement become more apparent at measurement time. Be prepared for some initial adverse reaction to affective testing.

Uses

All education has affective components, however nonexplicit. Two major affective goals of the general education program are that students shall *like them-*

selves and *like school.* In order to find out whether these general, ubiquitous goals are being achieved, attitude measurement must be employed. In higher education, measures of satisfaction have become commonplace. Their general use at lower levels has been rare. However, if instructional program evaluation is to include reference to goals of school liking and self-esteem, then attitude tests are unavoidable.

In many programs, specific attitude development is the target of focus. Social studies, for example, is relevant to the attempt to increase positiveness of student attitudes toward citizenship and participatory democracy. Reduction or elimination of ethnic, racial, or sex bias also is a target. Career programs usually attempt to improve attitudes toward craftsmanship and increase career maturity. Even at early grades, improving attitudes toward participation often is a goal. Where such goals exist, they must be measured—by affective tests.

Recommendations

Two recommendations about the measurement of attitudes and values will be made. The first is: **DO IT!** Live dangerously, but relevantly; where affective goals occur, measure them as part of your instructional program evaluation. Not to do so would be to do a less than complete job. You may be selling your program short otherwise.

The second recommendation is to find attitude tests, where possible, rather than trying to build them. Another source lists many compendia of such tests as well as explicit instructions on how to construct them (Tuckman 1975). Two particular sources worth singling out are: (1) the Instructional Objectives Exchange at UCLA (Box 24095, Los Angeles, California 90024), which publishes booklets of tests of attitudes toward self and toward school; and (2) the Educational Goal Attainment Tests published by Phi Delta Kappa,* which include many attitude scales in a multitude of areas for program evaluation at grades seven to twelve.

Learning-Related Behavior

Description

Students' attendance records; work habits; degrees of self-control, hostility, initiative, creativity, and so on, are all examples of learning-related behaviors. We are aware of, and concerned about, student behavior and "motivation" as major determinants and indicators of educational growth but seem not to build

---

* In fairness to the reader, it must be noted that I am an author of these tests and, hence, am partial to them.

these into our instructional program evaluations. Such behavior is an obvious area of inclusion and, in fact, is typically measured by schools under the rubric of "deportment." Most report cards are filled with it, particularly at the elementary level, and many school districts require teachers to make such ratings for the permanent records. (An illustration of the measurement of learning-related behavior is found in Case Study 1, Appendix A, under the heading "Self-Discipline." This instrument itself also appears at the end of the study.)

Characteristics

It may be argued that learning-related behaviors represent important prerequisites to the kinds of learning previously covered, and that their omission would represent a serious oversight. However, their mere inclusion is not enough, because such subjective judgments by teachers are extremely sensitive to bias and distortion by the rater. Teachers usually are given no specific instructions on what the behaviors look like or how they are to be judged. Leaving each teacher to formulate his or her own definitions and rules encourages idiosyncratic ratings that may reflect the teacher's set or predisposition more than the student's acts. Hence, behavioral information is relevant and often available, but its reliability under present circumstances of collection is in serious question.

Other than asking teachers to report on student behaviors, these behaviors can be reported on by the students themselves. (Such measurement of student behavior is used in the Educational Goal Attainment Tests, mentioned earlier as a practical way of getting this information.) Keep in mind that self-judgments of behavior fall heir to the same sources of distortion as do self-reports of attitudes (described in the preceding section).

Uses

The uses of the measurement of learning-related behaviors are threefold. First of all, such measurement is necessary to *determine whether those behaviors deemed necessary by teachers are occurring.* If the objectives of an instructional program include some that apply to behavior, then the systematic measurement of that behavior is the only way to determine whether such objectives are being met.

Second, the systematic measurement of student behavior may help to *increase the sensitivity of teachers to behavior.* In other words, they will become more aware of exactly how students behave and under what circumstances.

Third, such measurement can potentially help make teachers *more effective measurers.* It is important that teachers separate their roles of shaper of student behavior and recorder of student behavior insofar as possible. Behavioral measurement, of course, calls on teachers to serve as recorders of student behavior, a role at which they are perhaps less adept and for which they have been less well trained.

Recommendations

Again, three points are offered that are intended to improve behavioral measurement, assuming that there are student behavior goals to be measured. First, teachers must be called on to *provide the greatest degree of specificity possible* in describing desired student behaviors. Rather than saying just "cooperative," teachers must say "assists the teacher when called on to do so," "helps classmates when asked," "follows directions when given," and so on. The likelihood of accurate measurement increases as specificity increases.

Second, better and more complete instruments for measuring student behavior must be developed. It is not sufficient to provide merely a list of behavior words for teachers to use. Phrases and sentences, better than words, are needed; and they should be accompanied by the kinds of specification called for above. Districts probably will have to construct these kinds of measures themselves. Make sure to include a well-defined scale for teachers to report the degree to which the desired behavior or its antithesis occurred.

Third, teachers must *receive training as observers.* Reliable observation by observers requires training. They must discuss and agree on what they are looking for and how they can tell if and to what degree it occurs. Then they should observe together (using intervisitation or training video tapes) and compare judgments. Only through repetitions of the discussion-observation-discussion cycle can they develop skills of reliability and consistency.

Specifying and Measuring Outcomes

The first step in instructional program evaluation is *specification* of the outcomes to be measured. This means preparing the measurable objectives that constitute the goals of the program to be evaluated. This list should be prepared by program developers and teachers together, with an emphasis on completeness and acceptability. Moreover, *an effort should be made to include objectives in all of the five outcome areas described here.* The more detailed and complete the specification of outcomes is, the easier each succeeding step will be.

No attempt will be made here to provide guidelines for the second step, item writing, since they are available elsewhere.* However, chapters 9, 10, and

---

* See *Measuring Educational Outcomes: Fundamentals of Testing* (Tuckman 1975) for a complete and detailed description of specific item writing rules and guidelines in the various outcome areas.

11 of this book describe district strategies and a timetable for developing and using tests for instructional program evaluation. Hence, discussion and description of this highly operational step will be deferred until the last section of this book. But it is important to reemphasize that objectives must be prepared before the items are written.

The third step involves creating evaluation designs. Models for such designs were described in detail in the preceding chapter and so need not be discussed here.

This chapter, so far, has attempted to show instructional program evaluators that the essential considerations should be the specification and measurement of intended program outcomes. No evaluation can proceed without deciding on desired program objectives and developing or finding an appropriate means for their measurement. Much of the measurement may be currently available within existing district measurement practices, as this chapter has pointed out. Paying attention to the guidelines for choosing measures offered in this chapter can help the program evaluator keep the process *maximally on target.*

Deciding what is to be measured is a first step—represented by the preparation of objectives. These objectives should span the five outcome areas if your instructional program is indeed multifaceted. Once you have decided what to measure, you are faced with the task of measuring it. To assist you in this regard, an auditing system has been designed and is described next. For efficiency of discussion, the fivefold outcome categorization will be collapsed to three.

Auditing and Evaluating Program Outcomes

Let us assume that objectives have been specified in each of the three major outcome areas, namely: (1) *knowledge* (achievement of specific knowledge and comprehension); (2) *higher cognitive* (mental ability, thinking, problem solving); and (3) *affective* (attitudes and behavior). This, of course, is a necessary first step. Let us also assume that measuring instruments either have been located or designed for measuring each of these categories of objectives, which, as we have seen, is a second step. Thirdly, let us trust that an evaluation design has been chosen and/or appropriate procedures established for generating comparison or criterion data. (More on these steps is presented in chapters 9, 10, and 11 in conjunction with the operational guidelines for the different types of evaluation.)

We now are ready to proceed with the evaluation using the *audit* procedure described below. The purpose of the audit procedure is to report achieved outcomes and to place these side-by-side with intended outcomes to determine the degree of instructional program success. This purpose is most easily ac-

Measure	Achieved group score	Comparison or criterion score	Increment or decrement
Reading Total			
Vocabulary			
Comprehension			
Language arts			
Total			
Structure			
Usage			
Spelling			
Mathematics			
Computation			
Concepts			
Application			
Science			
Social studies			
_____			
_____			
_____			
_____			
_____			

FIGURE 5.1   *Specific Achievement Output Audit Form*

complished through the use of audit forms, such as appear in Figures 5.1 and 5.2. These forms are to be considered samples because instructional program objectives will vary to some extent from district to district. (Lines also have been left open in each form to add further objectives.)

Specific Achievement

The sample *Specific Achievement Output Audit Form* shown in Figure 5.1 has been designated to accommodate the achievement categories measured by most published achievement tests. A finer breakdown of objectives has not been provided because information at too great a level of specificity makes drawing conclusions difficult. That is, the more detailed the analysis of target areas, the more demanding the requirement for synthesis in drawing conclusions.

In Figure 5.2, a copy of the *Specific Achievement Output Form* appears with numbers entered to illustrate the application of the form. Results for all

Measure	Achieved Group Score[1]	Comparison or Criterion Score[2]	Increment or Decrement
Reading Total	5.21	4.94	+0.27
Vocabulary	5.14	4.96	+0.18
Comprehension	5.49	5.14	+0.35
Language Arts			
Total	5.62	5.23	+0.39
Structure	6.14	5.33	+0.81*
Usage	5.39	5.00	+0.39
Speech	5.68	5.52	+0.16
Mathematics			
Total	5.42	5.21	+0.21
Computation	5.57	5.36	+0.21
Concepts	5.42	5.18	+0.24
Application	5.00	4.82	+0.18
Science	*Not Tested*		
Social studies	*Not Tested*		
Study skills	5.27	5.16	+0.11
Total battery	5.38	5.16	+0.22

[1] This year's sixth graders
[2] Last year's sixth graders
*Probability that this is a chance difference is less than .05

FIGURE 5.2 *Specific Achievement Output Audit Form Illustrated for Sixth Graders in a Sample School District (Grade Equivalent Scores on a Published Test of Basic Skills Achievement)*

sixth graders in a school district are shown under "achieved group score." (The process was applied to all twelve grade levels and it is possible to make out forms for each grade level, but only one appears here for illustration.) In using this approach, you would fill out separate forms or separate entries for each grade level on each category of specific achievement objectives.

The "comparison" column in Figure 5.2 shows the results from the sixth-grade glass of the previous year. In the interim period, the school district adopted a new instructional approach and wished initially to evaluate its short-term impact on basic skills. Using prior results at the same grade level, as in Figure 5.2, is an application of the *cross-sectional design*—one of the ex post

Measure	Achieved group score	Comparison or criterion score	Increment or decrement
Mental ability— total			
Mental ability— verbal			
Mental ability— nonverbal			
Application skills			
Analysis skills			
Synthesis skills			
Evaluation skills			
Total problem solving			

FIGURE 5.3 *General Achievement (above dashed line) and Thinking and Problem Solving (below dashed line) Output Audit Form*

facto designs described in chapter 11 (and in Case Study 3, Appendix A).* Any of the designs described in chapters 9, 10, and 11 can be used for generating comparison data.

The important points to keep in mind in auditing outcomes in the specific achievement area are that: (1) outcomes to be achieved in specific cognitive areas have been specified as objectives; (2) procedures for their measurement have been identified; (3) this measurement then has been carried out to yield outcome data; (4) comparison data have been collected through the use of an evaluation design; and (5) program and comparison data have been laid side-by-side and discrepancies have been noted. On the basis of these discrepancies (and the results of the input survey described in the next chapter) ameliorative and improvement efforts could be undertaken.

---

* We also might have looked at actual gain versus expected gain if we were using the longitudinal design described in chapter 11.

Measure	Achieved Group Score[1]	Comparison or Criterion Score[2]	Increment or Decrement
Mental ability— total	98.7[3]	99.1	−0.4
Mental ability— verbal	96.4	97.0	−0.6
Mental ability— nonverbal	101.0	101.2	−0.2
Application skills	71.4[4]	70.3	+1.1
Analysis skills	69.8	68.8	+1.0
Synthesis skills	65.4	65.5	−0.1
Evalutation skills	70.2	70.0	+0.2
Total problem solving	69.2	68.6	+0.6

[1] This year's sixth graders
[2] Last year's sixth graders
[3] IQ deviation score
[4] Percentage score

FIGURE 5.4   *General Achievement (on a Mental Ability Test) and Problem Solving (on a Homemade Essay Test) Output Audit Form Illustrated for Sixth Graders in a Sample School District*

General Achievement

The top half of Figure 5.3 shows the output audit procedure for general achievement based on scores on a mental ability test. Results on the test are reflected in the completed form in Figure 5.4. The rough equivalence of the program group and the comparison group on a characteristic as stable as mental ability or intelligence testifies that any differences obtained in specific achievement are based on program effects and not on ability differences between groups. Had the groups not been found to be equivalent on intellectual outcomes, these mental ability differences would have to be considered in evaluating specific achievement results. Without pretest data, it would be difficult to know whether mental ability differences preceded the program or were the result of it.

The principal purpose of the general achievement audit is more to establish or reinforce equivalence of mental ability input (by not changing, mental ability input and output become indistinguishable) than to identify differential program effects. However, it would be better to conduct this audit at entry into the program rather than on exit from it to be sure that the differences precede the program.

Thinking and Problem Solving

The bottom halves of Figures 5.3 and 5.4 show the blank output audit form and completed form, respectively, for higher cognitive outcomes. These outcomes have been labeled using levels three to six of Bloom's Taxonomy (Bloom 1956). Where more specific higher cognitive objectives are available, these can be placed in the audit form in lieu of the broader categories presented. As mentioned before, there are no all-purpose tests currently available to measure these categories of thinking and problem solving, but we will assume that individual tests have been built or located by the district.*

In Figure 5.5, an alternative set of categories for specifying thinking and problem-solving outcomes has been provided, based on the conceptual approach for teaching social studies developed by Hilda Taba (Taba 1974). In either case, obtained outcomes on a program group are compared to a criterion or comparison group results and all discrepancies are noted. This audit procedure allows for the recording of outcome levels of the different types of measures along with comparison results that can be used to assess the meaning of the outcome.

Attitudes

Reporting and comparing attitude results are shown in Figures 5.6 and 5.7 (top halves). Again, a district should use the form to specify the attitude outcomes related to its program; only the most general attitude outcomes have been listed here. Adequate instrumentation is available for measuring each attitude outcome. However, districts may readily generate their own instruments in order to maximize the appropriateness of the tests for the assessment of intended outcomes (see, for example, Anderson 1981).

As in previous outcome categories, illustrative results for the program year are reported as achieved scores, whereas results for the preceding (preprogram) year constitute the comparison (seventh-grade data have been used

---

* See Tuckman (1975) for a description of procedures for measuring these outcomes.

Measure	Achieved group score	Comparison or criterion score	Increment or decrement
1. Stating the facts contained in a given decision, outcome, event or set of conditions.			
2. Stating and explaining categories for grouping the facts stated above.			
3. Identifying and explaining events or conditions that may have caused a given decision, outcome, event or set of conditions.			
4. Predicting likely reactions of different parties to a given decision, outcome, event or set of conditions.			
5. Constructing and explaining alternative courses of action to those actually taken in response to a decision, outcome, event or set of conditions.			
6. Stating personal situations that fit a given decision, outcome, event or set of conditions.			

FIGURE 5.5 *Alternative Thinking and Problem Solving Output Audit Form for Taba Objectives*

in this instance; these data appear in the top half of Figure 5.7). The resulting comparison yields an indication of areas of greater and lesser success on a relative basis.

For the most part, in the illustration in the top half of Figure 5.7, little difference between groups is noted—suggesting that the instructional program

Measure	Achieved Group Score	Comparison or Criterion Score	Increment or Decrement
Attitudes towards self			
Attitudes towards school			
Attitudes towards learning			
Attitudes towards others			
Attitudes towards civic participation			
Attitudes towards ambiguity			
Attitudes towards internal control			
Career maturity attitudes			
Attitudes towards aesthetics			
Self-control			
Cooperation			
Mutuality			
Participation			
Initiative			
Neatness			
Resource use			
Following instructions			
Completion of work			
Interest in learning			
Creativity			

FIGURE 5.6   *Affective Domain (Attitudes appear above dashed line and Behavior, below dashed line) Output Audit Form*

Measure	Achieved Group Score[1]	Comparison or Criterion Score[2]	Increment or Decrement
Attitudes towards self	73.1[3]	66.0	+7.1*
Attitudes towards school	70.9	65.4	+5.5
Attitudes towards learning	74.4	66.6	+8.1*
Attitudes towards others	64.7	64.1	+0.6
Attitudes towards civic participation	64.6	63.7	+0.9
Attitudes towards ambiguity	60.5	59.2	+1.3
Attitudes towards internal control	63.9	61.3	+2.6
Career maturity attitudes	64.1	67.7	−3.6
Attitudes towards aesthetics	66.2	69.2	−3.0
Self-control	8.5[4]	8.2	+0.3
Cooperation	8.0	7.0	+1.0*
Mutuality	7.8	7.5	+0.3
Participation	9.0	8.5	+0.5
Initiative	8.8	9.0	−0.2
Neatness	6.5	6.0	+0.5
Resource use	7.2	6.1	+1.1*
Following instructions	7.6	6.9	+0.7
Completion of work	7.5	7.4	+0.2
Interest in learning	8.1	7.0	+1.1*
Creativity	6.8	6.9	−0.1

[1] This year's seventh graders
[2] Last year's seventh graders
[3] Percentage score
[4] Based on a 10 point scale
*Probability that this is a chance difference is less than .05

FIGURE 5.7 *Affective Domain* (*Attitudes Measured by Educational Goal Attainment Tests and Behavior Measured by Teacher Observation Form*) *Output Audit Form Illustrated for Seventh Graders in a Sample School District*

Measure	Group Score	Comparison or Criterion Score	Increment or Decrement
1. Citizenship behavior			
2. Positive human relations			
3. Nonconformity			
4. Ethical behavior			
5. Self-improvement behavior			
6. Job behavior			
7. Career and self-awareness			
8. Creative expression			
9. Family participation			
10. Resource management			
11. Health and hygiene			
12. Exercise and diet			

FIGURE 5.8   *Out-of-School Behavior Output Audit Form (Measures are taken from the Educational Goal Attainment Tests)*

being evaluated has had only a small effect on attitudinal outcomes. Where these outcomes have not been preset in goal areas or objectives, this finding would produce little concern. Note, however, that in two of the perhaps most critical attitudes, those toward self and toward learning, the program group

Measure	Achieved Group Score	Comparison or Criterion Score	Increment or Decrement
1. Listing main topical ideas and supporting information on a given page.			
2. Constructing an outline for a set of main topical ideas.			
3. Locating three books dealing with a given topic.			
4. Making a reference card listing main information on a given bibliographic source.			
5. Expanding an outline into paragraph form.			
6. Using graphs and charts to supply requested information.			
7. Developing a written report using library resources and an outline.			
8. Presenting a written report to the class.			

FIGURE 5.9 *Study Skills Behavior Output Audit Form*

scored significantly higher than the comparison group. In these presumable target areas, the program seems to have been a success.

Behavior

The bottom halves of Figures 5.6 and 5.7 deal with in-class (and hence observable) student behaviors. (Figure 5.8 covers out-of-class behaviors, which, by virtue of their inaccessibility to observation, would likely be measured by self-report; Figure 5.9 covers achievement-relevant behaviors, namely, study skills.)

By now the pattern of use of the audit procedure is familiar. This year's class-achieved scores versus those of last year's class (as one basis for comparison) are contrasted and discrepancies noted. Results are based on teacher reports usually using district-built approaches to the measurement of behavior (as perhaps is done on report cards).*

In this illustration (bottom half of Figure 5.7), teachers rated in-class behavior for six students, chosen at random, each month on each of the specified behavioral categories. At the end of the year, ratings were averaged over months and over students. Results showed program students to be significantly more cooperative and more interested in learning and to use the resources more.

Conclusion

The audit approach is recommended to school administrators who are responsible for instructional program evaluation. It provides a format for systematically recording and reporting performance results in five outcome areas as well as focusing attention on the comparison of these results with prior results (either through longitudinal, cross-sectional or summative design) or their contrast with preset performance criteria. The identification of resulting discrepancies can form the basis for subsequent resource allocation.

This auditing approach can be used as a reporting and interpreting procedure in conjunction with the three types of evaluation described in chapters 9, 10, and 11. In every instance, evaluators are encouraged to audit outcomes in each of the five outcome areas described.

---

* See Tuckman (1975) for guidelines.

CHAPTER 6

Surveying the Inputs and Processes from the Classroom

In order to know exactly what it is you are evaluating, inputs and processes must be closely examined and described. Since the results of an evaluation serve either to reinforce current practices or to cause them to be altered in the direction of more nearly attaining the goals, it is necessary to determine what current practices are—that is, the *level of implementation* of the current instructional program. This approach has been called *input evaluation* or *process evaluation*. However, its purpose is not to evaluate the quality of the program but to determine the degree to which the program is being carried out as intended. Thus, it is not an evaluation. Moreover, the distinction between the terms "input" and "process" is fuzzy and hence barely worth making. This chapter will refer hereafter to the combination of inputs and their operation.

The purpose here is to do an *input/process survey*, that is, to determine the nature and characteristics of currently *operating* inputs as processes (that is, their level of implementation or use), which then can be compared to desired or intended input levels, which might be called input specifications. We will look only at classroom-based inputs as processes, namely: (1) instructional materials and activities; (2) subject matter coverage and emphases; (3) classroom environment and organization; (4) teaching style; and (5) student characteristics. Context variables such as administrative structure or school building characteristics will not be considered because they are removed from the immediacy of instructional effects and because this book focuses on instructional program evaluation.

A final point before we begin our description. We will focus on supervisors as data collectors for the input/process survey because they must observe in classrooms and this involvement may help them fulfill their role. In describing what transpires in classrooms, observers typically use techniques such as coding individual acts, surveying ongoing behavior, or rating impressions. The coding process breaks behavior down into too small segments and requires considerable training and concentration to perfect. Rating, on the other hand, often is too global and impressionistic. Hence, we will settle mainly on a technique called *behavior sampling* as the primary data collection procedure (in all cases except for two, teacher style and environment, for which the impressionistic quality of rating seems well suited and will be retained).

The behavior sampling survey approach works in the following way. A sampling plan is developed in terms of number, duration, and timing of visitations, and a number of students (between four and six) are randomly selected *before* each visitation from the class roster. (Two alternates also are selected at random in case of absences among the first six.*) In any given visitation, the observer records the instructional material used by each student in the sample, the instructional activity engaged in by each, and so on, and makes an entry on the appropriate entry form. (Each form will be described in more detail, in turn.) Over time, the series of entries made should begin to show a pattern indicating the nature of the inputs operating as process across and within classrooms. Even though each classroom may display some uniqueness, an overall trend may be detected across a school or district. Thus, in this procedure, the level of concentration required of an observer is much less than that of coding, and the level of inference demanded is much less than that of rating. Instead, actual behavior samples are collected by survey procedure. The role of this procedure in instructional program evaluation is illustrated in Figure 6.1.

We will now apply this procedure to each input/process category.†

---

* An alternative method for selecting sample students would be to superimpose a 6 x 6 grid on a "picture" of the classroom, number each of the 36 cells, randomly select six cells, and then observe the six students occupying those cells.

† The measurement techniques and instruments presented in this chapter represent *possibilities* for the evaluator's consideration. However, there are other *alternatives* that can be obtained from other sources.

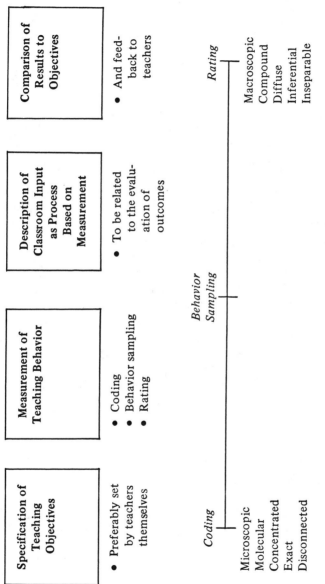

FIGURE 6.1 *The Role of the Determination of Classroom Inputs and Processes in Instructional Program Evaluation*

Instructional Materials

Instructional materials include such items as published and unpublished print materials, multimedia auditory and visual materials (e.g., audio and video tapes), technological materials (e.g., computers), participatory materials (e.g., games), manipulable materials (e.g., kits), and others. The supervisor would make six visits to the classroom (at different times of day and days of week), each time having preceded the visit by selecting six children at random from the class roster. Upon entering the classroom, the supervisor would locate these children, identify the instructional materials each child is using at that moment, and designate this by an entry in the Instructional Materials Survey Form, shown in Figure 6.2. In other words, if on the first observation three of the students were using textbooks and three were listening to a lecture being given by the teacher, than a "3" would be placed in column 1 alongside "Textbooks" and "3" in column 1 alongside "Spoken." No other entries would be made until the second observation.

At the completion of the six observations, a total of thirty-six entries will have been made (using six *different* children at each observation). The pattern of these entries can be compared to what the desired or intended input state is in terms of instructional materials. If, for example, the school's emphasis is on multimedia use and the survey shows little or no evidence of the use of multimedia instructional materials, then it must be concluded that intentions and designs for instruction either are not being transmitted to teachers or are not being carried out by them. Consequently, it would be inaccurate to conclude from the evaluation of outcomes that those results reflected broad multimedia usage when, in fact, such usage was not observed. Hence, the input/process survey serves to determine the status or level of implementation of inputs as process so that the school or school district can be sure what it is evaluating and can know how to interpret and target the results of the subsequent outcome evaluation. In other words, the input/process survey can tell the district what to change.

Instructional Activities

Various instructional activities can take place in a classroom, ranging from listening to the teacher, to painting a picture, to daydreaming. The pattern of such activities over time and students can be determined by using the behavior sampling approach and the Instructional Activities Survey Form shown in Figure 6.3. As in the collection of data on instructional materials, instructional activities data are collected by making six visits, determining what activities each of six randomly chosen students (different ones each visit) are engaged in, and entering this on the survey form. To facilitate the process, the observer (usually

	Observation					
	1	**2**	**3**	**4**	**5**	**6**
Print published						
Textbooks						
Workbooks/worksheets						
Reference books						
Other books						
Print unpublished						
Handouts						
Multimedia						
Filmstrips/films						
Photographs/drawings						
Audio tapes/records						
TV						
Technological						
Computer						
Kits						
Devices						
Participatory						
Games/plays						
Simulations						
Group assignments						
Manipulable						
Hands-on kits						
Usable displays						
Apparatus/manipulanda						
Spoken						
Other						
Exhibits						
Nothing						
Total	6	6	6	6	6	6

FIGURE 6.2 *Instructional Materials Survey Form*

a principal, department chairperson, or other supervisor) can observe the same six students each time as were used to generate data on instructional materials. For these students, you could simultaneously determine both their instructional activity and the material they are using. In other words, different students should be sampled from visit to visit, but the same students should be used for all survey forms in a given visit.

Again, the results serve as a basis for specifying the inputs that are in operation as process at the time of the outcome evaluation. If the teacher does most of the talking, for example, the operational input system obviously is

	Observation					
	1	2	3	4	5	6
Listening to teacher						
Listening to peer						
Reading assigned materials						
Reading reference materials						
Reading for pleasure						
Writing on programmed materials						
Writing in a workbook or worksheet						
Writing creatively (or on a report)						
Writing a test						
Talking (re: work) to teacher						
Talking (re: work) to peer						
Talking (socially) to teacher						
Talking (socially) to peer						
Drawing, painting, or coloring						
Constructing, experimenting or manipulating						
Utilizing or attending to AV equipment						
Presenting a play or report in a group						
Presenting a play or report individually						
Playing or taking a break						
Distributing, monitoring, or in class routine						
Disturbing, bothering, interrupting						
Waiting, daydreaming, meditating						
Total	6	6	6	6	6	6

FIGURE 6.3   *Instructional Activities Survey Form*

teacher-centered. If the expectation was for a student-centered approach, then the absence of teacher-independent activities indicates that the input system is not operating as intended. Unfavorable outcomes, then, would suggest a more complete implementation of the intended inputs.

Instructional Organization

The third facet of the classroom input/process system is organizing instruction in terms of grouping and location; for this, refer to Figure 6.4. Using the same behavior sampling procedure as the preceding surveys, determine the size of the group within which the student is working and the location of that group in the classroom or building and enter both on the Instructional Organization Survey Form (Figure 6.4) in the proper location. Taken in total, the results will indicate whether large group or small group activities predominate and the extent to which instruction is or is not classroom-centered.

Again, for efficiency purposes, the same students who were sampled for information of instructional materials and activities also should be sampled for instructional organization.

	Observation					
	1	2	3	4	5	6
Group size:						
1						
2						
3–5						
6–10						
11–20						
Whole class						
Total	6	6	6	6	6	6

	Observation					
	1	2	3	4	5	6
Location:						
Own classroom						
Seat						
Interest center						
Small group						
Other classroom						
Resource Center						
Library						
Outdoors						
Field site						
Total	6	6	6	6	6	6

FIGURE 6.4 *Instructional Organization Survey Form*

Subject Matter

The fourth facet of the classroom input/process system is the subject matter being covered. Even though teachers might be asked to provide this information directly, it is recommended that behavior sampling again be used to assure reasonable validity of the observations. The observer can easily determine the subject-matter area within which a sampled student is working simply by looking at the topic of the materials being used. Thus, the subject matter can be determined with high reliability of judgment. Cochran and Tuckman (1976) report reliabilities of 1.00 on a series of measures using behavioral sampling. That is, in *every instance* both members of a pair of observers working independently made the same judgments, testifying to the objectivity of the approach. It is important, though, that a sufficient number of observations be made over time to assure that they are *representative* of the typical classroom pattern. At least six observations should be made (of six students each time). However, each observation requires relatively little time, which is one advantage of behavior sampling.

The Subject Matter Survey Form (Figure 6.5) should be used in the same manner as the three preceding it and with the same students. Relative subject

Instructions: During each observation, visit a sample of six students randomly chosen from the class roster before entering. Determine which subject matter area each is working on and enter the number of students engaged in each subject matter area in the appropriate box below.

	Observation					
	1	**2**	**3**	**4**	**5**	**6**
Reading						
Language arts						
Mathematics						
Social studies						
Science						
Art/Music/Drama						
Career education						
Foreign language						
Affective education						
Guidance						
Other						
None						
Total	6	6	6	6	6	6

FIGURE 6.5   *Subject Matter Survey Form*

matter emphasis will become apparent from the results, which will give some indication of time spent on task.

Teaching Style

Until now, we have focused on a sampling of student behavior to determine the nature of the classroom experience as experienced by students. In order, how-

MY TEACHER IS:

1. DISORGANIZED	ORGANIZED
2. CLEAR	UNCLEAR
3. AGGRESSIVE	SOFT-SPOKEN
4. CONFIDENT	UNCERTAIN
5. COMMONPLACE	CLEVER
6. CREATIVE	ORDINARY
7. OLD FASHIONED	MODERN
8. LIKEABLE	"STUCK-UP"
9. EXCITING	BORING
10. SENSITIVE	ROUGH
11. LIVELY	LIFELESS
12. ACCEPTS PEOPLE	CRITICAL
13. SNOBBY	MODEST
14. CONFUSED	ORDERLY
15. STRICT	LENIENT
16. IN CONTROL	ON THE RUN
17. TRADITIONAL	ORIGINAL
18. WARM	COLD
19. RUDE	POLITE
20. WITHDRAWN	OUTGOING
21. EASY GOING	DEMANDING
22. OUTSPOKEN	SHY
23. UNCHANGEABLE	FLEXIBLE
24. QUIET	BUBBLY
25. AWARE	FORGETFUL
26. "NEW IDEAS"	SAME OLD THING
27. IMPATIENT	PATIENT
28. UNCARING	CARING
29. DEPENDENT	INDEPENDENT
30. UNPLANNED	EFFICIENT

FIGURE 6.6 *The Tuckman Teacher Feedback Form, Student Edition (TTFF)*

ever, to describe the style of the teacher specifically, we must look directly at the teacher. To do this, we will switch from a behavior sampling approach to the more impressionistic and global rating approach because of the impreciseness and subjectivity inherent in measuring teacher style.

To describe teacher style, the Tuckman Teacher Feedback Form, Student Edition (shown in Figure 6.6) and Scoring Form (shown in Figure 6.7) are recommended. The first, usually referred to as the TTFF, has been described in detail elsewhere (Tuckman 1976, Tuckman and Yates 1980). It provides the

---

Person Observed _____ Observer _____

Date _____

A. ITEM SCORING INSTRUCTIONS

 I. Each response choice on the answer sheet contains one of the numbers 1-2-3-4-5-6-7.

  This gives a number value to each of the seven spaces between the 30 pairs of objectives.

 II. Determine the number value for the first pair, Disorganized-Organized. Write it into the formula given below on the appropriate line under Item 1.

  For example, if the student darkened in the first space next to "Organized" in Item 1, then write the number 7 on the dash under Item 1 in the summary formula below.

 III. Do the same for each of the 30 items. Plug each value into the formula.

 IV. Compute the score for each of the 5 dimensions in the Summary formula

B. SUMMARY FORMULA AND SCORE FOR THE FIVE DIMENSIONS

 I. *Organized Demeanor*

Item		Item		Item		Item		Item		Item		Item	

$$((\ 1\ +\ 14\ +\ 30)\ -\ (2\ +\ 4\ +\ 16\ +\ 25)\ +\ 25)\ \div\ .42$$

 II. *Dynamism*

Item Item   Item Item Item

$$((20\ +\ 24)\ \quad\ -\ (3\ +\ 11\ +\ 22)\ +\ 19)\ \div\ .30$$

 III. *Flexibility*

Item Item Item Item

$$((15\ +\ 23)\ -\ (10\ +\ 21)\ +\ 12)\ \div\ .24$$

 IV. *Warmth and Acceptance*

Item Item Item Item Item Item Item

$$((13\ +\ 19\ +\ 27\ +\ 28)\ -\ (8\ +\ 12\ +\ 18)\ +\ 17)\ +\ .42$$

 V. *Creativity*

Item Item Item Item Item Item

$$((5\ +\ 7\ +\ 17)\ -\ (6\ +\ 9\ +\ 26)\ +\ 18)\ \div\ .36$$

FIGURE 6.7 The Tuckman Teacher Feedback Form, Student Edition Scoring Sheet

data collector with impressions of teacher style on five dimensions: organized demeanor, dynamism, flexibility, warmth, acceptance and creativity. Average levels across teachers or teacher samples can be reported as a way of describing the teachers in a school or district.

The advantage of the TTFF, Student Edition, over the earlier edition is that it is completed by the students themselves, who are, in fact, constant observers of the teacher. Ratings are averaged across students. These results then contribute to the description of the status of district inputs, which are related to instruction. The TTFF is deemed one of the simpler and more efficient instruments for generating this information.

Environment

Environment is used here to describe how the teacher uses classroom space; the concept, therefore, bears a similarity to the variable of instructional organization previously described. For purposes of measuring teacher use of space, an instrument called the Flexible Use of Space Scale or FUSS* is recommended. (See Figures 6.8 and 6.9 for a copy of the Scale and a guide to its use.) The Scale was developed for elementary school use and therefore is limited in its demonstrated applicability to the lower grades. Like the TTFF, it utilizes the more global rating approach as opposed to the more specific behavioral sampling procedures used in the earlier survey forms.

The observer should complete the FUSS or an equivalent version designed for upper grades during the two visits in which he or she completes the TTFF. This FUSS or equivalent form would provide information about the traditionalness versus openness of space utilization.

Other rating instruments that can be used to describe the level of implementation or use of input/process approaches as regards classroom environment, particularly as reflected in Case Study 1, Appendix A, appear at the end of Case Study 1.

Student Factors

Obviously, learning outcomes partly depend on student characteristics or factors as described in preceding chapters. Thus, the input picture would not be complete without some information about the students' status before the evaluation. Since student performance or output is a continuing process, last year's output becomes this year's input. Also, stable and enduring student characteristics are more reasonably considered input than output regardless of when

---

* I am grateful to David Cochran for his collaboration in developing this instrument and the instructional activities and organization forms previously described. Further description may be obtained in Cochran and Tuckman (1976).

Classroom Observed _____ Observer _____

Date _____ Time _____ Score _____

FLEXIBLE USE OF SPACE SCALE (FUSS)

I. PHYSICAL ARRANGEMENT

A. Diffusion of Desks

| limited | moderate | extensive |

B. Use of floors for work areas

| limited | moderate | extensive |

C. Decoration of walls and bulletin boards

| limited | moderate | extensive |

D. Decoration of ceiling

| limited | moderate | extensive |

E. Existence of display areas

| limited | moderate | extensive |

F. Existence of partitions

| limited | moderate | extensive |

II. MOVEMENT

G. Degree of student movement

| limited | moderate | extensive |

H. Degree of teacher movement

| limited | moderate | extensive |

Score: limited = 1; moderate = 2; extensive = 3

FIGURE 6.8 *Flexible Use of Space Scale (FUSS)*

they are measured since they more clearly represent partial causes of learning at any moment in time rather than results or outcomes of it. For this reason, it is a moot question whether student factors are treated under input or outcome. In fact, to make sure they are considered, they are covered in both categories.

Possible student input factors are listed in Figure 6.10. (One factor, mental ability, was covered as an outcome or control variable in chapter 5 under the General Ability Outcome Audit.) Clearly, the contribution of student inputs is not easy to determine without comparison data. The comparative approach was covered in chapter 5.

Aspect	Limited	Moderate	Extensive
I			
A. Desks	Desks in rows; formal arrangement designed for whole-class instruction	Desks in groups or U shape; arrangement to facilitate some grouping	Desks spread out; no desks; arrangement to facilitate diversity of activity
B. Floors	No one working on the floor; no signs that the students use the floor as work area	1–3 students working on the floor; some evidence of students being allowed to use the floor, e.g., rugs or mats	Several students using the floor; evidence of much use of floor, e.g., materials on the floor, many mats, rug areas in use
C. Walls & Bulletin Boards	Minimal decorations, empty boards, no use of walls for decoration	Bulletin boards filled; some use of walls as display areas	All bulletin boards filled; walls filled; great use of students' work on bulletin boards and walls
D. Ceiling	Nothing on ceiling for decoration	Some items hanging from ceiling as decoration, e.g., 1–3 mobiles	Many hanging objects; great use of students' work to decorate the ceiling
E. Display Areas	0–2 display areas; little use by the students; displays not to be used by students	2–4 display areas; some use by students for performing activities	Many display areas; areas used as interest or learning centers; displays intended for performing activities
F. Partitions	No partitions; partitions not used to separate learning centers	1–2 partitions; partitions used to separate learning centers	3 or more partitions; partitions used to separate learning centers
II			
G. Student Movement	Little student movement; most students working in seats or in group with teacher; move with permission only	Students move within limits; some out-of-seat activity; use of some areas other than desks for work	Free movement; students move to areas around room; much out-of-seat activity
H. Teacher Movement	Little teacher movement; teacher centered in front of room or with a group	Teacher moves to some extent; still maintains primary focus in one area	Teacher moves freely throughout the room; works with several individuals or groups

FIGURE 6.9 *Guide for Flexible Use of Space Scale (FUSS). (From the book, SCHOOL ADMINISTRATOR'S HANDBOOK OF TEACHER SUPERVISION AND EVALUATION METHODS by Dr. Ronald T. Hyman. © 1975 by Prentice-Hall, Inc. Published by Prentice-Hall, Inc., Englewood Cliffs, New Jersey 07632.)*

> Achievement scores for preceding year (GE's) on:
>
> Reading _____
>
> Mathematics _____
>
> Language arts _____
>
> Social studies _____
>
> Science _____
>
> Mental ability (most recent testing) _____
>
> No. of males _____
>
> No. of females _____
>
> Age _____
>
> Socio-economic status _____
>
> Grade point average _____

FIGURE 6.10   *Reporting on Mean Student Input Status*

Conclusion

A district or school need not feel compelled to use all of the input/process data collection procedures described in this chapter. The more procedures used, however, the more detailed and explicit will be the determination and description of classroom inputs and process and hence the more explicit the interpretation of outcome results. The more you know about how your classrooms are functioning, the more you will know about exactly what is working and what is not working when you see the outcome results. In other words, you will be able to feed back or relate outcomes to inputs—and that is what instructional program evaluation is all about.

Any of the instruments can be altered so they better fit the situation for which you are using them, as can the procedures for using them to collect data. It is more important to follow the spirit of their intent than the letter. Appropriate customizing should increase rather than decrease their suitability.

Moreover, you can develop a new set of procedures and instruments to fit your specific input/process objectives if they differ widely from the ones offered in this chapter. The emphasis should not be on the specific forms used but on the fact of carrying out steps to determine the level of implementation of intended inputs as processes. Without this information, subsequent outcome evaluation results can be used only to choose between the simple options of program continuation or termination. With this information, outcome evaluation results can be related to the inputs and processes that have produced those outcomes and can be used to alter or improve on the subsequent level of implementation. What is being implemented should determine the procedures used to discover its level of implementation.

CHAPTER 7

Assessing the Type of Teaching

Of the many input factors that influence what students gain from instruction, the type or nature of teaching stands out as particularly noteworthy. Quite apart from the quality of the instructional program and the degree to which that program is actually implemented in the classroom, the teacher's style, approach, and behavior can have a considerable effect on student outcomes. Therefore, it is sensible to assess the teacher's approach as a means of separating its effect from the effect of the instructional program. This chapter will present some strategies for describing and assessing the behavior or approach of the teacher.

The Dimensions of Teaching

Remember, now, that we are not talking here about the level of implementation of the instructional program by the teacher as our essential consideration. We have already discussed how the level of implementation may be determined. Therefore, the dimension of "implements fully" to "does not implement at all" is not our dimension of concern here. What we are interested in is the general quality and character of teaching which can serve as a potential source of influence on outcomes over and above those produced by the instructional program. In order to deal with these aspects of teaching, we must identify some dimensions to describe the teacher's behavior.

Perhaps the simplest teaching dimension, at least from a conceptual point of view, is the evaluative one, that is, the "good-bad" dimension. The problem with this dimension, from a practical standpoint, is that it is difficult to identify the criteria on which its overall evaluation is to be based. If we talk about an evaluation of the teacher from the student's point of view, then it is more accurate to label this dimension as "popular-unpopular" or "liked-disliked" rather than "good-bad," since the evaluation represents students' judgments. If we rely on an observer or visitor to the classroom to make this judgment, then our purposes would be better served by dealing with more observable qualities of teaching rather than something as subjective and elusive as "goodness."

In an attempt to be more descriptive we can specify and attempt to assess such dimensions of teaching as the following:

1. *Directiveness:* the extent to which the teacher controls classroom events in contrast to allowing students to control them
2. *Planning:* the amount and degree of preparation by the teacher to conduct a lesson, including the specification of intended outcomes and activities for attaining them
3. *Activity:* the extent to which the teacher moves and actually performs physically in the classroom
4. *Considerateness:* the degree of warmth, caring, and humaneness that the teacher conveys based usually on his or her liking for students and the extent to which this liking is projected
5. *Knowledgeability:* the amount of knowledge or information that the teacher possesses in the subject area being taught
6. *Demandingness:* how "tough" the teacher is in terms of assignments, expectations, tests, and material covered
7. *Commitment:* how strongly the teacher is committed to the profession of teaching and to the goal of helping students learn
8. *Enthusiasm:* the degree to which the teacher projects positive feelings and positive expectations about teaching and learning in the course of teaching
9. *Openness:* how much the teacher is willing to accept criticism and suggestions, especially from students
10. *Flexibility:* the extent to which the teacher will change a plan or an intention to meet new contingencies

This list of dimensions is not meant to be exhaustive. If, however, we were to assess the teacher on each of these dimensions, we would have a reasonably complete picture of how the teacher functions in the classroom.

Measuring the Dimensions of Teaching

We will now turn to a consideration of procedures and techniques that can be used to measure various dimensions of teaching such as those listed above.

Teacher Appraisal Interview

A certain amount of useful information about a teacher can be obtained by directly questioning that teacher. While this might not be a valid way to determine how that teacher performs in a classroom situation, it can help you determine such factors as the teacher's commitment to teaching and the teacher's philosophy and attitudes regarding such concerns as the degree to which students are capable of controlling themselves and the likelihood of students, particularly from different backgrounds, succeeding at the task of learning.

In conducting such an interview one must be careful to reassure teachers that the purpose of the interview is to complement instructional program evaluation and not to assess the teacher's competence as a basis for subsequent personnel decisions. The latter function is usually carried out in a manner prescribed by the teacher's contract.

Before conducting the interviews, the interviewer should prepare a brief set of questions that will serve as a guide in each interview. These questions should be focused on soliciting descriptions of self from the teacher. Some of the kinds of questions that might be asked are listed below.

- To what extent do you think learning is a function of the quality of teaching and to what extent is it a function of the learner's motivation and readiness?
- How would you teach a class if half of the students in it were so-called slow learners and half were working at or above grade level?
- Show me a typical lesson plan you have developed and describe to me how you went about developing it.
- What would you say are the principal rewards for you in the career of teaching? Can you give me some concrete illustrations?
- How do you decide what level of difficulty at which to set your course requirements? Have you ever changed them during a course? If so, describe the circumstances.
- If we asked your students to describe you, what positive comments might they make? What negative comments?

During the interview, the interviewer could either take notes or tape record the teacher's responses. From these responses, judgments could be made regarding the various dimensions of teaching. More detailed information on the evaluation interview process may be obtained from Fear (1978).

Testing the Teacher

One way to gain information about teachers is to test them. Achievement tests can be used to yield information about teachers' grasps of subject matter, while attitude tests can be used to determine such things as their philosophies of teaching or their sentiments about students. However, since teachers are not normally tested, except perhaps when they are seeking entrance to the teaching profession, they may view such testing as intrusive and threatening. In order to proceed, it will probably be necessary to anticipate such reactions and deal with them in advance.

Many states are currently involved in testing the competency of teachers (see Northern 1980) so that usable measures for this purpose are available. In the realm of attitude testing, such measures as the *Minnesota Teacher Attitude Inventory* can be used to probe the teacher's feelings about students and their nascent capabilities.

There are also instruments available for measuring teachers' attitudes toward specific teaching models such as the so-called open classroom (see, for example, Traub et al. 1972). If the instructional program incorporates or makes use of a model for which an attitude test is available, it would be wise to have those teachers using the program take the test so that their initial attitude toward the model can be assessed. (A subsequent administration of the test could be used to see if using the model has changed teachers' attitudes toward it.)

If no formal attitude scale is available for measuring teachers' attitudes toward a particular teaching approach or topic, then the generalized version of the semantic differential shown in Figure 7.1 can be used for this purpose. Note that the semantic differential (Osgood et al. 1957) makes use of very general adjectives such as good-bad, light-heavy and active-passive to measure the following three dimensions: (1) evaluative, (2) potency, and (3) activity. The instrument is applied to whatever object or subject appears at the top, be it "direct instruction," "teaching," or "students."

In summary, then, teachers can be tested to determine their knowledge of subject matter or their attitudes toward instructional approach, career, students, or any other relevant topic. However, be aware that such testing cannot be used to describe the teacher's behavior, only what the teacher brings to the classroom.

Observing the Teacher

One of the most commonly used ways to determine the manner of teaching is to place an observer in the classroom to rate or record his or her impressions of the teacher's behavior, style, and approach. While it is not possible directly to determine a teacher's attitude or philosophy by observing that teacher in ac-

Vocational Education

(E)	1. dirty	__:__:__:__:__:__:__	clean
(A)	2. sharp	__:__:__:__:__:__:__	dull
(E)	3. good	__:__:__:__:__:__:__	bad
(P)	4. strong	__:__:__:__:__:__:__	weak
(P)	5. rugged	__:__:__:__:__:__:__	delicate
(E)	6. unpleasant	__:__:__:__:__:__:__	pleasant
(E)	7. honest	__:__:__:__:__:__:__	dishonest
(A)	8. passive	__:__:__:__:__:__:__	active
(E)	9. beautiful	__:__:__:__:__:__:__	ugly
(P)	10. light	__:__:__:__:__:__:__	heavy
(P)	11. large	__:__:__:__:__:__:__	small
(A)	12. slow	__:__:__:__:__:__:__	fast

E—Evaluative scales
A—Activity scales
P—Potency scales

FIGURE 7.1 Sample Version of the Semantic Differential for Measuring Teacher Attitudes Toward, in this case, Vocational Education.

tion, it is possible to make reasonably accurate judgments of how that teacher functions in the classroom situation.

In order to maximize both the reliability (or accuracy) of observations and their validity it is helpful to use a systematic approach such as a coding or rating scheme. A coding scheme is made up of a set of behavioral categories; the observer records instances of each category as the instances are observed. A rating scheme is made up of a set of scales; the observer records his or her impression of the teacher's behavior on these scales. Coding has the potential to be more practical and interpretable. This distinction between coding and rating has already been made at the beginning of chapter 6 (see particularly Figure 6.1), in an effort to understand the role of behavioral sampling in measuring level of implementation of an instructional program. In gathering general impressions of teaching, apart from level of implementation, which is our concern here, we will focus on the rating scale approach as a more practical means than the coding approach. Construction of rating scales for this purpose are described in the next section of this chapter.

Using Students as Observers

Student ratings are employed in the assessment of teaching primarily at the college level, but there is no reason to suspect that they cannot be used at the high school level, and even lower if special designs for use with younger children are employed. Clearly, a major advantage of using students as observers is their continuous presence in the classroom and exposure to the teacher.

Student ratings are often criticized as reflections of little more than a teacher's popularity and hence much influenced by the course's demandingness, or lack of it. Work such as that by Ware and Williams (1977) indicates that student ratings forms measure more than a single dimension of teaching. Very often, as many as four discrete dimensions of teaching are identified, including liking for the way the course was taught, liking the content of the course, feeling that the course provoked interest and attention, and general liking of the whole experience. Needless to say, the element of popularity can never be entirely removed from this form of evaluation; however, it is certainly legitimate to expect an effective teacher to appeal to his or her students, at least in some respects.

A final type of criticism of student ratings is that students are whimsical, inconsistent, and unreliable judges who often judge a course by how well they are doing in it. However, most of the evidence fails to support this view. Student ratings have been found to be reasonably consistent and reliable and to agree fairly well with other sources of judgment of the quality of teaching (Aleamoni and Hexner 1980). Overall, it seems reasonable to conclude that student ratings represent one useful way to acquire information about the impact of teaching.

Specific student rating scales that may be employed to evaluate teaching will be described later in this chapter.

Student Achievement

One can argue, perhaps cogently, that the ultimate criterion for the effectiveness of teaching is not how the teacher behaves or how well liked the teacher is but *how much the students learn.* The difficulty with this approach is that the amount of learning by students is a function of many factors, only one of which is the quality of teaching. Other factors—such as students' prior learning in the subject area, student aptitude, student motivation, the intrinsic difficulty of the subject matter, and the nature of the test used to measure the amount of learning—all influence the outcome. While we have to believe that the teacher does make a difference, the degree of difference is only a percentage of the total gain in learning.

Within the above limitation, it is possible to make some evaluation of teaching based on student achievement. Assuming that student achievement can be measured at the start of a course (Time 1) and again at the end of the course (Time 2), the following formula (Millman 1981) can be used to calculate the proportion of the total gain that the class could possibly have made on the test that was, in fact, accomplished from Time 1 to Time 2.

$$\frac{(\text{Mean Test Score Time 2}) - (\text{Mean Test Score Time 1})}{(\text{Maximum Possible Test Score}) - (\text{Mean Test Score Time 1})}$$

The use of the above formula presupposes that the test is a fair measure of what the teacher actually taught and that the same students were present for testing at Time 1 and Time 2. Also, since the evaluation is based on the results of a single class, we cannot use it to evaluate a teacher in comparison with other teachers or to conclude that the class made a larger gain than might have occurred for a different teacher. Without comparison data, it is hard to evaluate the magnitude of the percentage gain except to say that bigger is better. Of course, if more than one teacher is teaching the same subject matter, we can compare the percentage gain each teacher's class achieves in order to see which has gained more and, within the limitations described above, attribute this difference to the quality of teaching.

Observational Measures of Teaching

There are two sources that can be recommended for locating an observational measure of teaching which is appropriate for your definition and purposes. The first of these is a six-volume compendium entitled *Mirrors for Behavior: An Anthology of Classroom Observation Instruments,* compiled by A. Simon and E. C. Boyer and published in 1967 by Research for Better Schools of Philadelphia, Pennsylvania. A more recent (1977) work is *Evaluating Classroom Instruction: A Sourcebook of Instruments* by G. D. Borich and S. K. Madden (published by Addison-Wesley of Reading, Massachusetts).

It is far wiser to locate a measure or approach that has been used before than to try to construct your own. If you can find one that comes close to meeting your needs, you may want to make some small modifications, recognizing of course that these modifications may alter the psychometric properties of the measure. (For a discussion of psychometric properties of a test, see chapter 8. A number of teacher behavior measures also appear at the end of Case Study 1, Appendix A.)

If you are determined to construct your own measure for describing teacher behavior, then you should follow the steps described below.

First, prepare a list of objectives of teaching which contains statements of acceptable or, at least, potentially observable teaching behaviors. Your list may contain some of the following. The teacher

- holds student attention
- maintains discipline or control
- covers or follows a lesson plan

- engages students in activities
- answers student questions

You may want to show your list to some teachers and have them react to each statement before you decide which to keep, which to eliminate, and which to change. You may also want to group your statements into clusters having to do with areas such as instruction planning, instruction delivery, evaluation of student performance, classroom management, interpersonal relations, and personal qualities. This breakdown may help you both in generating statements and in avoiding or minimizing redundancy.

Second, take each statement or objective and try to write as many behavioral indicators of it as you can. (Again, you want to seek teachers' input.) For example, given the objective of maintaining classroom control or discipline, your indicators may be such observables as:

- most students stay "in contact" with the task during the entire lesson
- the teacher is on task during the entire lesson
- there are few instances of student acting out, either behaviorally or verbally
- students don't wander around aimlessly
- the teacher doesn't allow inappropriate student behavior to go unnoticed and unreprimanded
- students, when reprimanded, return to or get on task.

Third, use these indicators or observables to form the basis of a measuring instrument. You may accomplish this by adopting one of the following strategies: (1) Make a count of the number of times each indicator is observed during a thirty-minute observation period. (2) Affix a numerical frequency or observability scale to each indicator—such as never, seldom, occasionally, often, always; or totally typical, quite typical, somewhat typical, somewhat atypical, quite atypical, totally atypical (the numbers 1–5 could be used for this purpose). Rate each teacher observed on each indicator using the scales. (3) Create a checklist of observed behaviors which are derived from the list of indicators and check each one in evidence during the period of observation.

Once you have constructed your measure, you should try it out. In effect, trying it out means testing what is called its *inter-rater reliability*. This refers to the extent to which two or more observers, working simultaneously but independently, generate essentially the same results on the instrument. An instrument that lacks this feature is of relatively little value, since we cannot trust its results as reflecting anything more than the whims and biases of the observer.

Have two observers sit in the same classroom at the same time and each complete the instrument. Compare the results of the two observations. If the degree of correspondence or agreement is about 75 percent (and certainly no worse than 65 percent), you may conclude that the instrument may be used reliably.

However, before performing this test, it is fair to have the two observers practice together and discuss the meanings of the various indicators and scales so that there is, at least, the possibility that they may use and interpret them in the same manner. Thereafter, whenever the instrument is to be used to describe, classify, or evaluate teaching, the observer or observers should be trained in the use of the instrument, unless, of course, such training has already occurred.

Because of the enormous potential influence of observer variability, idiosyncrasy, and bias on judgments of teaching, the pre-training of observers, up to some standard of judgment or agreement, is an essential prerequisite to the use of any observational instrument or system. The observer is a greater source of error in judgments of teaching than is the instrument that the observer uses. Therefore, observer training is as important as careful development of instrumentation in the process of describing and evaluating teaching by means of observation.

Case Study 1 in Appendix A illustrates the use of outside observers to describe the teaching process in classrooms participating in an open classroom project. A series of observation scales were developed for use in this evaluation and appear at the end of the write-up. At the time of the second or post-intervention observation, two observers were used and their ratings compared to produce the inter-rater reliabilities shown in Table 1 of the write-up.

Student Rating Scales

The topic of student ratings of instruction is covered in depth and detail by Aleamoni (1981). He cites research that supports the following conclusions: (1) student ratings of the same instructors and courses are highly stable from year to year; (2) a teacher's quality of teaching cannot be predicted on the basis of a teacher's intellectual ability or scholarly productivity nearly as well as it can be judged directly on the basis of ratings of teaching; (3) students are discriminating judges, that is, their judgments reflect more than just a teacher's popularity; (4) ratings of teachers by alumni tend *not* to differ from those of current students; (5) carefully constructed student rating forms are both reliable and valid.

Taken together, these conclusions strongly support student rating scales as both practical and accurate measures of teaching. Their use, however, has been largely confined to the college setting.

Critics of student ratings have contended that they are highly influenced by a number of extraneous variables such as class size, student sex, instructor sex, whether the course was an elective or a requirement, whether the students are majors or nonmajors, the grade level of the course, the rank of the instructor, and the grades the students receive or expect to receive in the course. Alea-moni (1981) reports that research has not shown a consistently strong relation-ship between any of these extraneous variables and student ratings of instruction. Again, this supports the use of student ratings for the purpose of evaluating the impact of teaching.

There are a great number of scales available for student description and evaluation of teaching. (One of them, the *TTFF, Student Edition,* appears in this book on pages 89–90.) Most colleges and universities routinely use these instruments and many have developed their own. Standardized evaluations, such as the *Student Instructional Report* distributed by the Educational Testing Service, have received widespread use. Many of these instruments could be used at the high school level. They typically contain about twenty items and ask each student to rate his or her overall liking of and evaluation of the course, along with such specifics as the instructor's quality of presentation and of orga-nization, the humaneness and accessibility of the instructor, the degree to which the course content was valuable and interesting, and the quality and timeliness of tests and feedback.

Were you to ask just one student to offer these judgments of teachers and teaching, you would not have much confidence in his or her accuracy—and rightly so. Each student's individual judgments can be expected to reflect per-sonal and unique perceptions, expectations and experiences. However, when such judgments are collected from fifteen to thirty or more students in a class and results are averaged to reflect a group judgment, individual idiosyncrasies become blended, statistically, into a total that is believed to represent the real impact of the experience and not biased perceptions of it.

Consider the following twelve questions, which may be asked of elemen-tary school children regarding the quality of the teaching they receive:

- Do you like coming to school?
- Do you like your teacher?
- Is your classroom fun?
- Is your teacher fair?
- Is your teacher nice?
- Are you learning a lot of new things in class?
- Are you afraid to tell your teacher that you don't understand some-thing?
- Does your teacher yell a lot?
- Is school boring?
- Do you hope you get the same teacher again?
- Do you like learning to read?
- Does your teacher spend enough time teaching you things?

This list of questions is not meant to be exhaustive but only to suggest the kinds of questions that may be used with young children to determine the impact of teaching.

If you decide to make up such a list of questions for use with children, the following suggestions should be taken seriously. First, the items should be read aloud to children so that differences in reading ability do not affect their response. Second, because of the potential for influence or intimidation, the person reading the items should not be the teacher. Third, students should answer each question in writing so that each student can answer independently. For this purpose, an answer sheet should be prepared with each item number coupled with a picture for easy reference. Fourth, there should only be two response choices, YES and NO, and these may be picture-coded as well with the same picture always representing YES and another always representing NO.

Some Suggestions

One certain source of variability in student outcomes is the style or type of teaching. Completely apart from the nature of an instructional program and the degree to which it is implemented, the style and type of teaching will have an important influence on whether and how much students learn.

Describing and assessing teaching is a regular and ongoing part of most educational programs. If the evaluation of innovative and experimental educational programming is going to be done in your school or district, then systematic determination of the style and type of teaching must also be done, so that the effect of programs can be separated from the effect of teachers.

To accomplish this, the following recommendations are offered:

1. Make regular classroom observations of teaching using a systematic and tested classroom observation form.
2. Have students rate their teachers and courses at least once a year using a valid student rating form.
3. Establish criteria for evaluating the style and type of teaching so that the data collected about teaching can be used to determine the quality or effectiveness of teaching.
4. Evaluate the standardized achievement of students once a year, using the formula provided in this chapter, and compare grade levels over time (longitudinally) and simultaneous classes taught by different teachers (cross-sectionally) using the evaluation designs provided in an earlier chapter.

These four approaches, taken together, will enable you to assess the style and quality of teaching and to determine its impact on student achievement on a regular, ongoing basis. Then, when any new instructional programs are introduced, their impact can be assessed in terms of effects achieved over and above those which are the result of teaching.

CHAPTER 8

Evaluating the Quality of Criterion-Referenced Tests

It is important that persons in a district charged with instructional program evaluation be familiar with procedures for determining the quality of a criterion-referenced test. Such tests, often of the home-grown variety, are coming increasingly into play in program evaluations; unless they are of high quality, they will introduce error into the evaluation process. The evaluator faces enough potential pitfalls without adding bad tests as another. Information on evaluating test quality will be presented by example. A test of competency in writing behaviorial objectives, actually used in a program run to train local district evaluation personnel, will be evaluated as a vehicle for introducing the topic of test quality evaluation.

Interest in and use of criterion-referenced tests in education for purposes of monitoring student progress and evaluating instructional program effectiveness are increasing. We need to acquaint both test builders and potential test users with procedures for assessing the psychometric qualities of these tests as a prerequisite to deciding on their use. The purpose of this chapter, then, is to explain and illustrate test evaluation by examining a test (shown in Figure 8.3) to determine whether and to what extent it meets the five test criteria of appropriateness, validity, reliability, interpretability, and usability described by

Tuckman (1975) in the Checklist for Criterion-Referenced Tests. The objective here is to suggest, by way of illustration, how the properties of a criterion-referenced test can be determined, using a device such as the checklist. (The checklist, Figure 8.1, should be studied closely before proceeding.)

Appropriateness

The criterion of appropriateness is concerned with whether test items fit the objectives that they are intended to measure. By laying the objectives (shown in Figure 8.2) and the test items (shown in Figure 8.3) side by side, we get the following:

Obj. 1   Items 1–4, 5A–11A
Obj. 2   Items 5B–11B
Obj. 3   Items 12–15
Obj. 4   Items 16–17

The existence of a well-written set of objectives makes the appropriateness question a reasonably easy one to answer. Since no objective has gone unmeasured and no items are unpaired with an objective, the level of appropriateness seems quite high.

Objective 1 requires that one or more instructional objectives be given, some properly written with action verbs and some improperly written without them; the student must identify those that are properly written. Clearly the corresponding items have this feature. Objective 2 calls for the students to distinguish between objectives that state criteria and those that do not state criteria for minimum acceptable performance. The items measuring the second objective fit this requirement. The items* measuring objective 3 meet its stated requirements, as do the items for objective 4.

As for the particular action verbs called for in the objectives in Figure 8.2, "identify" is specified as the behavior in the first three objectives and the paired items present alternatives that require students to select or identify those meeting certain criteria. The last objective requires construction, and students are given two items in which they must construct or write an objective.

Regarding appropriateness of the test items in meeting the criteria set forth in Figure 8.2, Objectives, each objective includes an evaluation criterion, such as the presence versus the absence of an action verb in objective 1, which becomes the basis for constructing short-answer items to measure the first three objectives, and for scoring performance on the items measuring objective 4.

---

* These items actually only describe performance as contrasted with the kinds of items that require an actual performance.

                                                              YES   *NO*

I. IS MY TEST *APPROPRIATE?*

   1. Does It Fit My Objectives:
- *Are* there 2 items or more for each and every objective and 0 items that fit no objectives?
- *Do* the number of items per objective accurately reflect the relative importance of each objective?

   2. Does It Reflect the Action Verbs:
- *Does* each item for a given objective measure the action called for by the verb in that objective?
- *Have* I used the item forms most appropriate for each action?

   3. Does It Utilize the Conditions:
- *Does* each item for a given objective employ the statement of givens or conditions set forth in that objective?

   4. Does It Employ the Criteria:
- *Is* the scoring of each item for a given objective based on the criteria stated in that objective?

II. IS MY TEST *VALID?*

   1. Does It Discriminate Between Performance Levels:
- *Do* students who are independently judged to perform better in the test area perform better on the test?
- *Do* different students with different degrees of experience perform differently on the various items?

   2. Does It Fit Any External Criterion:
- *Does* success on the test predict subsequent success in areas for which the test topic is claimed to be a prerequisite?
- *Do* students who receive appropriate teaching perform better on the test than untaught students (or does a student perform better on the test after teaching than before)?

   3. How Do My Colleagues View the Coverage:
- *Do* my colleagues in the topic area or at the grade level agree that all necessary objectives and no unnecessary ones have been included?
- *Do* they agree that the items are valid for measuring the objectives?

FIGURE 8.1 *A Checklist for Criterion-Referenced Tests. (From* Measuring Educational Outcomes: Fundamentals of Testing *by Bruce W. Tuckerman © 1975 by Harcourt Brace Jovanovich, Inc. Reprinted by permission of the publishers.)*

                                                              YES   *NO*

4. Does It Measure Something Other Than Reading Level or Life Styles:
   - *Are* the demands it makes on reading skill within students' capabilities?
   - *Is* performance independent of group membership or any other socio-economic variable?

III. IS MY TEST *RELIABLE?*

1. Are There Paired Items That Agree:
   - *Do* students who get one item of a pair (per objective) right also get the other right and those who get one wrong get the other wrong?
   - *Have* nonparallel items been rewritten?

2. Is Item Performance Consistent with Test Performance:
   - *Is* each item consistently passed by students who do well on the total test?
   - *Have* inconsistent items been removed?

3. Are All Items Clear and Understandable:
   - *Have* student responses been used as a basis for evaluating item clarity?
   - *Have* ambiguous items been removed or rewritten?

4. Have Scoring Procedures Proved to be Systematic and Unbiased:
   - *Have* multiple scorings yielded consistent results?
   - *Are* scoring criteria and procedures as detailed and as suitable as they can be?

IV. IS MY TEST *INTERPRETABLE?*

1. Do I know How the Scores Relate to Relevant Performance:
   - *Is* my test referenced in terms of some criterion (e.g., my objectives)?
   - *Can* I tell what a high score and a low score mean? Or, can I report the specific objectives on which proficiency has been demonstrated?
   - *Can* the results for an individual student be used as a specific indication of level or degree of proficiency?

2. Do I Know What Defines Acceptable Performance?
   - *Have* I pre-established cutoff scores (e.g. passing grade) and if so, on what basis?

YES   NO

- *Do* I have some concrete and verifiable way to say whether a particular performance suffices in terms of objective specifications of acceptability?

3. Does the Test Provide Diagnostic and Evaluative Information:
   - *Does* it tell me the areas in which a student needs help?
   - *Does* it tell me the areas in which the class needs help?
   - *Does* it tell me the areas in which instruction needs improvement?

4. Does it Provide Useful Relative Information:
   - *Does* it provide the kind of data that I can compare meaningfully with results of past and future testings?
   - *Can* the results be interpreted on a norm-referenced basis if that is desired?

V. IS MY TEST *USEABLE?*

1. Is it Short Enough to Avoid Being Tedious:
   - *Does* it stop short of creating fatigue? stress? boredom?
   - *Have* I tried to make it as short as possible within the limits of reliability?

2. Is is Practical for Classroom Use:
   - *Can* it be used conveniently in a classroom?
   - *Is* it within the limit of available teacher time?
   - *Can* it be used to test all students?
   - *Is* it realistic about the kinds of equipment and physical set-up it requires?

3. Are There Standard Procedures for Administration:
   - *Are* there clear, written instructions?
   - *Can* it be administered by someone other than me?
   - *Can* it be given in a nonthreatening, nondiscriminatory way?

4. Can Students Comprehend It and Relate to it:
   - *Is* it written at a level students can understand?
   - *Is* it interesting, clever, or provocative?
   - *Is* it written to engage students?

OBJECTIVES

1. Given one or more instructional objectives, the student will identify those stated in performance terms (i.e., those that state a behavior to be demonstrated) based on the presence or absence of an action verb.

2. Given one or more instructional objectives, the student will identify those that define minimum acceptable performance based on the presence or absence of a criterion.

3. Given one or more performance (test) items, the student will identify those appropriate to the evaluation of the objectives based on the presence or absence of the necessary conditions, actions, and criteria.

4. Given a goal statement, the student will construct an instructional objective representing that goal, including a statement of conditions, actions, and criteria.

FIGURE 8.2   *A Set of Sample Objectives for a Unit Writing Instructional Objectives*

Overall, the sample test can be considered high in appropriateness, an outcome easily determined given such clear and complete objectives from which to judge.

Validity

To demonstrate validity, *the matter of whether a test measures what it is supposed to measure,* the test was administered to a group of seventeen teachers and educational administrators participating in an in-service seminar in educational planning.

The criteria for establishing validity from the checklist in Figure 8.1 were applied to the sample test. The first criterion was based on a comparison of test scores to scores on an independent criterion, namely degree of relevant experience. In the case of the sample test and validation group, there was not an available independent criterion to use, such as a supervisor's rating of each student's ability to write instructional objectives. In lieu of this, each student was asked to rate his or her degree of experience in writing instructional objectives on the 1–10 scale shown below, with 1 representing no experience and 10 representing a lot of experience.

no									a lot of
experience									experience
1	2	3	4	5	6	7	8	9	10

Given criterion validity, the test should elicit better performance from students with more experience in the area of its objectives than from students with less experience. The scores that each student received on the sample test, Figure 8.3, were compared to the self-ratings of experience. (Students were not aware of what would be done with the self-descriptive ratings when they made them, hence should not have been motivated to distort them in any particular way.) The degree of correspondence was determined by means of a rank-order correlation (see Tuckman 1978, pp. 244–247, for this procedure). The resulting correlation was .76, indicating that students more experienced in writing objectives did better on the test than those less experienced. Since the test was intended to be a measure of a person's capability to write objectives and to evaluate those written by others, the high correlation establishes some validity for the test; that is, it indicates that what the test measured (its outcome) is what it was intended to measure (its purpose).

A second validity criterion could be applied by examining subsequent performance in either the long or short term. Here, students were given one form of the sample test before instruction (a pretest) and earned a class average of twenty. (The maximum possible score on the test was thirty.) Test answers then were gone over and scored, an hour of instruction was provided, and then a parallel, or alternate form, of the test was given. On the posttest the class earned an average score of twenty-six, a 30 percent gain over the original average and a net result of 87 percent out of the maximum possible. This pretest-to-posttest gain not only indicated the success of the instruction but also supported the validity of the test, that is, the extent to which it reflected proficiency in the writing of objectives. Were it not a measure of such proficiency, it would not have yielded such gains as a result of instruction.

The third validity criterion involved an attempt to validate the objectives themselves. For this purpose, discussion with colleagues was recommended in the Checklist for Criterion-Referenced Tests (Figure 8.1). Since the students who took the test were themselves professional educators, their opinions were solicited in lieu of those of colleagues. The students supported and reinforced the four given objectives but recommended two additional objectives. One stated that, given the action part of the objective statement, the student would be able to state the givens or conditions. This aspect of objective writing was one that many students had particular difficulty with and hence felt should be explicated as a separate objective.

TEST

Are the objectives below stated in performance (behavioral) terms? Does each at least name an act the learner would be performing when demonstrating that he or she has achieved the objectives?

	YES	NO
1. To be able to list the principles of secondary school administration.	____	____
2. To know the plays of Shakespeare.	____	____
3. To *really* understand the law of magnetism.	____	____
4. To be able to identify instructional objectives that indicate what the learner will be doing when demonstrating achievement of the objective.	____	____

Given below are two characteristics of a statement of instructional objectives.
A. *Identifies the behavior to be demonstrated by the student.*
B. *Indicates a standard, or criterion of acceptable performance.*
For each objective, indicate whether *each* of these characteristics is present. If present, write *yes* in the blank; if absent, write *no*.

	A	B
5. The student must be able to fill out a standard accident report.	____	____
6. The student must be able to write a coherent essay on the subject "How to Write Objectives for a Course in Law Appreciation." The student may use all references noted during the course, as well as class notes. The student must write the essay on paper provided by the examiner.	____	____
7. Besides each of the following psychological principles, the student must be able to write the names of the authors or experiments on which the principle is based.	____	____
8. Given a list of objectives, the student should be able to evaluate each.	____	____
9. The student must be able to list the important characteristics of branching and linear self-instructional programs.	____	____

FIGURE 8.3 *A Test to Measure a Student's Proficiency in Identifying and Preparing Instructional Objectives. (From the book,* Preparing Instructional Objectives, *1st Ed. by Robert F. Mager. Copyright, ©, 1962 by Pitman Learning, Inc., Belmont, CA 94002.*

A   B

10. The student should be able to name and give an example of each of six programming techniques useful for eliciting a correct response. To be considered correct, items listed by the student must appear on the handout entitled "Programming Techniques" issued by the instructor during the course. ____ ____

11. The student must be able to develop logical approaches in the solution of personal problems. ____ ____

Here is a rather poorly stated objective:

The student must be able to understand the laws pertaining to contracts. Indicate whether or not the following test situations would be considered appropriate for testing to determine if the objective had been achieved.

	Appro-priate	*Not Appro-priate*

Test Situations

12. Given a legal contract and a list of contract laws, the student is asked to indicate which of the laws, if any, are violated by the wording of the contract. ____ ____

13. The student is given 50 multiple choice questions on the subject of legal contracts. ____ ____

Which of the test situations below would be appropriate for eliciting the kind of behavior by which you could tell if the student had achieved proficiency on the following objective:

Objective: *Given a properly functioning audiometer of any model, the student must be able to make the adjustments and control settings necessary to administer a standard hearing test.*

	Appro-priate	*Not Appro-priate*

Test Situations

14. Describe the steps followed in administering a standard hearing test. ____ ____

15. Discuss the role of the audiometer in the hearing clinic. ____ ____

Below are two goals. State each in the form of a complete instructional objective, including all necessary parts.

Goal	*Instructional Objective*
16. Selecting a well-balanced meal.	
17. Understanding a short story.	

Test Answers: (1) yes, (2) no, (3) no, (4) yes, (5)A yes, (5)B no, (6)A yes, (6)B no, (7)A yes, (7)B no, (8)A no, (8)B no, (9)A no, (9)B no, (10)A yes, (10)B yes, (11)A no, (11)B no, (12) app, (13) app, (14) not app, (15) not app, (16) e.g., Given a list of foods, the student will select a meal with at least twice as much protein as either carbohydrate, or fat, (17) e.g., Given a particular short story, the student will analyze it in an essay of 500–1000 words, the analysis to include mention of the following: names of main characters, outline of plot, philosophy of author.)

The second suggestion dealt with the issue of the origin of the goal statements that serve as the basis for writing objectives; that is, on what basis does the teacher formulate a content outline as a prerequisite to writing objectives. Discussion of this point yielded the observation that a teacher must be able to *analyze* a subject, unit, or curriculum into its component elements or goals before objectives can be written. There is no question that such analysis is a prerequisite to the actual preparation of objectives for instructional or measurement use. However, this would seem to represent a task separate from the actual writing of objectives and, therefore, would apply to an earlier unit other than the one that the sample test dealt with. Discussion among colleagues thus served both to validate given objectives and to suggest additions to the list of objectives and could not have occurred had the objectives not been specified.

The students' reactions to the items themselves were mixed, but this aspect was deferred to the discussion on reliability.

The final validity criterion dealt primarily with reading level and other biasing factors associated with the test. To examine the reading level of the test, Fry's (1964) readability formula was used. A sentence count of the test per 100 words yielded a result of eight sentences. In essence, then, this kind of test uses quite short sentences, which is often the case in short-answer tests. However, a syllable count per 100 words yielded 182 syllables. Frequent use of words such as "instructional" and "objective" pushed the syllable count up, to put the test at the college reading level. Because the test is used with graduate students, this high reading level was deemed not to be a problem. As far as other sources of bias, none was seen as particularly likely given the educational level of the students taking the test.

Considering the four validity criteria, the sample test was considered to be of sufficient validity for continued use.

Reliability

Reliability refers to the consistency of a test over time or over items. The more consistent a test is, the more accurate it is as a measuring instrument.

Determining Parallel-Item Agreement for Each Objective

Let us consider the items per objective and see the extent to which there is reliability based on agreement between parallel items. Figure 8.4 shows the performance of twelve students on the posttest version of the sample test. Although seventeen students took the test, all reliability analyses were done on twelve of the seventeen, the six highest scorers and the six lowest scorers. The middle scorers were eliminated, as is often done, to focus on the students among whom item discriminability should be greatest.

Except perhaps for the items measuring objective 3, agreement between the items ostensibly measuring the same objectives seems to be high. However, demonstrated mastery of an objective does not seem to be clearly an all-or-none phenomenon, as has often been argued, possibly because it is difficult to write exactly parallel items, particularly in terms of difficulty. Consequently, Figure 8.4 shows that student performance reflects a degree of mastery, with some students, for example, getting two out of seven (2/7), some three out of seven (3/7), some four out of seven (4/7), some five out of seven (5/7), and so on. It is more meaningful therefore, to talk about *degree of proficiency* rather than *mastery.*

Based on the parallel-item analysis, the test seems to be reasonably reliable in all instances, with some possible weakness in the measurement of objective 3. Items 12–15, therefore, need a careful reexamination.

Carrying Out an Item Analysis

Figure 8.5 represents a different way to approach reliability—that of item analysis. Distributions of incorrect responses are shown and indices of discriminability and difficulty are calculated. The formulas used for calculating these indices are:

$$\text{Index of Discriminability} = \frac{\text{No. of top 1/3 who get the item right}}{\text{No. of top 1/3 + bottom 1/3 who get the item right}}$$

$$\text{Index of Difficulty} = \frac{\text{Total no. who get the item wrong}}{\text{Total no. who take the test}}$$

The item analysis approach to reliability has typically been used with norm-referenced tests, whereas parallel-item agreement can be expected to

Number of Students in Each Category

No. right/total no. of items	4/4	3/4	2/4	1/4	0/4	
Items 1– 4	6	5	1	0	0	Obj. 1A*
Items 12–15	4	2	4	1	1	Obj. 3

No. right/total no. of items	7/7	6/7	5/7	4/7	3/7	2/7	1/7	0/7	
Items 5a–11a	3	2	3	2	1	1	0	0	Obj. 1B
Items 5b–11b	1	6	3	1	1	0	0	0	Obj. 2

No. right/total no. of items	2/2	1/2	0/2	
Items 16–17	9	2	1	Obj. 4

*Objective 1 has been divided into two objectives based on item format.

FIGURE 8.4 Analysis of Parallel-Item Agreement by Objectives of the Items from the *Test to Measure a Student's Proficiency in Identifying and Preparing Instructional Objectives*

Student rank no.	Top Third Scorers						Bottom Third Scorers						Index of Discriminability	Index of Difficulty
	1	2	3	4	5	6	12	13	14	15	16	17		
Total score	29	29	28	27	26	26	23	22	22	21	19	18		
Item														
1				x									.45	.08
2													.50	.00
3													.50	.00
4	x			x	x		x		x		x		.50	.50
5a									x				.55	.08
5b											x		.55	.08
6a								x	x			x	.67	.25
6b			x							x	x		.55	.25
7a					x			x			x	x	.62	.33
7b		x			x	x					x		.50	.33
8a			x		x		x			x	x	x	.67	.50
8b			x		x				x	x		x	.57	.42
9a						x		x				x	.67	.25
9b								x					.55	.08
10a													.50	.00
10b								x					.55	.08
11a						x		x	x	x	x	x	.83	.50
11b							x			x	x	x	.75	.33
12										x			.55	.08
13				x		x		x	x	x	x	x	.80	.58
14							x	x	x	x		x	.85	.42
15							x			x	x	x	.75	.33
16								x			x	x	.67	.25
17												x	.55	.08

x indicates an incorrect response; blanks are correct responses

FIGURE 8.5   *Item Analysis of the Sample Test*

work best with criterion-referenced tests (Tuckman 1975), of which the sample test is an example. Since .50 represents the point of no discriminability (that is, equal numbers of high and low scorers get the item right), if we use this as a basis for judging items, than we must conclude that most of the items do not discriminate. If we are dealing with a test built around a set of objectives, as the sample test is, and effective instruction is provided for attaining those objectives, our expectation should be that most students will achieve proficiency and hence pass most items. When students pass most of the items, the items come out low in discriminability and difficulty as calculated with the above formulas.

Most tests that teachers build using objectives are probably more like criterion-referenced tests but imperfectly so. Hence, clear but not perfect success-failure patterns will emerge. In fact, the items that discriminate the most between high and low scorers may be the ones least related to either objectives or instruction and hence least appropriate.

An Overall Determination of Reliability

If we go primarily by the distribution of correct and incorrect responses per item as it relates to an objective (for example, using the results in Figures 8.4 and 8.5 simultaneously without being concerned particularly about the size of the indices), we can see that item 4 poses some problems in that it is more frequently missed than the three items it is "paired" with. It would be wise to examine item 4 with an eye toward the possibility of changing it. Some discussions with students would be most helpful in deciding whether to change it and, if so, how.

On items 5a–11, the worst culprits are items 8a and 11a, missed by half the group, whereas 10a is missed by no one. (Item difficulties help you spot these items. Items that no one fails have difficulties of .00 and discriminabilities of .50). Items 8a and 11a caused considerable difficulty during scoring because so many students took issue with the scoring key. The terms "evaluate" and "develop" seem behavioral and throw students off. It is interesting to note, however, the extent to which item 11a discriminates: all but one of the high scorers get it right and all but one of the low scorers get it wrong. It would not be unreasonable to keep item 11a and to rewrite item 8a.

On items 5b–11b, the worst culprit is 8b—missed by five of the 12 students including more of the high scorers than the low scorers. Item 8 (both parts) seems to be a troublesome item and should be rewritten.

Items 12–15 are passed primarily by the high scorers and failed by the low scorers. Because of the consistency across the four items, they seem to be reliable. However, these same items posed some problem on the parallel-item analysis (Figure 8.4). This conflict suggests a possible failure in instruction on this objective rather than a failure of the test itself and will be reconsidered in the next section on interpretability.

Finally, items 16 and 17 show a reasonably high degree of consistency; nine of the 12 students got both items right. Reliability based on the consistency, or parallelism, criterion must be considered high for these items.

Overall, then, we can conclude that the sample test possesses a reasonably high degree of reliability with the exception, most notably, of items 4, 8a, and 8b. Otherwise: (1) on objectives for which proficiency appeared to be achieved by the total group (most students passed them), item agreement within an objective was high; and (2) on objectives for which proficiency did not appear to be achieved by the total group (most students did not pass them), items discriminated between high scorers (those showing proficiency) and low scorers (those not showing proficiency). Items 4, 8a, and 8b should be rewritten to make them more consistent with the other items measuring those objectives.

Interpretability

Interpretability refers to the extent to which a test provides a teacher with meaningful and useful information about the students who took it. If the scores cannot be understood and applied, then the test is of little value.

The sample test measured the proficiency of students in identifying and preparing instructional objectives. Since the last two items on the test called for the actual preparation of objectives, successful performance on these items can be assumed to reflect proficiency in the task of writing objectives.

Successful performance on the first fifteen items represents demonstrated proficiency in identifying acceptable and unacceptable components of an objective. Thus, a high score on the test would indicate that a student has demonstrated proficiency on the objectives and a low score would indicate a lack of proficiency. The *criterion*, then, for purposes of *referencing*, or interpreting test scores, is the degree of competence on the given set of objectives of which the student's test performance is indicative. Even though additional or outside criteria might be helpful, sufficient interpretability is provided by the objectives around which the test was built.

Because of the absence of any outside criterion, it is difficult to say what point or score separates acceptable and unacceptable performance. If the test had been administered to a group of professional curriculum writers experienced in preparing behavioral objectives, it might have been possible to use their performance as the basis for establishing a cutoff score. Since this was not true, we can adopt either the criterion of 80 percent success—allowing 20 percent error to account for carelessness, misunderstanding, or failure in some items themselves—or the more liberal 70 percent success criterion as an acceptable level of proficiency. On the sample 30-point test,* then, an 80 percent score of 24 would be considered a pass (i.e., acceptable proficiency). The more liberal (or less rigorous) 70 percent cutoff score would make 21 the passing score. The 80 percent or 70 percent performance criterion for proficiency—remember, this is 80 percent or 70 percent of the items and not 80 percent or 70 percent of the students—can be applied not only to the total test score (as we are doing here) but perhaps more meaningfully on an objective-by-objective basis (as will be done below) so that students may pass some but not all of the objectives.

---

* Items 1–4 and 12–15 are each worth one point, yielding a subtotal of eight points. Items 5–11 are worth two points each, one per part (subtotal equals 14 points). Items 16 and 17 are worth four points each with one point for each of the three objective parts and a one-point bonus if all three are correctly given (subtotal equals 8 points).

If we look at the performance of this class on the pretest, we find the distribution of scores that appear in the top half of Figure 8.6. If we apply the 80 percent criterion, eight students (almost half) passed the test before receiving instruction. Using the 70 percent criterion, this pretest passing number swells to 10. In fact, the distribution is biomodal (meaning that there are two *modes* or high points). One group clusters just below the 70 percent mark and the other clusters at the 80 percent mark. The posttest distribution (shown in the bottom half of Figure 8.6) reveals that on the overall 70 percent performance criterion, 15 of the 17 students "passed" the test after instruction, as compared to 10 before.

Let us now look at the performance of this class on the posttest (i.e., after instruction) on an objective-by-objective basis—the characteristic way that criterion-referenced tests are interpreted. These results are shown in Figure 8.7 for the top six scorers (students 1–6) and the bottom six scorers (students 12–17). We can first use these results to interpret and report on individual student performance. (We also have divided objective 1 into two objectives, 1A and 1B, bringing to five the total number of objectives.*) Acceptable proficiency on a particular objective was based on getting right 70 percent of the items that measured that objective.† Students 1, 2, 3, 4, and 6 demonstrated acceptable proficiency on all objectives. Each student's "report card" would list all five objectives as performances that he or she had achieved with this level of proficiency on these items. Students 5 and 12 each manifested proficiency on four of the five objectives; students 14 and 15 were proficient on four of the five objectives; student 17 was proficient on two; student 16 on one. Each student would receive a list of the objectives on which he or she had attained proficiency. Where objectives were missed, students could be given remediation or retraining and then be retested until they achieved proficiency.

We also can use Figure 8.7 to provide information about instructional success. Eleven out of twelve students achieved proficiency on objective 1A; nine out of twelve became proficient on objectives 1B and 4; eight out of twelve showed proficiency on objective 2; but only six out of twelve (half) were proficient on objective 3. Clearly, instruction for objective 3 was not adequate, particularly for the poorer performers (note that all six of the low scorers failed to achieve proficiency on this objective). When and if the unit is retaught, the instructor would be wise to provide more instruction aimed specifically at objective 3.

Thus, we can use our objectives as a basis for interpreting test scores in

---

* This separation was based on item format. Objective 1A is based on items 1–4, objective 1B on items 5a–11a.

† The more liberal 70 percent criterion rather than the more rigorous 80 percent one was chosen because of certain item unreliabilities discussed in the preceding section based on ambiguity that arose. Such unreliability creates "errors" that cannot be "blamed" on the student.

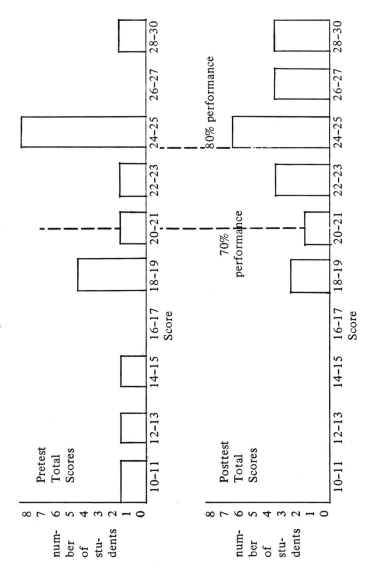

FIGURE 8.6 Distribution of Total Scores on the Pretest and Posttest of the Sample Test

125

Student	Obj. 1A (items 1–4)	Obj. 1B (items 5a–11a)	Obj. 2 (items 5b–11b)	Obj. 3 (items 12–15)	Obj. 4 (items 16–17)	Overall Performance Results (successes/total)
Student 1	X	X	X	X	X	5/5
2	X	X	X	X	X	5/5
3	X	X	X	X	X	5/5
4	X	X	X	X	X	5/5
5		X	X	X	X	4/5
6	X	X	X	X	X	5/5
12	X		X		X	4/5
13	X		X		X	3/5
14	X	X				3/5
15	X	X			X	3/5
16	X					1/5
17	X		X			2/5
Overall Performance Results	11/12	9/12	8/12	6/12	9/12	70%
Minimum Proficiency Criterion	3/4	5/7	5/7	3/4	2/2	

X indicates mastery

FIGURE 8.7 Analysis by Objectives of Individual Student Performance

terms of proficiency, both as a way of evaluating (1) student performance, and (2) instructional efficacy. We then can make decisions about student remediation and instructional improvement.

Because the sample test is a criterion-referenced test (that is, it was written to measure objectives), individual performance is most meaningfully interpreted in terms of degree of proficiency attained on individual objectives. If, for any reason, one chose to use a relative scoring procedure of total scores, two frequency plots in Figure 8.6 could serve as a basis. Scores of 26–30—the top third—could be given an "outstanding," 22–25—the middle third—an "average," and 18–23—the bottom third—a "below average."* Such reporting is of limited usefulness and information value either for student or teacher in this particular instance.

Since the criterion-referenced approach provides a basis for test interpretation in terms of objectives, it makes sense to report on the objectives that have been achieved with proficiency according to the given criterion and those that have not and then to provide additional opportunities for students to achieve proficiency on the objectives on which it was not achieved originally. In this way, no numerical grade or classification need be given (since this sometimes provokes feelings of failure and inadequacy). The objectives themselves form the basis for reporting and interpreting scores. They also form the basis for instructional program evaluation by helping the teacher discriminate between objectives the class has mastered and those that need to be taught differently.

Usability

The overall usability of the sample test in identifying and preparing instructional objectives was judged to be high. It took only between twenty and thirty minutes for students to complete the test—a time span sufficiently short to avoid fatigue or boredom. Since the test is entirely a paper-and-pencil instrument, its level of practicality for classroom use is high. Regarding administrative procedures, the test is largely self-administering, particularly with the adult population who used it. The only administrative difficulty was encountered on the last two items, the open-ended ones; some students had difficulty in understanding what was expected. For subsequent use, additional instructions should be written for these items. Finally, reading level posed no problem for the adult students, and interest was maintained throughout. Clearly, there was no problem in usability with this instrument for the adult group who used it.

---

* Of course, even though this is a relative basis for scoring, it is too limited and simplistic to be considered norm referencing in the true sense. For norm referencing, a norm group would be needed.

Conclusion

The sample test scored well on the five test criteria in terms of the performance of a group of students. More importantly, the five test criteria enumerated in the Checklist (Figure 8.1) seemed applicable as a basis for determining the properties of a given criterion-referenced test. Even though some of the techniques could be improved, the overall approach seems a helpful one for evaluating the quality of such tests. And within an instructional program evaluation, evaluators are encouraged to determine and demonstrate the quality of their tests. Moreover, test interpretability procedures generate the kinds of results that are best used for program evaluation.

Even though this chapter has focused on a single illustrative test to demonstrate the procedures used in test evaluation, the procedures themselves are generalizable for use with any criterion-referenced test. In fact, many of the procedures described can be used as effectively and as meaningfully for evaluating a norm-referenced test. Rather than concentrating on the theory behind these approaches, the emphasis has been on techniques that are practical for the evaluator.

PART III

Carrying Out the Evaluation

CHAPTER 9

Operational Guidelines for Doing Formative Evaluation

This chapter presents and describes an operational plan that a school district can use for the *formative evaluation* of its programs. This plan is summarized in a flow diagram in Figure 9.1.

The plan uses one of the three types of designs described in this book—formative evaluation. (Plans for the other two types of designs, summative and ex post facto, will be described in subsequent chapters.) The steps are listed in order in the figure, along with a suggested amount of time for each step. It is advisable that the district not attempt to operationalize a plan for all school levels simultaneously; rather, a projected year-and-a-half evaluation plan should be phased in and out as shown below. This will insure that the developmental load is not so excessive as to be its own undoing, while providing that an evaluation of the entire district be completed in a span of 3½ years.

	Middle Grades		
Elementary Grades		Secondary Grades	

| 0 | 6 mo. | 1 yr. | 1½ yrs. | 2 yrs. | 2½ yrs. | 3 | 3½ |

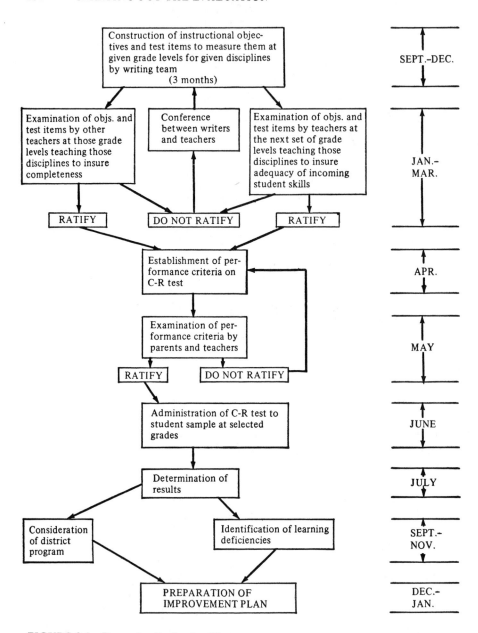

FIGURE 9.1   *Formative Evaluation Plan*

The remainder of this chapter will describe each step in the plan in order. The detailed operations required by each step, in most cases, are based on procedures already described in the book. (Also, refer to Case Study 1, Appendix A, for an illustration of a formative evaluation.)

Preparing Objectives and Test Items

The first step in formative evaluation is having the writing team construct instructional objectives and test items to measure these objectives at given grade levels for given disciplines. It is best not to start with all grade levels and/or all disciplines because of the large demands developmental activities make on the instructional staff and the possible disruptive influence of widespread, simultaneous change. It is more prudent and manageable to begin with a cluster of grade levels (for example, first, second, and third) and a limited number of subjects (for example, reading and mathematics) and then to branch out both in terms of grade levels (move into grades four, five, and six) and subjects (move into science, social studies, and language arts). Subsequent extensions would bring in the middle grades and lastly the high school.

Objectives and test items are best written by a writing team of teachers who volunteer for the task and are paid extra for all out-of-school hours devoted to it. The team should be assisted by central staff administrators and by consultants and should work according to a plan or schedule. Not all teachers will want to serve as writers, and they should not be pressured to do so. The writing team should be drawn from the ranks of teachers rather than exclusively from central staff or consultants. If the schedule can be started in July rather than September, the writing can begin in the summer, when teacher time is more easily arranged.

Writing Objectives

Many sources are available describing the preparation of instructional objectives. What is most important is providing the teachers with technical assistance in the form of consultant help. Moreover, emphasis in the preparation of objectives should be on substance rather than form. Members of the writing team should discuss and critique all objectives in order to make the set acceptable and complete.

A behavioral or instructional objective has three components: (1) the givens or conditions under which the behavior is to occur; (2) the behavior or action itself; and (3) the criteria that will be used to judge the suitability of the behavior. Often, however, objectives are written in shorthand form by listing just the behavior or action itself. The key element in this shorthand notation is the action verb, which characterizes the required learner behavior. (It is important to keep in mind that we are talking about observable and measurable

The action words that are used as operational guides in constructing the instructional objectives are:

1. *Identifying.* The individual selects (by pointing to, touching, or picking up) the correct object of a class name. For example: When asked, "Which figure is a triangle?" the student is expected to respond by pointing to a triangle; if the student is asked to point to an equilateral triangle, he or she is expected to point to an equilateral one. This class of performances also includes identifying object properties (such as rough, smooth, straight, curved) and kinds of changes, such as an increase or decrease in size.

2. *Distinguishing.* Identifying objects or events that are potentially confusing (square, rectangle) or that involve two contrasting identifications (such as right, left). For example: When asked to point to the square, the student is expected to respond by pointing to the square, not the rectangle.

FIGURE 9.2 Definitions and Illustrations of Action Verbs Useful in Writing Objectives. Drawings adapted from *An Evaluation Model and Its Applications: First Report* by the American Association for the Advancement of Science, Commission on Science Education.

3. *Constructing.* Generating a construction or drawing that identifies a designated object or set of conditions. Example: Beginning with pencil and piece of paper, the request is made, "Construct an isosceles triangle."

4. *Naming.* Supplying the correct name (orally or in written form) for a class of objects or events. Example: "What is the form I am pointing to called?"

5. *Ordering.* Arranging two or more objects or events in proper order in accordance with a stated category. Example: "Arrange these blocks in order of increasing size."

6. *Describing.* Generating and naming all of the necessary categories of objects, object properties, or event properties that are relevant to the description of a designated situation. Example: "Describe a pentagon." The student's description is considered sufficiently complete when there is a probability that any other individual is able to use the description to identify the object or event.

7. *Stating a rule.* Making a verbal statement (not necessarily in technical terms) that conveys a rule or a principle, including the names of the proper classes of objects or events in their correct order. Example: "What is a rule for telling when two triangles are congruent?"

8. *Applying a rule.* Using a learned principle or rule to derive an answer to a question. The answer may be correct identification, supplying a name, or some other kind of response. The question is stated so that the individual must employ a rational process to arrive at the answer. Example: "If you had a heavy rock how would you move it?" The student must know that the lever is a useful tool.

9. *Demonstrating.* Performing the operations necessary to apply a rule or principle. Example: "Use this marked stick to draw a line parallel to the edge of the paper." This requires that the student know the rule that parallel lines are equidistant.

10. *Interpreting.* The student should be able to identify objects and/or events in terms of their consequences. A set of rules or principles always will be connected with this behavior. Example: "What do these graphs tell us about the relation between variables a, b and c?"

behaviors that the learner is expected to be able to carry out.) Figure 9.2 lists and illustrates ten action verbs that can be used in preparing objectives. Each verb is illustrated by a simple geometrical example.

People are much more familiar with writing behavioral objectives for the cognitive domain than for the affective domain and therefore are more adept at it. Listed below are some *model objectives for the affective domain* that can be adapted to fit a variety of needs and situations.

1. Given an instrument or scale for measuring attitudes toward _____, the student will endorse the positive (self, school)
   items and reject the negative ones, thereby indicating positive attitudes toward _____. (self, school)

2. Given a _____ situation, the student will dem- (group work)
   onstrate the tendency to _____ as evi- (work coopera-
   denced by a self-report of _____, _____, tively)
   _____ and _____. (working well, getting along, contributing)

3. Given statements about one's own behavior, the student (practice good
   will indicate the tendency to _____ by re- health habits)
   porting _____, _____, _____ (good diet,
   _____. adequate sleep, cleanliness)

4. Given a(n) _____ situation, the student will (social)
   demonstrate the tendency to _____ as evi- (get along with
   denced by the nominations or selection by fellow students others)
   as _____. (likeable)

5. Given a(n) _____ situation, the student will (group task)
   demonstrate the tendency to _____ as evi- (work effec-
   denced by the report by other people of the student's tively)
   _____, _____, and _____ (participation,
   _____. contribution, interaction)

6. The student will demonstrate _____ for (or to- (positive
   ward) _____ as evidenced by values)
   _____, _____, and _____ (helping
   _____ in his/her drawings or writings. others)
   (the presence of others, warmth, detail)

7. Given a(n) _____ situation, the student will   (group task)
demonstrate the tendency to _____ as   (be self-
evidenced by teacher observations of the student's   directed)
_____, _____, and _____   (moving from
_____.   one task to
     another,
     completing
     work, seeking
     help when
     needed)

Constructing Test Items

Instructional objectives form the basis for a criterion-referenced test of intermediate difficulty that the writing team described above also could be asked to
prepare. Again, test-item construction (as the writing of objectives) is exten-
sively covered in various sources* and will not be detailed here. (Also, the steps
required in evaluating the test were described in the previous chapter of this
book.) However, some description will be given on constructing *test item specifications,* which should be used in writing test items. These specifications insure
the appropriateness of the test items written for measuring the stated objectives.

Test item specifications describe the *conditions, action, and criteria* that
are called for in an objective and thus must be operationalized in the test items
to measure that objective. For example, if the objective were to *add and sub-
tract fractions with common denominators,* then the conditions for measuring
this objective might include between four and six fractions all with the same
denominator, the denominator falling between two and thirty; the action would
be to compute their sum and reduce to lowest terms; the criterion would be a
correct sum expressed in lowest terms as a fraction or mixed number. One
could now write any number of test items that fit these specifications and hence
the objective.

If the objective were changed to *adding and subtracting fractions with unlike denominators,* then the conditions must specify what the acceptable denominators are, and even perhaps the requirement that the result exceed one so
that mixed numbers would become involved. The action would include finding
the least common denominator, converting all terms to it, and adding and subtracting the results. Criteria would include finding the correct LCD, making the
correct conversions, and obtaining the correct sums and differences.

Three other examples are shown in Figure 9.3.

---

* See also B. W. Tuckman, *Measuring Educational Outcomes: Fundamentals of Testing.*
New York: Harcourt Brace Jovanovich, 1975.

Objective: Given a list of compound words, the student will identify the component parts of each word.

Conditions	Action	Criteria
10 compound words, e.g., feedback handsome therefore	Separate each compound word into two words by making a slash through it.	Eight of 10 are correctly divided.

Objective: Given data resulting from scientific observation and a set of conclusions, the student will identify the conclusions drawn from and consistent with the data.

Conditions	Action	Criteria
A list of observations (e.g., magnet attracts iron filings; magnet attracts thumbtacks; magnet does not attract a penny) and a list of conclusions (e.g., magnets attract metal; magnets attract iron; magnets attract everything).	Circle the conclusion that fits the observation.	The correct conclusion is circled in each item.

Objective: Given a scale of attitudes toward school, the student will demonstrate positive attitudes toward school.

Conditions	Action	Criteria
40 statements (half positive and half negative) about school in terms of behavior of teacher, relation to peers, enjoyment of school environment.	Circle YES for those statements you agree with and NO for those you disagree with.	More than half of the positive items are marked YES and more than half of the negative items marked NO.

FIGURE 9.3 *Illustrations of Test Item Specifications for Three Objectives*

Obtaining Tests and Objectives

It is possible to acquire objectives and test items in some areas without writing them by tapping objectives "banks" or by purchasing criterion-referenced tests from testing companies. Such acquisitions clearly shorten the first step of objective and item writing. Where time and labor are particular considerations, districts are encouraged to attempt to buy rather than build the criterion-referenced tests that formative evaluation calls for. However, it must be realized that commercial sets are not likely to be as on-target to the district's needs as homemade ones. Also, the act of preparing objectives and test items is a valuable in-service experience for teachers in learning to delineate and specify the learning goals they want their students to achieve. Moreover, formative evaluation probably will be better accepted when the local teachers are more involved in it. Hence, for esprit, involvement, and a targeted product, teachers should be the writers; for speed, ease, and reasonably high test quality, objectives and item sets should be purchased.

Ratification

The objectives and items that are either written or purchased must be ratified to insure their *acceptability* and *completeness*. This is a simpler process when the objectives and test items are written by teachers because they will be more targeted than purchased objectives and items. Therefore, when objectives and items are to be purchased, alternative sets should be examined closely by a teacher team (comparable to the writing team described above) in order to identify the particular set or subset that most closely fits the district's goals and program.

Once objectives and items have either been written or selected by a teacher team, the ratification process can begin. The purpose of ratification is not only to maximize teacher involvement as a psychological strategy but also to insure the broad representativeness of the objectives and items in terms of the district's program. Ratification is an attempt to insure that the objectives and items are tailored to the district's needs. This is insured by asking teachers in the given disciplines at the same levels as the writers (or screeners), but who were not involved in writing (or screening) to judge the acceptability and completeness of the written or selected set.

Acceptability refers to whether a written or selected objective and item cover material that is taught or should be mastered by students in the district. *Completeness* refers to whether all material that is taught or should be mastered by students in the district is covered by objectives and items in the written or selected set. Hence, acceptability judgments seek to minimize "errors of commission" and completeness judgments seek to minimize "errors of omission."

Ratification should be a two-stage process. It should be done not only by teachers at the same grade level, but also by teachers at immediately adjacent grade levels. Middle-school teachers often complain about the inappropriateness of entry-level skills of students entering from the elementary grades. High school teachers voice the same complaints vis-a-vis the middle school. Similar criticisms abound from grade level to grade level. To minimize these difficulties of passage from grade to grade, first and third grade teachers should be asked to ratify second grade objectives and items, second and fourth grade teachers to ratify third grade, and so on. In other words, at each grade level there would be three ratification teams, one for that grade level, one for the preceding grade level and one for the succeeding grade level, all in the same discipline.

To summarize, examination of objectives and test items by teachers at the preceding and succeeding grade levels (articulation between grade levels) is important in a cumulative process such as learning. What is not learned at one grade level becomes a deficiency in the next level. When this failure to learn is based on curricular omission, then in effect it is being programmed in by the district. This happens when grade level articulation is lacking; succeeding grade levels assume prerequisites that are not being taught at prior levels. Articulation can result in either the missing skills being included earlier by agreement or in their being deferred so that mastery is not assumed. They then would be taught, again by agreement, at subsequent levels. The widest articulation gaps occur between grade levels housed in separate buildings (end of elementary—beginning of middle, end of middle—beginning of high). Again, to assure completeness and acceptability, objectives and test items should be examined, altered, and ultimately ratified by teachers of the same subject at the next highest and next lowest grade levels, particularly when either of those grade levels are housed in different buildings. When particular differences occur, conferences between writers and reactors should be held.

The consensus required by the ratification process can be built in many ways, including the one suggested here. It is better to use such a procedure than simply to conduct an open discussion on each objective and test item. The steps to use in the suggested ratification approach are:

1. Prepare a printed sheet describing the criteria for inclusion or exclusion that each teacher involved should read before beginning.
2. Prepare a printed sheet with each objective listed and a scale like this alongside each objective:

1	2	3	4	5
Definitely Excluded	Probably Excluded	Uncertain	Probably Included	Definitely Included

3. Ask each teacher to rate each objective on the five-point scale using the listed criteria.
4. Leave space for teachers to add additional objectives that they feel have been omitted.
5. Compute an average rating across teachers for each objective; automatically

include each objective receiving an average rating of four or higher; auto-matically exclude each objective receiving an average rating of two or lower.

6. Each objective receiving an average rating of more than two and less than four should then be discussed and then re-rated after discussion; objectives added by teachers also should be discussed and rated; those reaching the average score of four would then be included.

7. Repeat the same procedures for test items (although some of the criteria for inclusion/exclusion will be different from those for objectives).

The greater the number of teachers involved in the ratification process, the greater the communication between teachers across classrooms, grade levels, and buildings about the aims, objectives, and curriculum of the district. This communication is a positive side effect of the ratification process.

Setting Performance Criteria

Performance criteria or standards are needed as a basis for evaluating actual performance on the test items ratified in the preceding step. Such performance criteria must be both developed and ratified using procedures similar to those already described. When using a homemade test for the first time, no basis for comparison will be available. Typically, under these circumstances, 80 percent success on the items measuring an objective, unit, or course of study is preset as a standard. This criterion allows room for careless student mistakes or errors of measurement while remaining high enough to constitute a standard for mastery.

Another, more technical procedure, is illustrated below. After the first administration of a criterion-referenced test, it is possible to determine the scores that would be needed in each score category to represent a significant gain on the subsequent administration of the test. If you plan to test the same number of students the second time around and if you assume that the standard deviation or variation of the scores around the mean on the second testing will be the same as for the first testing, then the formula shown below can be used to calculate the gain required to obtain significance at the 95 percent level of confidence from the first to the second testing.

$$\text{Required Gain} = \frac{2.77\ \text{SD}}{\sqrt{N}}$$

SD: Standard deviation on first testing
N: Number of students tested on first testing

To illustrate the use of this formula, suppose that 100 third graders are given a test of their ability to add, and obtain a mean score of 20 (out of 40 problems) with a standard deviation of 8. In order for the group to make a significant gain on the next testing, their mean score would have to improve by:

$$\frac{2.77(8)}{10}, \text{ or } 2.2$$

A mean score on the second testing of 22.2 correct would constitute a significant improvement for the group.

A third source of a group standard* is unique to published criterion-referenced tests as compared to homemade ones. Because published tests are used beyond a single district, some test publishers provide an indication of the results in a national comparison group. The proportion of students getting an item or cluster of items correct, called the *p-value,* usually is reported. This is illustrated in the sample printout of results shown in Figure 9.4. When using a published criterion-referenced test, the p-values can be used as performance criteria or standards for evaluating the collective performance of district students, hence the effectiveness of your program.

The process of ratifying performance criteria is more a process of educating teachers and parents to the meaning of criterion-referenced test results. The clamor for test results has little purpose without a basis for evaluating the results. Evaluation means comparing actual results to desired results. When using criterion-referenced tests for formative program evaluation, teachers must understand how standards are determined so that evaluation conclusions will have credibility. The so-called ratification process is an excellent way to inform teachers and parents of the sources of performance criteria.

Collecting Data

You now are ready to administer your testing program to students. It is important to reinforce the point that the purpose of the testing described here is *not* to evaluate individual students but to evaluate the instructional program with an eye toward improving it. For this reason, it is not necessary to test all students on all objectives. Testing all students would be done only if: (1) it were easier administratively and politically to do this; or (2) the purpose of the testing program were a combination of individual assessment and program evaluation. If neither of these conditions applies, then it is more practical in terms of time, effort, and interference to divide the students in each class or grade level into random groups and give each group a portion of the testing program.

Formally, this approach is called *matrix sampling.* Let us assume that the

---

* Reference is made to a group standard rather than an individual standard since the purpose of testing is to evaluate the program and not the student. The program's worth must be measured on the basis of the performance of *all* students combined.

GROUP ITEM ANALYSIS — PAGE 3

WORD STUDY SKILLS — 54 ITEMS

PROCESS NO. 005-1543-001 — COPY I

TEACHER	MS WELLENS	NORMS GR 4.1 NATIONAL	GRADE 4
SCHOOL	LAKESIDE ELEMENTARY	LEVEL PRIMARY 3	FORM E
SYSTEM	NEWTON PUBLIC SCHOOLS	TEST DATE 10/12/82	

OBJECTIVES	ITEM NO	CLASS N	CLASS %	SCHL %	SYST %	NATL %	1	2	3	4	5	OMIT
PHONETIC ANALYSIS CONSONANTS 18 ITEMS												
Single letter sounds – /y/ (A)	19	22	88▲	82▲	79▲	57	1	22	2			0
Single letter sounds – /s/	25	16	64▲	52▲	48	43	5	16	4			0
Single letter sounds – /j/	31	19	76▲	62▲	60▲	52	2	3	19			1
Single letter sounds – /k/	37	15	60	57	54	51	15	5	5			0
Single letter sounds – /b/ (B)	43	15		47	46	47	9	1	15			0
Single letter sounds – /n/	49	12		52	44▼	50	6	12	6			1
Initial Clusters – consonant + 1 /bl/ (C)	21	18	72▲		69▲	51	3	4	18			0
Initial Clusters – s + consonant /sp/	33	20	80▲		86▲	55	2	3	20			0
Initial Clusters – consonant + r /dr/ (D)	45	21	84▲	72▲		51	2	21	2			0
Final Clusters – n + consonant /nt/	27	19	76▲	69▲		52	19	5	1			0
Final Clusters – n + consonant /nd/	39	12	48	43	40	36	4	12	7			2
Final Clusters – consonant + t /st/ (E)	51	17	68▲	50▲	38		17	3	5			0
Digraphs – /hw/ spelled wh	23	21	84▲	68▲	64▲		3	1	21			0
Digraphs – /sh/ (F)	29		72▲	57	53	50	2	2	18			3
Digraphs – /ng/	35		76▲	59▲	50	48	19	2	4			0
Digraphs – /TH/ spelled th	41	16	64	58	55	52	7	16	2			0
Digraphs – /th/ (G)	47	14	56▲	44	40	39	14	3				3
Digraphs – /ch/	53	12	38▼	47	43▼	53	3	5	12			5

CLUSTER SUMMARY — — — — — — — —

STUDENT'S RAW SCORE

(J)		SCHL	SYST	NATL		
Mean p Value		68	60	56	48	PERCENT CORRECT
Above Average	18	72	73	70	23	Above Average
Average	5	20	20	14	54	Average
Below Average	2	8	7	6	23	Below Average

SUBTEST SUMMARY — Mean p Value — 65 | 52 | 54 | 46 — RAW SCORE

TOTAL N: CLASS = 25 SCHOOL = 87 SYSTEM = 275

PERCENT CORRECT

(K) STANINE

▼ Denotes local p-value significantly lower than national p-value.
▲ Denotes local p-value significantly higher than national p-value.

FIGURE 9.4 *Objective-Referenced Report on the Stanford Achievement Test Showing p-Values (percentage of students in a given group answering the item or objective correctly; see columns labeled B, C, D and E). Reproduced from the Stanford/Achievement Test 1982 Edition, Objective-Referenced Interpretation. Copyright © 1981 by Harcourt Brace Jovanovich, Inc. New York, NY. All rights reserved.*

STUDENTS ARE LISTED ALPHABETICALLY

BALLARD	BLACKMAN	BURNS	CHANG	COHAN	CRAIG	FARLEY	GLADSTONE	GOLDMAN	GORDON	GROVER	HALL	JENNINGS	LONG	MILLER	PALLACE	PARIS	PETERS	RAYMOND	RIVARA	SANTOS	STEVENS	WANG	WHITTIER	WILSON
CHUCK	DENNIS	THELMA	MARY	JEAN	ROBIN	IRWIN	ELLEN	MIKET	MATT	GLENDA	BARBIE	PHIL	PAUL	BETH	STEVEN	CARL	VAL	SIMON	JOSE	CINDY	JODI	ELMER		
C	L	G	B	K	R	P	V	S	O	A	T	M	N	R	B	D	E	H	J	P	F	S	A	N
+	+	+	+	+	+	+	1	+	+	+	+	3	+	+	+	+	+	3	+	+	+	+	+	+
1	+	3	+	1	+	+	1	+	+	+	+	3	+	+	+	+	1	+	+	+	1	+	3	3
2	+	+	1	+	2	+	+	+	+	0	+	1	+	+	+	+	+	+	+	+	+	2	+	+
2	+	3	+	+	+	2	+	+	+	2	+	+	2	+	+	3	+	2	+	+	3	+	3	3
1	+	+	1	+	1	+	+	+	1	2	+	+	+	1	+	+	+	1	+	+	1	+	1	1
1	3	+	1	+	+	+	3	3	+	1	+	3	+	3	+	+	+	1	+	3	+	1	0	1
+	1	+	+	+	2	+		+	+	2	+	+	2	+	+	1	+	+	+	+	+	2	1	
1	2	+	+	+	+	+	1	+	+	+	+	+	+	+	+	+	+	2	+	+	2	+	+	
+	+	+	+	1	+	+	+	3	+	+	+	+	+	+	+	+	+	1	+	+	3	+	+	
2	+	+	+	+	3	+	+	2	+	+	+	+	+	+	2	+	+	2	+	+	2	+	+	
0	3	1	+	3	+	+	+	1	+	3	+	+	1	3	+	1	+	+	3	+	3	0	+	3
2	+	+	3	+	+	3	+	2	+	+	3	+	+	+	+	2	+	+	+	+	3	3	+	
+	+	+	2	+	+	+	1	+	+	+	+	+	+	+	1	+	+	+	+	1	+	+		
1	+	0	+	2	+	1	+	+	+	+	+	+	+	0	+	+	2	+	+	+	+	0		
+	+	3	+	+	+	+	3	+	+	2	+	+	+	+	3	+	+	1	+	+	3	2		
1	3	+	+	1	+	+	+	1	+	+	1	+	3	1	+	+	+	1	+	+	+	1		
+	2	+	3	+	+	3	0	+	+	2	+	0	+	3	+	+	+	2	+	+	0	+	3	3
1	0	2	+	1	0	+	+	+	0	+	2	+	2	+	+	0	+	0	+	1	+	2	+	2
6	11	12	12	13	14	13	12	12	14	11	17	11	14	14	15	12	15	12	12	15	13	10	9	7
33	61	67	67	72	78	72	67	67	78	61	94	61	78	78	83	67	83	67	67	83	72	56	50	39
	+	+	+	+	+	+	+	+			+			+	+	+	+	+	+	+	+			
	◊								◊		◊										◊	◊		
35	38	42	32	48	37	40	39	47	51	26	37	28	40	42	49	34	50	41	35	42	39	26	24	18
65	70	78	59	89	69	74	72	87	94	48	69	52	74	78	91	63	93	76	65	78	72	48	44	33
5	5	6	4	8	5	5	5	7	9	3	5	4	5	6	8	5	9	6	5	6	5	3	3	3

DATA SERVICES DIVISION  **THE PSYCHOLOGICAL CORPORATION**
HARCOURT BRACE JOVANOVICH, PUBLISHERS

Student Test Groups of 40 Each

		1	2	3	4	5	6	7	8	9	10	11	12
Reading Subtests	1	✓											
	2		✓										
	3			✓									
	4				✓								
	5					✓							
	6						✓						
Math Subtests	1							✓					
	2								✓				
	3									✓			
	4										✓		
	5											✓	
	6												✓

FIGURE 9.5 *An Illustrative Sampling Plan*

third-grade reading and math tests are each based on twenty-four objectives and that there are five items per objective. Hence, you have two tests of 120 items each, for a total of 240 items. Let us further assume that students can do about twenty items in a single sitting. Thus, we can consider each test to be comprised of six sittings, or subtests, making a total of twelve by combining the two. If the district has 480 third graders, then forty students could be given each of the twelve subtests, as shown in Figure 9.5.

How the forty students are chosen to take each of the twelve subtests is of critical importance. Each group of forty students must be as representative of the 480 at that grade level as is possible. If two classes were chosen at random for each subtest, the result would not be representative since the elementary schools in most districts are not mirror images of one another. If the decision was to give a single subtest to an entire class, then one or two classes in each school would have to be given each subtest, which would result in each student taking more than one test. This is acceptable but not consistent with the illustration.

To use the sampling plan shown in Figure 9.5, each third grader in the district would have to have an equal chance of taking each test. To accomplish this, you would have to take a list of all the third graders in the district by name and a table of random numbers and then randomly select forty students for each test group and then see that each got the subtest he or she was so assigned. This would be an arduous administrative task.

However, there is a shortcut for approximating the same result that does not require any student to take more than a single subtest. Print up each of the 12 subtests and label each so that each subtest can be identified. Then stack up the 40 copies of each test in sequential order; that is, Reading (R) 1, R2, R3, R4, R5, R6; Math (M)1, M2, M3, M4, M5, M6, R1, R2, R3, R4, R5, R6, M1, M2, M3, M4, M5, M6, and so on until all 480 tests have been so arranged. Then subdivide the pile of 480 into separate piles, one for each third grade classroom, so that each room gets a number equal to the number of students in that classroom. Where one classroom ends up in the sequence, the next begins. Put a rubber band around each packet, write the teacher's name on each, and distribute them. In this way, the students taking each test will be distributed across the entire district in an essentially random pattern.

In order to be sure that test results are an accurate reflection of student capabilities and are not influenced by test-taking conditions, it is essential that the test administration process be the same at all times. Have the teachers all administer the tests at the same time and in the same manner. Have students write their names on their test booklets or answer sheets so that they take the tests seriously. Because students in the same classroom will be taking different tests (and they should be told this in advance), they are likely to finish at different times. Make sure that students remain at their desks and work quietly when they have finished, in order not to disturb other students.

Determining and Interpreting Results

Analyzing data should be aimed at producing results in a form or forms that administrators, teachers, and parents (or taxpayers, in general) can understand. Remember that the purpose of the testing is instructional program evaluation and *not* student evaluation. (An additional purpose may be evaluation of the test itself, which was covered in the preceding chapter.) When presenting results, the emphasis should be on areas where program improvement is needed, since the identification of these areas is the purpose of formative evaluation.

Presenting item results will yield more detail than is necessary and useful; presenting total test scores will yield less. The proper unit of analysis for formative evaluation and criterion-referenced testing is the *objective*. (Refer to the discussion of *interpretability* in the preceding chapter for further discussion about reporting test results by objective.)

Let us assume that tests are designed to span a single grade level, and that in each major discipline for each grade level there are between twenty-five and fifty objectives. There is an advantage to keeping the number of objectives low to minimize fragmentation, so let us assume twenty-five objectives and four disciplines, resulting in a nice round number of 100 major objectives per grade level. (You probably also will want to include affective objectives that span the disciplines.) You may decide to have anywhere from two to ten test items per objective, depending on the scope and nature of the objective.

Essentially, your results should be presented in terms of: (1) *the percent of students "passing," or mastering an objective;* or (2) *the average score on those items measuring an objective by the students taking the test.* If you have established a mastery requirement per objective, such as two items out of two, or two out of three, or three out of four, then it is possible to label a student as having mastered or not mastered a particular objective. It then is possible to determine what percentage of the test-takers have mastered that objective (according to the individual mastery criterion). That percentage of test-takers actually mastering a given objective can be compared to the performance standard (either 80 percent or the p-value reported by test publishers) and the results reported. Those results will tell the various audiences not only the number of objectives in the set that were not mastered at criterion (that is, fewer than 80 percent of the district test-takers mastered them, or fewer test-takers in the district mastered them than in the national sample), but also exactly *which* objectives they were. This information provides the basis for program alteration, thereby hopefully program improvement. Hence, the aim of the results is not to embarrass or reward the district, but to give it the feedback necessary for improvement.

The second approach is not to set or assume any criterion for individual mastery, but simply to count up the number or percent of items gotten correct by each test-taker on an objective, and to obtain an average across all the test-takers. If there are five items measuring an objective, for example, the average number correct may be 3.1. This average then can be converted to a percent (in the example, 62 percent) and compared to the 80 percent or some other performance standard, or the average can serve as the basis for calculating the score required for next year to constitute a significant gain. (This procedure was illustrated earlier in the chapter.) If this is the second year of test administration, and the required significant gain score was determined last year, it can be compared to this year's result to determine whether positive progress had been made.

Decision Making

It is important to emphasize or reemphasize three points about formative evaluation:

1. Formative evaluation looks at programs, not students (although it uses student test results to do this).
2. Formative evaluation aims at program improvement.
3. Formative evaluation is most meaningful when done more than once.

A district's best source of comparison is itself. Does it move up? Does it improve? Do more students demonstrate mastery of more objectives? In between gaining answers to these questions, the district tries different approaches and emphases so that the formative evaluation can tell the district which techniques are working and which are not.

The results of formative evaluation provide the basis for the *identification of group learning deficiencies*. Evaluation results, when compared to standards or expectations, as illustrated above, will clearly show which objectives are being mastered and which not. Students may be learning to read, for example, but not to write grammatically; to perform operations on fractions but not on decimals; or to remember facts but not to design experiments. Patterns of substandard performance will reveal deficient areas, not for every student but for enough students for it to be problematical.

Knowledge of learning deficiencies, however, is not enough. There also must be a *consideration of the district program*—what is taught and in what manner. This is accomplished through procedures of *input/process evaluation,* as shown in chapter 6. Change cannot occur without a careful consideration of current practices so that those that are most likely connected to the deficiencies can be changed. Once you have identified weaknesses based on student performance as well as weaknesses based on level of program implementation, you are ready to prepare an improvement plan. That plan will be an attempt to overcome both types of weakness—program implementation and student performance. If, however, better implementation of the existing program seems insufficient to overcome problems in student performance, then, of course, you would be well advised to consider installing one or more new programs. This decision would be based on the results of the formative evaluation.

CHAPTER 10

Operational Guidelines for Doing Summative Evaluation

The approach described here for evaluating a specific intervention or program (rather than the overall program of the district) follows the basic model of summative experimental design described in chapter 5. This model includes the techniques of formulating goals and aims, constructing operational definitions of goals and aims in the form of objectives, selecting a design, developing measuring instruments, choosing comparison groups, collecting data, and conducting statistical analyses. This model is the most appropriate one for summative evaluation because: (1) it is a logical and consistent approach; (2) it allows one to establish cause-and-effect relationships; and (3) it provides the conditions for making systematic comparisons. Thus, this model enables us to determine whether a program achieves its aims better than some alternatives.

The overall evaluation model that is being suggested appears in Figure 10.1. It includes seven steps. The first step provides for *identifying the aims of the intervention* or experimental program. The second step involves *transforming these aims into an operational form* by stating them in *behaviorial terms*. Step three involves either *developing a test for measuring the program objectives* or *selecting such a test* in a manner that assures its content validity or appropriateness. The fourth step involves *establishing an experimental group* sample—that

153

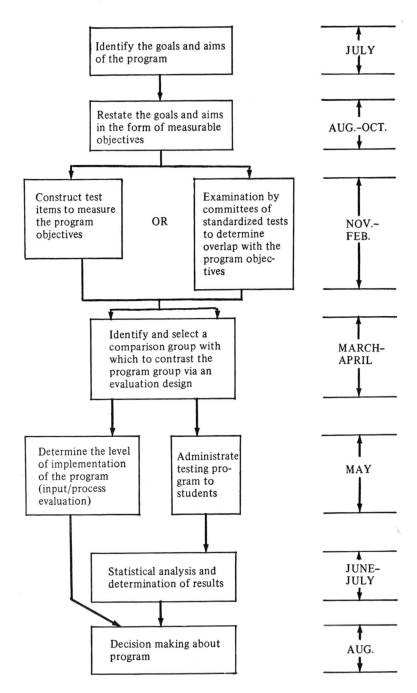

FIGURE 10.1 *Summative Evaluation Plan*

is, the group receiving the program—as one group, and a *comparison, control,* or *criterion* group as the second group. This step also undertakes to establish or determine the equivalence of the members of both groups on selection factors. In the fifth step *data collection occurs* and in the sixth, *statistical analyses are undertaken* as a prerequisite to drawing conclusions. *Decisions about the program* are made in the seventh and final step. Each step now will be described in some detail. (Also, Case Study 2, Appendix A, illustrates the approach to summative evaluation.) Refer also to the Program Evaluator's Checklist (Figure 11.6) in Chapter 11.

Goals and Objectives

Identifying the Goals and Aims of the Program

When a new instructional program is undertaken in a school system, whether this program is based on a specific course of study, a facility, or the introduction of a special piece of equipment, the program's developers or adopters have in mind aims or objectives on the outcomes they expect and hope for if the program is successful. These aims and objectives, which will be different for different programs, represent the goals or benchmarks of the program's success. Some educational programs locate their aims very specifically in the future adult life of the student. In vocational programs, for example, specific trade competencies and entry level and potential advancement level job skills often are identified as the aims or objectives to which the program is addressed. Other educational programs, on the other hand, may list as their aims or objectives mastery of the content that has been included in the course of study.

It is possible to distinguish between more immediate and more ultimate aims and objectives. However, the decision about aims or objectives should rest with the developer or user of the intervention rather than with the evaluator (although the evaluator may stimulate their articulation). It is up to the people who create or decide to try the program to decide what they expect from it. They must ask themselves: What is expected of students who have completed the program that is *not* expected of students who have *not* experienced the program, or who have experienced an alternative one?

Thus, the first step in the summative evaluation process, as in the other evaluation approaches, is to approach either the program developer or user, or both, and ask: What are the aims and objectives of this program? What is expected that students should be able to do after having experienced the program? In response to such questions, the developer or user may make statements such as: (a) the program will help the students develop an appreciation of art; (b) it will help them understand themselves better; (c) it will provide them with the skills for entering the carpentry trade; (d) it will make them more likely to be constructive citizens; (e) they will know more American history than they did before they started; (f) they will have a greater interest in science; and so on.

These statements exemplify the kinds of aims that program developers and users identify and how they are likely to be expressed. A specific short-coming can be seen with each of these statements. As stated, they will be diffi-cult to measure. Thus, in step one, the aims or goals of the program to be evaluated are identified, but only in general terms. In fact, they also may be identified in ambiguous terms. It is likely that the initial statement of the goals and aims will be in the kinds of vague terms that can be seen in these examples.

Operationally Defining the Goals and Aims: Behavioral Objectification

In the first step described above, the goals and aims have been identified. In a sense, this identification provides the hypothesis that states that these aims and goals may be more likely to be acquired by students after experiencing the in-tervention or program than had that program not been experienced, or if some other program had been experienced. The next step is to produce an opera-tional definition of the goals and aims that moves the evaluator one step closer to the concrete terms and dimensions that can be worked with.

In completing this second step, the evaluator asks the developer and the teachers implementing the program: "How can we tell whether the aims and objectives of the program or approach outlined in the first step have been achieved? What observable and measurable behaviors will the students per-form if these aims and objectives have been achieved that they will *not* perform if these aims and objectives have *not* been achieved?" The question is *not* how will the students be different after the program but what can we *see* about them that is different. It is impossible to get inside the head of students to determine whether they appreciate, understand, are interested in, or are motivated by something. We are limited in our judgments to overt actions and self-reports; that is, we can only study behavior. Any conclusions about thoughts, ideas, likes, fears, or skills can be made only from the observation of behavior (al-though we may, and often do, use tests to elicit this behavior).

Thus, the aims and objectives of the program being evaluated must be operationally defined in behavioral terms. They must be replaced by state-ments of behavior that are associated with them in order for evaluation to pro-ceed. This step, therefore, involves identifying and specifying behaviors that the program in question is intended to produce.

It is likely that a program of any size or duration will have more than one aim or objective. It may have many aims and objectives. Moreover, in trans-forming these objectives into behaviors that define them or imply their pres-ence, it often is necessary to deal with many behaviors associated with each aim and objective rather than thinking simply in terms of one behavior per objective. For this reason, we must think in terms of a series of behavioral objectives rather than one or a few objectives that will represent the aims of the evaluation as operationally defined.

Writing Objectives. How does one produce an operational or behavioral definition of an aim or goal? Although this material has been covered in the preceding chapter, it will be summarized briefly here. The major characteristic of such a definition is that it is written in specific behavioral terms; that is, it includes an action verb. Upon completion of the program, the student will be able to *identify,* that is, point to something that has the following properties; or on completion of the program, the student will be able to *describe,* that is, to tell one about those properties; or on completion of the program, the student will be able to *construct,* that is, to make something having the following properties; or the student will be able to *demonstrate,* that is, to use a procedure of a particular nature. To identify, describe, construct, demonstrate, and so on, represent the kinds of action verbs that indicate behavior and thus are required for behavioral objectives. (More examples of useful action verbs were given in Figure 9.2, chapter 9.)

In order to specify something in behavioral terms, one must use behavioral words, and action verbs are behavioral words. They specify *doing* rather than *knowing.* To *know,* to *appreciate,* to *understand* (and other words such as these) are not action verbs and therefore do not qualify for use in the statement of a behavioral objective.

In addition, the action verb of a behavioral objective must have a referent, which is its content. What is it that a student shall be able to identify? What is it that a student shall be able to describe? What is it that a student shall be able to construct, etc.? The specific content in which mastery or competence is to be shown through behavior represents the action referent of the behavioral objective.

The next element of the objective is specifying the exact conditions under which the behavior is to take place. *"Given a list of twenty items,* the student shall identify," or *"using the following pieces of equipment,* the student shall construct or demonstrate," are examples that specify the conditions.

Finally, we may, if possible, want to specify in a behavioral objective the criterion, such as the amount of time the student will have and how many correct responses the student will be expected to make in that amount of time. However, at this stage of behavioral objectification, it is not considered completely necessary to include this level of detail in the description. It will suffice to include an action verb, a statement of content, and any special conditions that need mention.

Since the English language contains many action verbs, it is useful to restrict one's usage to a finite and standard list. It then is possible to compare such objectives more easily. Of greater importance, however, is that by using one of a limited number of action verbs, one can be sure of writing a behavioral objective rather than a nonbehavioral one. The list in Figure 9.2 should be referred to for this purpose.

Thus, the second step in summative evaluation, as in other forms, is to transform statements of aims and goals, which represent the *outcomes* of the evaluation, into more concrete and observable statements of behavior; that is, to transform them into operational definitions or behavioral objectives. By doing this, it then becomes possible to enter into the third step of the process—measuring these goals and aims.

Measurement of the Program Objectives

Now that the program goals have been transformed into operational definitions in the form of behavioral objectives, it is necessary to devise or discover a measuring instrument to use for determining the extent to which those behaviors representing the objectives of the program have in fact been achieved. Building or finding a test that is appropriate for measuring a set of behavioral objectives is a relatively straightforward process. We ordinarily tend to think of tests as a basis for evaluating individuals and individual performance. However, when a group of individuals who have commonly experienced an intervention or training program are given a test, and their test data are pooled and examined on a group basis with proper comparisons (this will be discussed in the next section), it is possible to use such test data for evaluating the intervention or program.

A Test Must Be Appropriate

The critical quality that a test of a program's behavioral objectives must possess is content validity or appropriateness. That is, the test must reflect accurately on the intervention or program. It must be representative of those skills, competencies, aims, and objectives that have been set for the program. By systematically delineating each objective associated with the program and then mapping out measurement items for each objective, it is possible to guarantee that such test items, when taken together, will represent the program, and thus be appropriate (or content valid). This concept is illustrated in Figure 10.2.

As seen in this figure, breaking down an intervention or program into its separate units and identifying the competencies and skills to be obtained from each unit, and then developing test items to measure each competency or skill make it possible to build a measure high in content validity. If this process is not undertaken, the establishment of such appropriateness cannot be guaran-

Has Content Validity
(is appropriate)

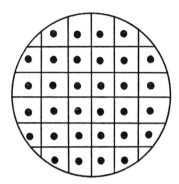

Lacks Content Validity
(is inappropriate)

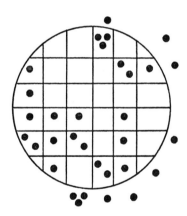

● Test item
□ Behavioral Objective or Requirement

FIGURE 10.2 *A Schematic Representation of Content Validity*

teed. There is no way to know whether, in fact, the test items that have been developed are or are not representative of the program objectives.

The tests that are developed to measure the program objectives often will require physical performance by the students. It is useful to think in terms of paper-and-pencil items that can accurately capture the measurement of competencies that involve performance. However, in attempting to replace performance items with paper-and-pencil items, be careful not to lose the essential characteristics that the item is intended to measure.

Figure 10.3 illustrates a few behavioral objectives and test items that have been written to measure them. Further information on preparing test items through the use of *test item specifications* was described in the previous chapter. Also, evaluating the quality of a test, once developed, was described in chapter 8.

---

1. Demonstrating a procedure for expressing improper fractions as mixed numbers.

   Express 1 1/16 as an improper fraction.

2. Describing the function of information conveyed in a purchase order.

   Circle the Letter Next to the Correct Answer

   A purchase order is used when:
   a. A retailer orders merchandise from a wholesaler
   b. A retailer orders services from a consumer
   c. A wholesaler orders merchandise from a retailer
   d. A foreman orders stock from an inventory

3. Demonstrating an interest in the study of science.

   List any books or articles that you have read on your own that have to do with science.

   Do you have a chemistry set? A microscope? Did you get these before or after your new science program?

FIGURE 10.3 *Sample Behavioral Objectives and Appropriate Test Items for Each Objective*

Locating a Test

A quicker and more efficient strategy than building a test is to find one already built that is appropriate for measuring your program objectives. Since so many tests are currently available, it is likely that tests can be found for measuring the final objectives that students in the program are attempting to master.

There are some principal sources through which to locate tests. Test publisher catalogues are one source; they come out annually and list the characteristics and costs of each test offered by that publisher. Another excellent source is the *Mental Measurements Yearbook,* published by the University of Nebraska Press. These volumes contain test descriptions and price information and also critical reviews. Various collections and compendia of available tests also are on the market, including particularly experimental and noncommercial tests. One collection is *Tests and Measurements in Child Development: Handbook II* edited by Orval G. Johnson and published by Jossey-Bass, San Francisco. This volume includes measures of cognition (e.g., readiness, language skills, specific achievement), personality and emotional characteristics, perceptions of environment, self-concept, qualities of care giving and home environment, motor skills, sensory perception, physical attributes, attitudes and interests, social behavior, and vocational qualities.

It is important to determine the properties of a test before using it, particularly its appropriateness, reliability, and validity. For published tests, this information usually is found in the test manuals (the test's objectives as listed in the manual, for example, can be compared to the program's objectives to establish the test's appropriateness for your purposes). If you must determine or estimate these properties yourself, use the procedures described in chapter 8.

Identifying a Comparison Group

Thus far, we have been working backwards. We began by identifying the outcomes, providing operational definitions for them, and developing or finding a test to measure them. An important aspect of the summative evaluation process is that it is not simply an attempt to describe what behaviors a student has acquired as a result of specific experiences, but to judge these acquired behaviors and their level of performance against some standard of goodness. Thus, evaluation implies comparison of some sort. The experimental approach is used to provide for summative evaluation in the establishment of a comparison group.

Control and Comparison Groups

Three kinds of groups can be used in contrast to the experimental or treatment group in order to assess the effect of the program or intervention. The first contrast group can be called a *control* group. A control group is a group of students who have not experienced the program or any other similar or related program. That is, using a control group enables the evaluator to answer the question: Would the program's behavioral objectives have been met even if the program had not occurred? Or: Can these objectives be expected to occur spontaneously, or be produced by some unspecified means other than the program?

The fact that students who complete a program now can do more of something than they could before they completed the program might be alternatively explained to have been caused by other factors, such as non-school experiences, student characteristics, or maturation. In order to assure that none of these factors is responsible for the change but that the intervention or program is responsible for the change, a group of individuals who have not experienced the program can be compared to those students who have, thus using the basic experimental–control group contrast.

Very often, however, problems in evaluation take a somewhat different form. It usually is true that problems in evaluation do not pose the question: Would the students have developed the behavior anyway? But often they do ask the question: Is the treatment or program producing the behaviors to a higher degree or perhaps more efficiently than alternative programs or interventions that have been used traditionally? When stated in this way, the problem becomes one not merely of control, but of *comparison.*

Thus, the second group to which the intervention or program group could be compared is a group of students who have presumably been trained to attain the same behavioral objectives in a different and in many cases more traditional way. Comparing the performance of the two groups using the test developed in the previous step would answer the question: Is the new way better than the old way?

Criterion Groups

Occasionally, our evaluation questions take a third form. In this third form, the standard is developed in reference to some ideal state that is to be attained. Thus, we might ask: Has the vocational student developed a level of job skills that is sufficient for reasonable success in the occupation for which he or she was trained? Or, if a program's objective is to give students more information about a particular subject matter in order to make them more proficient in using that subject matter in future learning, we could ask: How does knowledge of that subject matter by these students compare to knowledge of that subject matter by students who are succeeding at the next step in the educational process? Thus, we are asking for a contrast, not in terms of a control group that has had no experience, nor in terms of a comparison group that has had an alternative experience, but in terms of a *criterion* group, which is able to display the behavior in another context that the treatment or intervention has attempted to produce in its students.

At times, we are likely to look most naturally to the criterion group as a basis for contrast. We must then identify a group of individuals who have met the criterion toward which the intervention group aspires. Very often in vocational programs or professional programs, for example, in which we are attempting to prepare individuals to have on-the-job competence, a criterion group can be chosen from among people already employed who have shown this on-the-job competence.

Of course, identifying these "competent" individuals as a criterion group must be accomplished using a measuring instrument other than the one being developed to evaluate the intervention. Otherwise, you will just be comparing one set of results on a test to another set on the same test (which is a reflection of the test's reliability, not its validity). Thus, in order to identify those on-the-job employees who have achieved the criterion to which the intervention is aimed, we must use such strategies as asking for supervisors' judgments or looking at promotion rate, or salary, or some indication of mastery other than direct measurement of competence and skill. Once this group has been identified using another criterion, it then can be used to evaluate by comparison to the intervention or treatment group.

Selecting Samples

Another important point applies to the validity factor of selection. In selecting a control, comparison, or criterion group, potentially relevant individual difference characteristics (such as IQ or prior achievement) should be controlled for through the procedure of matching to avoid selection bias. It usually is not possible in this situation to randomly assign individuals to groups. Usually, individuals have come to participate in the procedure or its alternatives on a voluntary basis or on some other basis other than assignment exclusively for the purposes of the evaluation. The evaluation often is designed on an after-the-fact basis.

When random assignment to programs is not possible, it is necessary to try to match groups as closely as possible on many relevant variables or to *determine that groups are equivalent after assignment.* Age, for instance, is useful for selection matching. Certainly this would be true of sex, IQ, or some other measures of ability or aptitude; of whatever prior achievement data or measures of prior knowledge in the program areas are available; of socioeconomic status, and the like. It is important to match treatment and control groups, treatment and comparison groups, or treatment and criterion groups as nearly as possible on all potentially relevant individual difference measures. All groups should be pretested whenever possible on the test of the program objectives developed in the preceding step in order to establish that groups have initial equivalence (or, if they do not, to adjust statistically for differences).

Ideally again, potential students should be assigned on a random basis to program and control (comparison, or criterion) groups; however, this often is beyond the realm of possibility. When random assignment of students to programs cannot be accomplished, efforts should be made to match the programs on all potentially relevant individual difference measures. When this is not possible or practical, pretesting should be done or prior test scores used to assure that groups begin on an equal footing. An unequal starting point will make differences in the ending point difficult to evaluate. It will be hard to know whether individual differences or the program is responsible for any final difference.

Finding Comparison Groups

Comparison groups can be identified in any of three locations: (1) the same school as the program group; (2) the same district as the program group but in different schools; or (3) a different district from the program group. If some of the classrooms on a particular grade level in a school are not participating in the program, then it would be possible to use the nonparticipating classrooms as a comparison group. If classrooms have been grouped heterogeneously and decisions about which classrooms would and would not experience the program were made on a random basis, then this is an excellent strategy. If, however, nonprogram classrooms are systematically different from program classrooms in regard to students or teachers, then this strategy should be avoided. Using this approach also opens the possibility of word spreading from one room to another.

Classrooms in various schools in a district other than those in which the program is operating also represent a source of comparison. In choosing other buildings in the district be sure that the sending community is highly similar to that of the school or schools in which the program is housed. Pretests of students should be used to establish initial equivalence, and teacher characteristics should be examined to be sure that teachers in program and comparison classrooms are as equivalent as possible.

Schools or classrooms in other districts also can be used for comparison purposes. In going to schools in other districts, you again must make sure that their student populations are a reasonable match to your program students and also that their particular teachers are a match to your program teachers. To make a valid comparison of program and nonprogram experiences (that is, to reach conclusions about their comparison with *certainty*), it is necessary to limit differences in outcome that might occur as a result of either student input characteristics or teacher input characteristics (refer to Figure 4.1, chapter 4).

Student and teacher differences must be neutralized by selecting program and comparison students and program and comparison teachers who are as similar as possible. For students, similarity ideally should extend to pretest knowledge, IQ, socioeconomic status, age, and sex; for teachers, equivalence should exist on their judged capability and success in the district.

It is also sometimes possible to use a single group as both the treatment group and the comparison group. This approach is illustrated in Case Study 2, Appendix A.

Data Collection and Analysis

Administering the Tests

The measure of the objectives developed in the third step is then administered to all the students in the program, or a random sample drawn from among them if there are too many students to test conveniently, and all the students in the control, comparison, or criterion group or groups (again, selecting a random sample from among these if there are too many to test conveniently).

Very often, the summative evaluation will proceed most effectively if more than one group is used for contrast purposes. It may, for instance, be useful to include both a control group and a criterion group in order to determine the level of achievement that the program provides for as identified by or bounded by no experience at one end and operational competence at the other end. Thus, three groups might be tested.

Data Analysis

Wolf (1981) recommends a four-step procedure for data analysis. The first step is to apply descriptive statistics to the data set to yield such information as frequency distributions of outcome variables, along with means, medians, and standard deviations. This step is exploratory in nature and can be done by computer using such statistical packages as the *Statistical Package for the Social Sciences* (*SPSS;* Nie et al. 1975).

The second step is the formal data analysis involving a comparison between groups or treatments using analysis of variance (ANOVA) or analysis of covariance (ANCOVA) procedures. Porter and Chibucos (1974) describe two different applications each of ANOVA and ANCOVA to fit each of two different situations. Their analysis can be quite helpful in choosing between and among these procedures. In this second step, Wolf (1981) further suggests that one outcome variable be analyzed at a time in order to avoid obscuring important findings and to be sensitive to nonlinear relationships.

The third step is to try one or more alternative approaches to analyzing the data to provide different perspectives.

The fourth, and highly important, step is interpretation of results. Wolf (1981) divides this step into three stages. In the first, the results from the various analyses are compared. In the second, the internal meaningfulness of the results is assessed, usually in terms of effect size. The *effect size* (Glass, 1977) is the difference between treatment and comparison group means (or adjusted means, in the case of ANCOVA) divided by the standard deviation of the comparison group. Effect sizes of .3 or greater are considered important (Cohen, 1977). Wolf's third stage of interpretation is to determine the meaningfulness or potential impact of the results in terms of their bearing on the specific program being evaluated.

Alternative procedures for data analysis using different designs are provided by Cook and Campbell (1979) in the book, *Quasi-Experimentation: Design and Analysis Issues for Field Settings.* More detailed statistical approaches are provided by Winer (1971).*

Decision Making

The statistical results of the summative evaluation will show whether the program is achieving its goals as well as or better than a control, comparison, or criterion experience. For example, if the program is aimed at improving reading achievement and self-concept, the results will show whether reading achievement test and self-concept test outcomes for the program students exceed those of the nonprogram students. Obviously, three kinds of results are possible: no differences, program superior, and program inferior. On the surface, it would seem reasonable to continue the program if its outcomes are superior and to alter or discontinue it if its outcomes are equal or inferior to the comparison group. However, another factor must be considered—namely, level of program implementation.

The program may be producing lesser student outcomes than desired not because it is ineffective in its conception but because it is ineffective in its implementation. Often we conceive of a good plan but do not or cannot execute it well, and so its results are less than expected or hoped for. It is not the plan that is faulty, but its operation. Were it to be fully and satisfactorily implemented, it might result in the intended outcomes.

Determining the level of implementation of a program is done by completing an *input/process evaluation* using the procedure described in chapter 6. This activity will help you determine what the implementation characteristics

---

* See also Tuckman, B. W. *Conducting Educational Research,* 2d ed., N.Y.: Harcourt Brace Jovanovich, 1978.

of the program are in terms of materials, activities, subject matter, grouping, teaching style, and the like. These actual levels can be compared to desired levels to see whether the program is being implemented as called for in its own philosophy and specifications.

When the summative evaluation results show that the program is doing less than was intended of it, the decision may be to attempt to improve its level of implementation based on an input/process evaluation. Such improvement may take the form of increased supervision and feedback, additional in-service training, or perhaps supplementing supplies and materials. Rarely is the decision made on the basis of summative evaluation one of completely eliminating the program. More often than not, when results are poor, specifics of the results are combined with level of implementation information to form the basis for recommendations about *program improvement.* Hence, summative evaluation, although primarily an attempt to demonstrate causally that the program "works," also can contribute to program improvement when combined with input/process evaluation.*

An Illustration

Let us suppose that you had designed a one-semester secondary-school-level training program to prepare students to enter the occupation of key punch operator after high school graduation. Furthermore, you had put this program into operation with a group of thirty high school seniors and now were interested in evaluating the outcome. Let us apply the summative evaluation model to see how it would be used.

The first step would be to identify the goals and aims of the training program. Broadly speaking, these would be to provide the students with entry level job skills in key punching. More specifically, they would be to produce a student who could operate a key punch at acceptable rates of speed. A second objective might be to increase the interest of some students in staying in school after age sixteen.

The second step would be to construct an operational definition of (that is, behavioral objectives based on) the program's goals and aims—operating a key punch at acceptable rates of speed. Using our list of behavioral words, this operational definition might read as follows:

> Demonstrating a procedure for punching proper data into proper columns at the rate of 300 entries per hour after having planned and prepared a key punch for programmed control.

---

* Evaluating federally titled programs for "national validation" is primarily summative, aimed at demonstrating program success.

Moreover, a behavioral objective such as the one stated above might be seen as composed of four components, as follows:

1. Demonstrating a procedure for activating the proper functional control switches at the proper times.
2. Demonstrating a procedure for planning and punching a program card from punching and verifying instructions.
3. Demonstrating a procedure for mounting a program card on a program drum and removing it.
4. Demonstrating a procedure for punching a card from an original source document.

The second aim of the study—retention—might be stated operationally simply as decreasing the probability of dropping out, and increasing attendance.

Step three would require the creation of a test or measurement procedure to assess attainment of the objectives. The test of key punching skills would involve having a student sit at a key punch with some punch cards and some data, telling that student to punch the data on the punch cards using a program card, and then timing the performance. Scoring could be done for each of the four subtasks in terms of time or errors (or both) and then these scores summed for a total score. As for the retention measure, both drop-out rate and number of days absent could be used.

Step four would require the indentification of comparison groups. Let us assume that a company ran its own training program for key punch operators and it considered the program successful. Information could be collected about the age, IQ, and socioeconomic status of the trainees in this company program and compared to students in the test program to determine equivalency. Students in the company program could be used as a comparison group pending the result of this determination of equivalency. Another possibility would be to use persons successfully employed as key punch operators as a criterion group. The only shortcoming with this suggestion is that key punching skills improve with practice and employed key punchers are likely to have had considerably more practice than students. To eliminate the practice effect (that is, to control for it) would require the comparison of two student groups, as in the first suggestion.

To assess the retention value of the program, it would be necessary to identify a control group in the same school as the key punch student test group. A sample of thirty students equivalent to the test group students on age, IQ, and socioeconomic status but not enrolled in the key punch training program should be identified. These control students could be matched on a student-by-student basis or group basis with the program group or at least compared to them on pretest data to assure equivalence.

Attendance

	No. Absent 10 Days or Fewer	No. Absent 11 Days or More	
Keypunch Training Program	27	3	30
General Studies Program	15	15	30
	42	18	

Chi-Square = 9.60 p < .01 (therefore, program students are absent significantly less often than comparison students)

Performance

	No. Punching Above Criterion Rate	No. Punching Below Criterion Rate	
Keypunch Training Program	25	5	30
Adult Center Keypunch Program	14	13	27
	39	18	

Chi-Square = 5.14 p < .05 (therefore, program students perform significantly better than comparison students)

FIGURE 10.4   *Some Sample Results for the Illustration using the Chi-Square Test (with correction for discontinuity). This figure shows a comparison between training program students and control students (in a program of general studies) in terms of attendance. Significantly, more program students than control students were present in school more often. The figure also contrasts the performance of program students with those in a comparison program and shows that the former significantly exceed the latter.*

It must be recognized that the program and control groups may be different in terms of both initial motivation, if the training group represents volunteers, and continuing motivation, for reasons of identification with the training program and expectancy about its effects. In the latter case, it might be useful to try to find a control group to control for these identification and expectancy effects (for example, using students involved in a neighborhood social program or involved in a school activity as comparisons).

The last steps would involve the collection and analysis of the data and their interpretation and use. The performance test developed in the third step would be administered to the test group and comparison group, scored, and analyzed using a t-test or Mann-Whitney U test. Data on drop-out rate and attendance would be collected from both the test group and control group and analyzed via t-test, Mann-Whitney U test, or Chi-square test (this latter approach is shown in Figure 10.4).

Assuming that the test group outperformed the comparison group and out-attended the control group, you then could conclude that the high school key punch training program was effective in providing students with job skills and increasing their interest in school. On this basis, you would be likely to: (1) continue the program, even if local funds were required to operate it; (2) extend publicity about it and recruitment efforts in order to expand its enrollment; and (3) establish and evaluate pilot programs of a similar nature in other vocational areas.

CHAPTER 11

*Operational Guidelines for Doing Ex Post Facto Evaluation**

We now are ready to explore the third and last type of outcome evaluation to be covered—*ex post facto* evaluation. Thus far, we have covered formative evaluation, which is noncomparative, using only the group that is experiencing the program to be evaluated; and summative evaluation, which uses a designed experiment to compare the group to one experiencing some alternative. The approach in this chapter, ex post facto evaluation, covers comparative evaluation between the program group and some other group that has been tested previously. Because this second group already has been tested, the comparison must be made after the fact, that is, on an ex post facto basis.

We will consider two steps in ex post facto or after-the-fact evaluation. In the first step, comparative data are drawn from prior performance results in the same district as the one operating the program. This is called the *prior achieve-*

---

* Including the all-purpose Program Evaluator's Checklist.

ment approach. In the second, or _normative approach,_ comparative data are drawn from a national sample. The overall steps in an ex post facto evaluation plan are shown in Figure 11.1. Both approaches are based on the use of a standardized achievement testing program by the district and thereby are restricted to the types of outcomes measured by these tests.

Analyzing Prior Achievement

If a district has been using a measurement system such as an achievement testing program for a period of three to five years, it will have a prior achievement data base to use in ex post facto evaluation. The more measurements employed in the district on a continuous basis over time, the greater the possibility for employing the ex post facto approach.

Basically, the prior achievement approaches to ex post facto evaluation are longitudinal, cross-sectional, or some combination of the two. These approaches were described in purely methodological terms in chapter 4, and their application is illustrated in Case Study 3, Appendix A. This chapter will give some practical pointers about their use.

The _longitudinal_ approach involves examining the performance of the same students over time. If, during the period of time examined, the program has been instituted, its success will be reflected in score improvement subsequent to program onset. If the program has been experienced from the beginning of the examination period, steady score improvement should result. The difficulty with the longitudinal approach is that students experience progressive growth and maturation over time, which normally results in steady score improvement. Hence, it is difficult to interpret the meaning and significance of score improvement without some basis for comparison. (That is, the evaluator must separate improvement based on maturation from that based on the program.) This basis for comparison usually comes from national data; it will be discussed in the next section.

One type of longitudinal analysis that provides its own basis for comparison is across subject matter scores. Steeper growth curves in reading than in mathematics, in vocabulary than in comprehension, for example, can be informative for district planning.

For internal comparison purposes, the _cross-sectional_ approach can be used. In this approach, current students are compared to former students or classes are compared from one year to the next. Do this year's first graders obtain higher test scores than last year's? If the first-grade program has just been changed and if it is "working," we would expect this year's scores to exceed last year's scores. However, the cross-sectional approach also has a serious shortcoming. That is, that the average capability of different classes changes. Higher

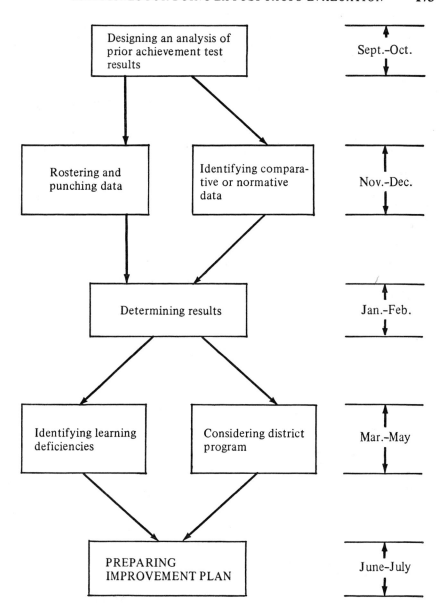

FIGURE 11.1 *Ex Post Facto Evaluation Plan*

scores for this year's than last year's first grade may not reflect program improvement; it may reflect a "smarter" group of children passing through the district. We refer to this influence as the student *selection* effort.

Thus, test outcomes reflect selection, maturation, and training. Unless the effects of both selection and maturation are controlled for, it will not be possible to attribute higher scores to training or program. The longitudinal approach controls for selection, since the same group of students are used throughout, but does not control for maturation. The cross-sectional approach controls for maturation, since the same age or grade level students are compared, but fails to control for selection.

It is fair to conclude that it is best to use an approach that combines both the longitudinal (a comparison of students with themselves over time or grades) and the cross-sectional (a comparison of students with other students over classes or school years). This can be done by comparing the rates of growth of different classes. The comparison of classes or years at a given grade level will be unaffected by maturation and the examination of growth rates of a class over time will be unaffected by selection.

Let us start out, for example, with a grade 1–5 school testing program.

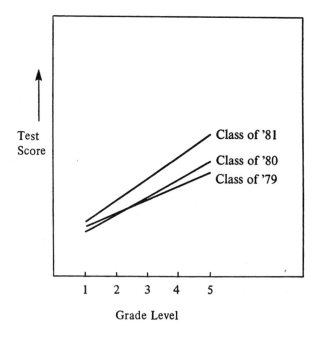

FIGURE 11.2 *Illustrative Growth Curves (longitudinal approach) for Different Classes (cross-sectional approach)*

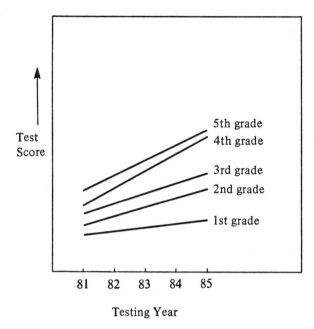

FIGURE 11.3 *Illustrative Year-by-Year Analysis (cross-sectional approach) for Different Grade Levels (longitudinal approach)*

From the time a class enters the testing program, it will take five years to complete it. Plotting the achievement test results will yield a growth curve for that class. Doing the same for succeeding classes will provide growth curves that can be compared. Curves that reflect the simultaneous consideration of grade level and class provide the basis for an adequate ex post facto evaluation. Two illustrations are provided in Figures 11.2 and 11.3. (Further illustrations will be shown later in the chapter and in Case Study 3, Appendix A.)

To summarize, therefore, the combined longitudinal and cross-sectional approaches require a data set of grade levels by testing years. Testing in five grades over five years, for example, will provide a 25-cell matrix of data. These data can be examined longitudinally and cross-sectionally by taking either: (1) each class starting from its earliest appearance in the data set and tracing its progress through the grades (as shown in Figure 11.2); or (2) each grade level and examining the test performance in it over each of the testing years (as shown in Figure 11.3). The critical aspect of this approach is that the two factors—*grade level* and *year of testing* (or class tested)—always will be examined together as they affect test scores. Changes from grade level to grade level by different groups or classes of students after differing amounts of exposure to the program represent a way of evaluating a program after the fact.

In order to have the potential for making comparisons, testing programs should be continued for at least three- to five-year periods. Moreover, the large testing companies will provide individual test results punched on computer cards for a reasonable cost. The availability of cards makes the examination of longitudinal and cross-sectional data very practical. It also eliminates the requirement for rostering and punching data.

Making Normative Comparisons

Using Growth Curves

Even after longitudinal and cross-sectional analyses are made, it is difficult to know whether outcomes are a result of program experiences or simply the result of selection ("smarter" kids) or maturation (normal growth) factors, without some external basis of comparison. It would be helpful to have growth curves from outside the district against which district results can be compared. An interesting approach to comparison is provided by one test publisher, Science Research Associates (SRA), in conjunction with its *Achievement Series and Iowa Tests of Educational Development.* SRA provides growth curves for comparison purposes with local results, as shown in Figure 11.4.

Figure 11.4 shows test results for the same class over a three-year span in reading, language arts, mathematics, and their composite. These local longitudinal results are shown by solid lines. In addition to plotting the mean standard score (the performance of the "average student"), the test publisher has plotted two other sets of standard scores: (1) scores that are one standard deviation above the mean (the top one/sixth of the students); and (2) scores that are one standard deviation below the mean (the bottom sixth). These separate curves allow a district to examine the performance of the better performing and poorer performing students in the district.

For comparison purposes, Figure 11.4 also contains results for the national standardizing sample or norming group, a representative group of students from across the country. (Curves for the top 5% or $+2\sigma$ and bottom 5% or -2σ also have been included for the norming group.)

What do the results in Figure 11.4 tell the district? On the composite score and reading score, district students are performing just slightly above the norming group; in language arts, they are at or slightly below the norming group. In mathematics, the average and top sixth students in the district are right at the norm. The bottom sixth in mathematics show a dramatic departure from the norm as students move from ninth to eleventh grade. At ninth grade, these students are slightly above the norm; by eleventh grade, they are well below it. Later, in the discussion on decision making, we will interpret these results.

SRA ASSESSMENT SURVEY
GROWTH SCALE CURVES

SRA Achievement Series—Iowa Tests of Educational Development

Grade 9 (1973)   Grade 11 (1975)

COMPOSITE

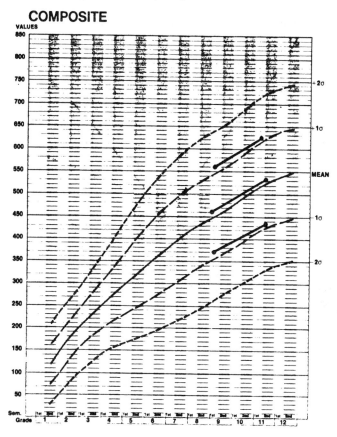

FIGURE 11.4   *Growth Curves Relating District Results to National Norms. (From SRA ACHIEVEMENT SERIES—IOWA TESTS OF EDUCATIONAL DEVELOPMENT © 1980 Science Research Associates, Inc. Reproduced by Permission.)*

SRA ASSESSMENT SURVEY
GROWTH SCALE CURVES

SRA Achievement Series—Iowa Tests of Educational Development

Grade 9 (1973)   Grade 11 (1975)

READING

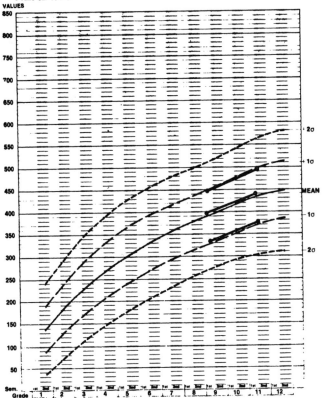

SRA ASSESSMENT SURVEY
GROWTH SCALE CURVES

SRA Achievement Series—Iowa Tests of Educational Development

Grade 9 (1973)   Grade 11 (1975)

MATHEMATiCS

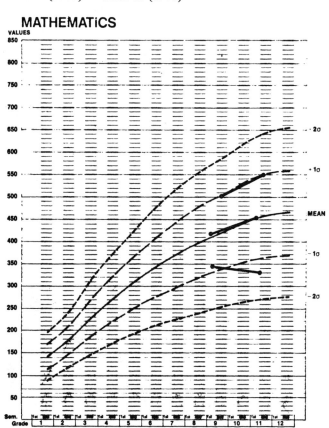

Printed in the United States of America.

SRA ASSESSMENT SURVEY
GROWTH SCALE CURVES

SRA Achievement Series—Iowa Tests of Educational Development

Grade 9 (1973)   Grade 11 (1975)

LANGUAGE ARTS

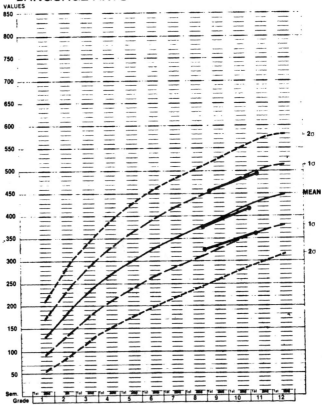

Printed in the United States of America.

Using Norms Tables

Even though it may be difficult for districts to generate normative growth curves, such as those shown in Figure 11.4, on their own, there are reasonably simple procedures for accomplishing the same procedure by using the norms tables provided in the manuals of standardized tests. The procedure described here was developed initially for the evaluation of Title I programs and is described in the monograph *A Practical Guide to Measuring Project Impact on Student Achievement,* prepared for the U.S. Department of Health, Education and Welfare in 1975.* (This procedure is used when no control, comparison, or criterion group is otherwise available to the district. When such groups are available, the summative evaluation approaches described in the preceding chapter can be used.)

In this procedure, the group of students experiencing the program in the district takes a standardized achievement test on a pretest and posttest basis. This group may, in fact, be made up of all the students in the district at one or more grade levels. If the district is using a standardized testing program on a yearly basis, then any testing may be considered the pretest with the immediately succeeding testing serving as the posttest. However, both testings should be done with the same level of the same test and the time of year when the test is administered (e.g., October or April) should be the same time at which its results were standardized. Thus, two successive years of testing yields pretest and posttest results. (These results should be presented as standard scores in the form of the mean standard score and standard deviation for the test group.) The question, then, is *whether the actual or obtained change from pretest to posttest represents a significant gain relative to the norming group.*

To get norming group results for comparison purposes, look up in the test manual norms table the *percentile* equivalent of the mean pretest standard score obtained by the district group. Then go to the norms table for next year's group (the posttest group) and see what standard score corresponds to the same percentile as the one obtained on the pretest by the district group. This second standard score represents the posttest results for the equivalent norm group, or what you might have expected the district group to have done if their growth corresponded to that of the norm group. If the actually obtained mean posttest standard score is higher than the expected one, that is, the obtained posttest score is higher than the one taken from the norms table based on the pretest percentile score, then it may be possible to conclude that the district improvement is significant.

To test whether the obtained result is significantly higher than the expected one, use the formula shown below:

---

* This document is sold by the Superintendent of Documents, U.S. Government Printing Office under stock number 017–080–01460–2.

$$t = \frac{\bar{Y}_A - \bar{Y}_E}{\sqrt{\dfrac{S_A{}^2 + S_p{}^2 - 2r_{pA}S_A S_p}{N - 1}}}$$

where $\bar{Y}_A$ = actual mean posttest score
$\quad\ \bar{Y}_E$ = expected mean posttest score
$\quad\ \ S_A$ = actual posttest standard deviation
$\quad\ \ S_p$ = actual pretest standard deviation
$\quad\ \ r_{pA}$ = correlation between actual pretest and posttest scores
$\quad\ \ N$ = number of students tested in pretest and posttest combined

Let us take an example to illustrate this approach since, unlike the other approaches described in this book, there is no case study in the appendix to illustrate it. This illustration uses the norms table shown in Figure 11.5 for the *National Educational Development Tests.*

Assume that you are evaluating an English program operating in the entire seventh grade of the one middle school in the district. Since all district seventh graders are in the program, there are no nonprogram students available to serve as a control or comparison group. You therefore have chosen to do an ex post facto standard using the national norming group of a standardized test for comparison purposes.

After examining the available tests, you chose one that: (1) did its norming at the same time of the year that you wanted to do your testing; (2) measured content or objectives that conformed to those of your program; (3) had a single level test suitable for testing both pre- and post-; and (4) provided both percentile score norms and standard score norms. Some tests are normed in the spring, some in the fall. (Few are normed twice.) If you plan a spring testing, use a test that did a spring norming. (Note that the norms in Figure 11.5 are labelled 7–1, 7–2, 8–1, 8–2, which indicates that seventh and eighth grade norms were obtained in the first and second semesters of the school year—that is, probably October and May.) This illustrative norms table also shows that the test is suitable for both ending seventh graders (the pretest group) and ending eighth graders (the posttest group) and that both standard scores and percentile scores are available.

Continuing our example, the chosen test is administered to all 100 seventh graders in May; they obtain an average standard score of twenty-five (with a standard deviation of five), which is equivalent to the fifty-seventh percentile. (See the circled numbers in Figure 11.5.) The question now becomes: What growth or change would we expect on a normative or nationally averaging basis? We can answer this question by again referring to the norms table (Figure 11.5) and looking at the boxed numbers. In the absence of program effects, we would expect the ending eighth graders to perform at the same percentile level (fifty-seventh) as the seventh graders. If this were to happen,

TABLE 1. NEDT national percentiles, first and second semesters

PERCENTAGE OF STUDENTS RECEIVING LOWER SCORES

NEDT STANDARD SCORE	English Usage				Mathematics Usage				Social Studies Reading				NEDT STANDARD SCORE
	7-1	7-2	8-1	8-2	7-1	7-2	8-1	8-2	7-1	7-2	8-1	8-2	
48													48
47													47
46													46
45													45
44													44
43													43
42													42
41												99	99	41
40				99			99	99			98	98	40
39			99	98			98	97		99	98	98	39
38		99	98	98		99	98	97		98	97	96	38
37	99	98	98	97		98	96	95	99	98	97	96	37
36	98	97	96	96	99	97	95	94	98	97	95	94	36
35	97	96	95	94	98	95	92	90	97	95	94	92	35
34	96	95	94	92	97	94	90	87	96	94	92	90	34
33	95	93	91	89	97	93	89	85	94	91	88	86	33
32	92	90	87	85	95	91	87	82	92	89	86	83	32
31	90	87	84	82	93	87	81	76	91	87	83	80	31
30	87	83	80	76	91	85	79	72	88	83	78	73	30
29	84	80	75	71	89	82	75	68	85	80	75	70	29
28	81	76	72	67	86	79	71	64	81	75	69	63	28
27 [26.5]	75	70	65	60 ←57	78	70	61	53	78	72	66	59	27
26	70	65	59	54	73	65	57	48	71	65	59	53	26
(25)	63	(57)	51	45	68	60	52	44	66	60	54	48	25
24	56	51	46	40	61	53	45	37	62	56	50	44	24
23	51	45	39	33	47	40	33	26	51	46	40	35	23
22	41	35	30	25	39	33	27	20	43	39	34	30	22
21	33	29	24	19	31	26	21	15	28	25	22	19	21

○ Actual Pretest
□ Expected Pretest

FIGURE 11.5   *Norms Table for the* National Educational Development Tests. (*From NATIONAL EDUCATIONAL DEVELOPMENT TESTS, 1977-78, Interpretive Manual for Grades 7-8.* © *1971, 1969, 1967, 1966, 1963, Science Research Associates, Inc. Reproduced by permission.*)

the eighth graders (our posttest group) would obtain a mean standard score of 26.5.

Let us suppose that ending eighth graders (the posttest group) obtained a mean standard score of 28, again with a standard deviation of five.* Thus, our

---

* A standard score is one based on the mean and standard deviation of the norming group with raw scores transformed to fit a preset mean and standard deviation. For the *Na-*

TABLE 1. NEDT national percentiles, first and second semesters

PERCENTAGE OF STUDENTS RECEIVING LOWER SCORES

NEDT STANDARD SCORE	English Usage				Mathematics Usage				Social Studies Reading				NEDT STANDARD SCORE
	7-1	7-2	8-1	8-2	7-1	7-2	8-1	8-2	7-1	7-2	8-1	8-2	
20	21	18	15	12	23	19	16	12	20	18	17	15	20
19	14	12	10	8	16	14	12	10	13	12	11	11	19
18	8	7	6	5	11	9	8	6	13	12	11	11	18
17	5	4	3	2	11	9	8	6	8	8	7	7	17
16	3	3	2	2	6	5	4	3	8	8	7	7	16
15	2	2	1	1	6	5	4	3	4	4	4	4	15
14	1	1			3	2	2	1	4	4	4	4	14
13					3	2	2		2	2	2	2	13
12					1	1	1		2	2	2	2	12
11									1	1	1	1	11
10													10
9													9
8													8
7													7
6													6
5													5
4													4
3													3
2													2
1													1

results would indicate a higher posttest score than expected. We could use the formula on page 182 to determine if the obtained posttest score, 28, was significantly higher than the expected one, 26.5. Given pretest and posttest standard deviation of 5, an N of 200 (100 seventh- and 100 eighth-grade test-takers) and assuming a correlation between pretest and posttest scores of .70,† the formula yields a t-value in excess of 5. This is quite statistically significant; that is, the probability that it is due to chance is extremely slight. Although a difference of 1.5 standard score points may not sound like a lot on an individual basis, moving the average score of a group of 100 students by this amount is a considerable achievement.

Decision Making

Clearly, using a norms table to provide comparison data is an effective approach when program data from only a single group are available. A district

---

tional Educational Development Tests, these numbers are about twenty-four and five respectively. A percentile score is the percentage of students receiving lower scores than a given score.

† This correlation should, of course, actually be computed; but based on reliability correlations reported in the NEDT manual, it probably will fall in the range of .70.

can look at growth and class comparison data from within as well as normative results from outside to help make decisions about program effectiveness.

As in the case for both formative and summative evaluation, decision making in conjunction with ex post facto evaluation must consider the level of program implementation as revealed by input/process evaluation. If the program appears to be yielding improved achievement over and above that based on maturation alone or on selection effects, then the decision to continue the program would be justified. If no improvement occurred following the program, then the answer may lie in improved program implementation rather than in the total abandonment of the program.

Refer, for example, to the results shown in Figure 11.4. Here, the bottom sixth of the eleventh-grade student body showed a worsening in mathematics achievement relative to the norming group. Decision making requires considering the district program before deciding on an improvement plan. Lower sixth students in the illustrative district characteristically stop taking any mathematics at the end of ninth grade. Obviously, the district cannot afford to let so many of its students end their math instruction if they hope to maintain normative performance levels throughout high school. Thus, a logical decision might be to institute a required "refresher course" in mathematics in the tenth grade.

The Program Evaluator's Checklist

Figure 11.6 contains the *Program Evaluator's Checklist.* It is intended to summarize all that has preceded and to help remind the program evaluator of all the steps that are to be taken or considered in the complete instructional program evaluation. It summarizes the full range of evaluation approaches, not merely the ex post facto, even though it appears at the end of this chapter.

The checklist covers: (1) outcomes, (2) inputs/process, (3) design, and (4) decision making. It lists all the points and considerations that have served as the tenets or basic principles of this book. Evaluators are encouraged to study it closely and apply it to any and all standard tasks in order to insure that all the necessary steps have been taken. If questions arise about particular steps, refer to the parts of the book that cover them.

I. OUTCOMES

A. Specification

1. Have you specified *specific knowledge and comprehension* outcomes? In behavioral form?

2. Have you specified *thinking and problem-solving* outcomes? In behavioral form?

3. Have you specified *attitude and value* outcomes? In measurable form?

4. Have you specified *learning-related behavior* outcomes? In measureable form?

B. Measurement

1. Have you constructed appropriate test items to measure your *specific knowledge and comprehension* outcomes? and/or, Have you selected a published test and determined its appropriateness for measuring your *sk&c* outcomes?

2. Have you constructed appropriate test items to measure your *thinking and problem-solving* outcomes?

3. Have you constructed appropriate test items to measure your *attitude and value* outcomes? or, Have you selected a published test and determined its appropriateness for measuring *a&v* outcomes?

4. Have you constructed appropriate scales to measure your *learning-related behavior* outcomes?

C. Ratification

1. Have your outcomes been ratified by teachers at the target grade level? by teachers at adjacent levels? by parents?

D. Criteria

1. Where necessary, have test criteria levels been prespecified? Have they been ratified by the groups in Step C?

II. INPUTS/PROCESS

A. Specification

1. Have you specified the critical parameters and details of the *instructional approach*?

FIGURE 11.6 *Program Evaluator's Checklist*

2. Have you specified the critical parameters and details of relevant *teacher behavior*?

3. Have you specified the critical parameters and details of the relevant *environment* or milieu?

4. Have you specified the critical parameters and details of the *subject matter*?

5. Have you specified relevant *student input* factors, such as general knowledge and comprehension, pretest perforance, and socio-economic status?

B. Costs

1. Have you determined the cost of implementing the *instructional approach*?

2. Have you determined the cost of producing desired *teacher behavior* through training and supervision?

3. Have you determined the cost of establishing and maintaining the desired *environment*?

C. Process Determination

1. Have you determined that the *instructional approach* is operating as intended?

2. Have you determined that *teachers* are *behaving* as intended?

3. Have you determined that the *environment* is functioning as intended?

4. Have you determined that the specified *subject matter* is being covered?

5. Have you measured the *student input* factors that have been specified?

III. DESIGN

A. Specification

1. Has the type of design been specified: formative, summative, and ex post facto? (based on purpose and availability of data)

2. If summative, has the specific design been laid out?

3. If ex post facto, has a longitudinal, cross-sectional, or combined approach been selected?

B. Units and Levels of Analysis
    1. Have the units and levels of analysis been chosen?
    2. Are the units and levels of analysis chosen consistent with with both inputs and outputs?

C. Experience Effects
    1. Has a control or comparison group, not experiencing the program, been identified?
    2. Have other experience factors (other than the program being evaluated) been equalized across experimental and control groups (e.g., teacher effects)?

D. Student Effects
    1. Have students from experimental and control groups been compared to determine their equivalency? (If not equivalent, have adjustments been planned?)

E. Procedures
    1. Have all development, measurement, and implementation steps been planned in terms of procedures, sequence, and intended date of completion?
    2. Have all statistical procedures, both descriptive and inferential, been specified?

IV. DECISION MAKING

A. Change
    1. Have plans been made for comparing outcome results to input/process results to help locate the source of any deficiency?
    2. Have considerations been given to program replacement or substitution?

B. Implementation
    1. Have plans been made for feeding back the evaluation results to teachers in order to have an impact on program implementation?
    2. Have plans been made to use the evaluation results for subsequent district planning and resource allocation?
    3. How can the results be fed into the supervision and inservice teacher training process to improve level of implementation?
    4. Have plans been made to communicate results to parents in conjunction with planned changes based on the results?

CHAPTER 12

Qualitative/Case Study Evaluation

Thus far, this book has focused on the evaluation of programs based on the systematic and objective measurement of program inputs, processes, and outcomes. While it is not possible to be either totally systematic or totally objective, the measurement procedures described have been aimed at mirroring program variables as objectively as possible and representing these variables as numbers or quantities. However, there are occasions when evaluators are called upon to use their own judgment rather than measuring instruments to depict accurately a program's variables. It is to such qualitative or case study evaluation that we now turn.

Characteristics of Qualitative Evaluation

According to Bogdan and Biklen (1982), qualitative research has the following five features: (1) the natural setting is the data source and the researcher the key data collection instrument; (2) it attempts primarily to describe; (3) the concern is with process as much as with product or output; (4) its data are analyzed inductively as in putting together the parts of a puzzle; and (5) it is essentially concerned with what things mean, that is, the why as well as the what.

This type of research or evaluation methodology, also referred to as *ethnography,* is said by Wilson (1977) to be based on the fundamental beliefs that (1) events must be studied in natural settings, that is, be field based and (2) events cannot be understood unless one understands how they are perceived and interpreted by the people who participated in them. Thus, *participant observation* is used as the major data collection device.

The application of the qualitative or ethnographic approach to instructional program evaluation has been termed *responsive evaluation* by Stake (1975) and *naturalistic evaluation* by Guba and Lincoln (1981). Both labels apply well to the *site visit* or *case study* approach, which will be described in detail in this chapter. In both, the evaluator visits the site or field location of the program to engage in *fieldwork* or participant observation. In both, the evaluator talks to or interviews everyone in and around the program and makes observations of the program in operation. In both, the evaluator attempts to identify the *concerns* about the program held by its various clients, participants, and audiences; and in both the evaluator attempts to assess the program's *merit* and *worth.* To accomplish this, the evaluator must determine whether the program meets the needs of its adopters within the context of the local situation.

Guba and Lincoln (1981) point out some methodological concerns associated with this approach, including the need to set boundaries and find a focus in order to insure that the process is credible, fitting or appropriate, consistent, and confirmable or neutral. To attempt to meet these criteria, which collectively provide qualitative evaluations with "rigor," the approach described here will be structured as much as possible in a way that is consistent with the purposes of evaluation as previously set forth in this book. In this structured form, the type of qualitative evaluation described here is less like the ethnography approach and may more appropriately be called *case study evaluation.*

Specifying the Questions to Be Answered

The ultimate questions of worth and merit to be answered in a qualitative or case study evaluation do not differ basically from those to be answered in a quantitative evaluation of whether the program is meeting its goals. The aspects that do differ are the kinds of data needed to answer those questions and the way those data are to be collected. Even though the evaluator is going to serve as the "measuring instrument," the process need not be entirely unstructured. To attempt to maintain neutrality and to use limited time in a most efficient way, the process should be structured to some degree. This means that some of the types of questions to be answered should be specified in advance, as should the general data collection procedures that will be employed to answer these questions. Building some structure into the qualitative or case study evaluation process will enhance its confirmability. *Confirmability* in this instance means that other evaluators would be likely to arrive at the same conclusions using essentially the same procedures.

The types of questions needed can be drawn from those shown in the Program Evaluator's Checklist at the end of the preceding chapter. These questions must relate to the data collection procedures described later in this chapter and must enable you to determine (a) what the program objectives are and (b) to what extent these objectives have been achieved. It may be helpful to think of program objectives in terms of the four categories (i.e., specific knowledge and comprehension, thinking and problem solving, attitudes and value, and learning-related behavior) here as it was in doing the kinds of formative, summative, and ex post facto evaluations already described.

It is also important to try to determine what the program's inputs are, including costs, and whether these inputs have operated as intended, i.e., what course the process of program implementation has taken. Again, it may be helpful to consider both input and process (that is, the implementation of input) in terms of the categories in the checklist, namely: instructional approach, teacher behavior, environment, subject matter, and student input.

In dealing with inputs and processes, it would be wise to consider their specification, costs, and implementation not only from the perspectives of intentions and actuality but also from the perspective of program management. Thus, you may want to ask:

- Was there a plan for managing inputs and their implementation?
- What were the specifics of the plan?
- What was the feasibility of the plan?
- To what specific extent was the plan carried out?

In other words, one should examine and evaluate not only the specification, cost, and implementation of inputs but also the efficacy of the plan by which this was done. Was there a plan? Was it specific? Was it feasible? Was it followed? These are management questions that should be explored, in addition to: What were the inputs? What were the costs? Were the inputs implemented? Part of the plan will be the program budget, which is a plan for dealing with the cost of inputs and their implementation. Part of the plan will (or, at least, should) be the evaluation plan, which is a plan by which program directors intend to determine whether their program has achieved its desired results.

Thus, the questions basically take the form of:

- What was intended?
- What was actually done?
- What were the results?

Furthermore, these questions may be applied to both the *input/ process/outcomes* themselves and to the management of *input/process/ outcomes* as well.

Data Sources

Data sources which may be used in this case study approach are usually of three types: (1) interviews of various people, such as program managers, administrators, teachers, students, and parents; (2) documents, such as proposals, progress reports, public relations materials, and curriculum guides; (3) observation of the program in action. The purpose of collecting data in any of these three ways is to acquire information related to the questions posed in the preceding section. Each of these data sources will be discussed in turn.

Interviews

One fundamental way to find out about a program is to ask questions of the people who are involved in it in some way. Each person's answers will reflect his or her perceptions, interests, and slants. Since different people will have differing perspectives, what may emerge is a reasonably representative picture of the program's operation.

In order to maximize your *neutrality* in using this approach and the *consistency* of your findings, it is helpful to have two components: (1) an interview schedule and (2) a sampling plan.

To get varying perspectives on the same questions, it helps to ask the same questions of different people. These prepared questions are embodied in what is called an *interview schedule.* In selecting the questions, you should avoid asking about proposed intentions; instead you should focus on what has actually been done. Information about proposed intentions and about formal outcomes can be obtained from source documents (see below). However, it is likely that interviews will be your major source of information about implementation. Below is a sample list of such implementation questions. These questions have been posed here in generalized form for illustrative purposes. In an actual case study evaluation, they would be tailored to fit the specifics of the program in question.

1. Describe the implementation of the inputs listed in the proposal. How have you departed from your intended plan, if at all? Why have you departed? What particular problems have you encountered?
2. Describe the implementation of the management plan listed in the proposal. How have you departed from your intended plan, if at all? Why have you departed? What particular problems have you encountered?

3. Describe the implementation of the budget listed in the proposal. How have you departed from your intended plan, if at all? Why have you departed? What particular problems have you encountered?

This line of questioning would be suitable for the *project manager* or managers. Based on their answers, further lines of related questions could be asked. These additional questions need not be preplanned in specific form but would emerge from answers to preplanned questions. After one has gained experience in interview situations, it becomes easier to detect worthwhile but unanticipated lines of questioning.

The same specific questions that are posed for the program directors may not be suitable to ask other respondents, such as teachers, students, or parents. Such respondents may not be aware of the intended implementation plans and hence would not be in a position to contrast intentions and actualities. However, they would be in a position to describe actualities from their own perspectives, and you can then make the contrasts yourself. Moreover, they would not be likely to be aware of such matters as the management plan and the budget; their awareness would be limited to the implementation of inputs in observable areas such as curriculum development and delivery of instruction. Again, the examples below must be, of necessity, extremely general. In the real situation it would be advisable to make them as specific as possible.

For teachers:

1. Describe how you were made aware of program goals.
2. What were you expected to do as part of the implementation of the program?
3. Were you trained and/or assisted in carrying out your role and if so, how? Was it adequate?
4. What did the program provide for students that was different from the regular program?
5. Did the program operate smoothly and efficiently in the classroom? If not, why not?
6. Was the program well managed? If not, why not?

Needless to say, all of the above questions could be preceded by the phrase, "In your opinion . . ." However, when a number of teachers are questioned, a pattern may begin to emerge.

It is also useful to ask questions of students if they are old enough to respond reliably to the interview format. They, after all, are the recipients of the program under evaluation and are in a position to provide data on the delivery of that program. So, *students* could be asked:

1. Describe the program to me. Tell me about the topics that were covered and how the material was presented to you.

2. Did your teacher seem comfortable and well prepared in presenting the material?
3. Were there any incidents, either good or bad, that occurred while the program was being carried out that stand out in your mind?
4. Did you enjoy the program? Was it interesting? Did you learn from it? More than from your regular program?

The first two student questions deal with process or implementation and thus are somewhat parallel to those questions asked of teachers. The third question represents use of an approach called the *critical incident technique* in which respondents are asked to recall critical or outstanding incidents that can be used by evaluators in forming hypotheses about program implementation or outcomes or for illustrative purposes in citing results or conclusions.

The last set of questions represents a way of evaluating program outcomes based on the subjective reactions of the program recipients. We can identify three levels of program evaluation from the perspective of the recipient as follows:

1. Was the intended program provided (i.e., did you get what you "paid for")?
2. Were you satisfied with what you received?
3. Did your knowledge and/or competence improve as a result?

The last set of questions is an attempt to discover whether the students were satisfied with the program. Even when we ask students whether they learned or improved, we are really only asking for their opinion of a program's worth, which essentially is a reflection of their satisfaction. If we want to test whether their knowledge and/or competence improved as a result, then we have to measure their level of relevant knowledge or competence at the conclusion of the program, compare it to their level prior to the program, and contrast the difference with that of a group of students who did not experience the program. Satisfaction, on the other hand, is subjective by definition and can only be "measured" by asking the student for a self-assessment.

Finally, it is often useful to interview *parents*. If a program is having an impact of great enough magnitude, parents will be aware of it. Their impressions are worth garnering since the future of the program may depend on them. Some questions that may be asked of parents are listed below:

1. Are you aware of the program which is being carried out in the school on a trial basis? If so, how did you find out about it? (If not, it would be pointless to ask any further questions.)
2. What are your impressions of its strengths or successes? How did you arrive at these judgments (be as specific as possible)?
3. What are your impressions of its weaknesses or failures? How did you arrive at these judgments (be as specific as possible)?

Documents

A second source of information about a program is the documents which program designers, managers, and directors have prepared. These documents are usually of the types described below.

A *proposal* is a written description of the proposed program objectives, inputs, processes (i.e., implementation plan), management plan, and budget. It usually contains background material describing the problem, content, and setting as well as the philosophy on which the program is based. Often it contains a needs assessment or statement of the need to which the proposed program is a response. A careful reading of the proposal will give you a lot of information useful for understanding the program and for planning the evaluation and designing the evaluation instruments.

Materials are often an important ingredient of a program and may be developed as a part of the program. Such materials are often detailed sets of objectives, lesson plans and instructional guides, teachers' manuals, textbooks or handouts, and accompanying testing devices. Where such materials are in print form, as is usually the case, they may be considered to be documents. As such they represent inputs to the instructional process which must undergo implementation in order to produce desired outcomes. They may be evaluated as to their (1) suitability or appropriateness in relation to stated program objectives, (2) completeness of teaching/learning materials, (3) subject matter coverage in terms of both accuracy and suitability for the grade level in question, (4) comprehensiveness—that is, readability and understandability. In document form, materials may be evaluated as inputs. To evaluate their implementation, however, requires sources of data other than documents.

Reports take the form of progress reports, final report and evaluation reports. Such reports often contain clues about the manner of program implementation and the kinds of problems encountered. Such reports may also contain formal evaluations of the program using formative, summative, or ex post facto approaches, including statistical analyses of student performance data collected for evaluation purposes. If so, this is likely to be the evaluator's only formal source of information about program outcomes and must be examined in great depth.

Observations

Observations, the third qualitative data source, were also described as a quantitative data source. In fact, they may be either qualitative or quantitative depending upon the manner in which observational data are collected. If formal observation instruments are used, like coding or counting systems or rating scales, then the product of observation will be numbers—hence quantitative evaluation. If observation means looking around with only a general scheme to guide you and with fieldnotes as the product of such observation, then it would be considered qualitative. Given the limited amount of time that the evaluator will be on site, and the basic nature of the qualitative or case study approach, observational data will not be highly structured and will take the form of field-notes.

What should be observed is the program in action. This means sitting in classrooms, generally in as unobtrusive a manner as possible, and watching teachers "deliver" the program to students. It does not mean asking questions, because that is "interviewing." (Questions can be asked either before or after observing.) It just means looking. But it need not be totally unstructured look-ing. It usually means looking for something, primarily looking for whether the program is being implemented in (a) the way set forth in the proposal and ma-terials and (b) a way that is conducive to student learning. It may also mean looking for some of the pitfalls, problems, or weaknesses which have emerged from the interviews or reports. It will also mean looking for things that strike you and about which you will want to ask questions during the interviewing.

The critical aspect of observation is looking, taking in as much as you can without influencing what it is that you are looking at. Be forewarned, however, that what goes on before your eyes, as evaluator, will represent—at least in part—a performance intended to influence your judgments. This is inevitable. The more observations you make, especially without forewarning, and the more unobtrusive you remain, the less you are likely to influence what is going on before you.

Conducting the Evaluation

The next section of this chapter will deal with specific procedures for conduct-ing the qualitative or case study evaluation.

Obtaining the Documents

The first step in conducting a qualitative evaluation is *to obtain copies of all available program documents and study them carefully.* This is the best and most objective way to orient yourself to the program that you are about to evaluate. In reading the documents, you will want to take particular note of (a) the pro-gram's intended objectives; (b) the implementation plan, including the man-agement plan; (c) any suggestion of problems encountered or changes necessitated; and (d) any formal evaluation data.

The information that you are able to glean from the documents will assist you in preparing your own plan for your case study evaluation, which will be a combination of standard evaluation approaches with those geared to the specif-ics of the program you have agreed to evaluate.

Preparing for the Site Visit

The collection of data in a qualitative/case study evaluation is accomplished during what is called a *site visit*. This is ordinarily a one- to three-day period during which the evaluator is present at the program site. Of course, there may be more than a single visit, and the evaluation may be conducted by more than a single evaluator. However, for illustrative purposes we will assume both a single visit and a single evaluator. In order to use the time on site most efficiently and effectively, it is necessary to plan as specifically as possible the way your time there will be spent. To do this you need to develop a *visitation schedule* and interview instruments.

A visitation schedule includes a listing of all the people you want to see and the amount of time you want to spend with each. It should also specify time to be set aside for classroom observations. For the sake of efficient use of your limited time, it should be made up of specific appointments for you to see specific persons, such as the project director and teachers involved in the project, and time set aside for you to make observations or to see people without a specific appointment. A sample visitation schedule for a one-day site visit appears below:

8:00– 9:00   Interview project director

9:00– 9:30   Interview superintendent

9:30–10:00   Interview assistant superintendent for instruction

10:00–11:30   Make unannounced classroom visits (visit three classrooms for thirty minutes each)

12:00– 1:00   Have lunch with project teachers

1:00– 1:30   Meet with a group of project students

1:30– 2:00   Meet with president of faculty union

2:00– 2:30   Make unannounced classroom visit (choose one classroom unannounced based on impressions gained during visit)

2:30– 3:15   Interview project director

3:15– 3:45   Interview group of parents

All of the formal appointments on the above schedule should be made in advance by the project director to ensure that everything that is planned can be accomplished. It is advisable to have both an entry interview and an exit interview with the project director. While you are on site, your interviews and observations will raise questions that you may wish to present to the project director before leaving. The exit interview gives you the opportunity to follow such emerging leads by asking questions you had not thought to ask in the entry interview.

Again, it is important to emphasize that you should prepare the visitation schedule and make all necessary appointments in advance. Time is at a premium and you cannot afford to waste any. If the project director made up a schedule for you, review it in advance and make sure it fits your specifications. Make sure as well that it provides you with time to make notes and arrange your thoughts.

You must also prepare your interview questions in advance, although you need not attempt to write every question you might ask. After reading the documents and reviewing what was said earlier in this chapter about interview questions, you should be able to prepare a general line of questions to be used for your interviews. Each interview on your schedule may require a separate set of questions in which case each should be sketched out.

You will also want to prepare a mechanism for recording responses to interview questions. You may want to tape record each interview so that note taking will not be necessary. If you choose to tape, you must request in advance permission from each interviewee, and you may only record in those instances where permission is granted. In place of or in addition to recording, you should prepare a notebook for taking what are called fieldnotes. Systematic pre-marking of the notebook pages with interview questions or question numbers will facilitate the taking and interpreting of fieldnotes.

It is also a good idea to prepare a plan for observation. This plan may be a set of questions that you hope to answer as a result of the observation. Or it may be a listing of critical incidents or a description of what students and teachers are doing during the time you are present. In your notebook, you should prepare a page for each observation's fieldnotes, listing the day, time, and teacher, and providing markings to indicate what entries to make while you are observing.

It is important to emphasize that the site visit is the data collection phase of the case study evaluation. It is imperative that you be prepared and organized. It is most helpful for you to have (a) a specific, preset list of appointments and (b) a procedure or mechanism for taking fieldnotes, which constitute your observation and interview data.

"Analyzing" the Data and Preparing the Report

The fieldnotes that you bring back with you in your notebook and in your head, plus any information gleaned from program documents, represent the data for the qualitative evaluation. Analyzing it means using it to answer the questions which the evaluation should attempt to answer.

What Are the Program's Objectives? A formal statement of these should appear in the proposal.

Do Developed Materials Fit the Program's Objectives? To answer this question, you will have to examine the materials, which you should have on hand, in the light of program objectives.

Do Teachers and Parents Know What the Program Is Trying to Do? If you ask teachers and parents this question and make good notes of their responses, you should have less trouble answering this question.

Is There an Implementation Plan? If there is, you should find it in the proposal.

To What Extent Was the Implementation Plan Carried Out? This is a difficult question to answer. It is best answered by trying to break the implementation plan down into its component pieces and trying to determine if and how each component piece was implemented. If, for example, the implementation plan calls for the training of teachers, then teachers should be able to tell you about this training component.

Was the Program Operating As Intended? The answer to this question will be largely dependent on the answer to the previous one, but it is possible for you to obtain direct evidence here as well. Between the written documents and the information provided by the program director in the interviews, it should be possible to form a fairly detailed image of how the program was intended to operate. Classroom observations, in particular, and interview responses by all respondents should tell you whether this intended image has been met in reality. Determining this is critical to the evaluation, since it will be the basis for determining whether intended program outcomes could legitimately be expected.

Where Did Program Operations Fail to Meet Intentions and Why? Results of a qualitative evaluation can be used to get a program back on track. If, in answering the preceding question, you found that the program was off track, you must now try to specify where and how this slippage occurred if the information you provide is to be useful. The "where" will be answered when you detect that the program is off track. The "why" is much harder to answer. You should have gotten clues from the program director, teachers, and even parents and students. You will have to follow those clues through your notes and see where they lead you. (If you use these questions as the basis for constructing your interview questions and if you keep them in your head at all times while you are on site, then you will be able to pick up clues and follow up on them as part of your interviewing and observing. For example, if teachers tell you that the training period was shortened, then in your exit interview with the program director you can ask him or her why that was done.)

Was There a Management Plan and Budget and Was It Followed? The management plan should appear in the proposal or should have been provided by the program director. It should specify how the program was to be managed, i.e., what activities were to be completed by what dates and at what cost. Interviews with the program director should help you to determine whether the plan was followed, but in order to get this information you may have to ask for the dates that specific milestones (i.e., accomplishments) were attained. Look for clues in your interviews with teachers, parents, and students which suggest that events did not occur on time and follow up on them in your exit interview with the program director.

Was There Evidence That the Program Met Its Objectives? This question is what you might call the "bottom line." All that has preceded it is aimed at maximizing the likelihood that the answer to this question will be "yes." The most direct form of evidence would be a report of a formative, summative, or ex post facto evaluation using quantitative measures of the objectives. If this has been done and such a report exists, then it is up to you to evaluate this report in terms of the reliability and validity of the measures employed and the validity of the evaluation design. The extent to which the quantitative results can be taken seriously will depend upon your critique. If such data are not available, then it will be up to you to try to answer this question in the best way you can, given your data. In essence, you will be answering the following kinds of questions. In the judgment of program director, superintendent, teachers, students, and parents, did the program meet its objectives? Did your observations yield any evidence which suggests whether the program was meeting its objectives? Was there any other basis for determining whether or not the program was meeting its objectives?

Preparing the Report

The last step in the qualitative evaluation, as in any type of evaluation, is the preparing of the evaluation report. Any impact that the evaluator is likely to have will be based on this report. Moreover, there may be some concern about the inherent objectivity of this type of evaluation. Specifically, there may be those who believe that the evaluator has drawn conclusions prior to the site visit and the data collection process. In order to combat this type of suspicion (cynical though it may be), it is necessary for the evaluator to provide as much detail as possible of both evaluation methodology and conclusions. Insofar as possible, conclusions should be supported by descriptive documentation of the sort described above under "analysis" of the data. Detailed fieldnotes will make it possible to provide such documentation.

The evaluation report should contain, therefore, at least two sections. The first section should cover *methodology*. It should describe and provide (a) dates, times, and schedules of site visits; (b) lists of interviewees; (c) interview questions asked; and (d) lists and descriptions of observations. It should also list and describe any other source of information used, such as program documents.

The second section should describe *conclusions* reached and the data on which each conclusion was based. Often, the best procedure is to begin with the conclusion, either underlined or in capitals or bold type. It should be followed by a detailed statement of the data base which supports the conclusion. So, for example, if you conclude that the program has not been implemented as planned, you should describe those aspects of the program that have not been implemented and the sources of information that were used to detect this failure to achieve full implementation. You may want to describe your observations related to this point as well as specific interview data which suggest that certain aspects of the program have failed to be implemented and why.

In similar fashion, you should offer all of your conclusions with an indication of the evidence on which each has been based.

CHAPTER 13

Issues and Advice

Current Issues in Program Evaluation

As in any area of evolving methodology dealing with human behavior and its improvement, there are differences of opinion on how to proceed as well as concern about some potential by-products of the approach. We now will briefly discuss some of the more salient of these issues.

Individual Student Exit Requirements

One of the chief by-products of instructional program evaluation is a set of de-tailed data on most, if not all, individual students. Although these data are collected as the basis for the assessment of program effects, they nevertheless tell us much about the performance capability of each student. Given a pervasive orientation toward evaluation and standard setting, there are citizens who contend that these data should be used for deciding whether students are qualified to be certified for course completion or, more dramatically, for graduation.

It must be emphasized that this is *not* a central issue of instructional program evaluation but a by-product of its heavy emphasis on data collection and documentation. Moreover, it is a different issue, philosophically, from program evaluation. Program evaluation locates the locus of instructional outcomes in the program and seeks to uncover whether these outcomes are improved for groups of students by the program experiences. The exit requirement approach places the burden of accountability on the students rather than on the schools and penalizes the student, rather than the educational system, for failure.

Evaluators must be careful to focus their craft on the program effects they set out to evaluate—this is their domain of expertise and responsibility. Administrators must exercise caution in not implementing an exit requirement plan under the guise of program evaluation since neither then will be likely to succeed. Student evaluation and program evaluation must be kept separate both philosophically and operationally. In the long run, it would appear that of the two approaches program evaluation has the greater potential payoff for student improvement since it examines and directly seeks to improve the school's attempt at facilitating learning. It focuses not on laying blame and punishing but on finding avenues for greater student gains.

Teacher Evaluation

This discussion can be repeated almost verbatim for teacher evaluation. A district may choose to use the results of program evaluation, especially when they are unfavorable, to evaluate teacher performance. To do so, however, assumes that teachers, individually and collectively, are the sole cause of learning outcomes. This is a shortsighted assumption and at much variance with the facts. To use program evaluation results as a basis for improving level of program implementation via teacher supervision and in-service training is entirely appropriate. It assumes, correctly and reasonably, that teachers are a component of the program. In fact, they are usually its implementers. To use these results as the basis for personnel decisions not only fails to take other factors into account but also may result in totally alienating teachers from the program evaluation process.

Teachers must not only cooperate in the program evaluation process in order for it to be done successfully but also be open to its results if program improvement is to occur. Turning the process "against" them will only doom it to failure.

Predetermination of Outcomes

Although the emphasis in this book has been on determining outcomes in the form of goals and objectives before conducting the evaluation, it must be noted that at least one evaluation authority, Michael Scriven, advocates "goal-free evaluation." He contends that awareness of goals biases the perception of evaluators, causing them to uncover the expected and overlook the unexpected. Most evaluation writers have not endorsed this approach since it seems to be an example of "missing the forest for the trees." There is so much to look for that the evaluator must have some guidance in the choice of measures.

Hard versus Soft Data

Our final concern deals with the degree of objectivity and authenticity of the evaluation data collected. So-called hard data require an emphasis on objectivity; test scores are an illustration. In return for objectivity (for data not being influenced by the data collector), the process must involve some degree of contrivance or alteration of the normal stream of classroom behavior. Soft data, on the other hand, are more subjective and wholistic since they are drawn from the normal stream of classroom behavior. Although the evaluator need not introduce himself or herself into the data collection process, he or she will influence the accuracy of the recording of behavior since its detection and classification is a judgmental process.

In the approach of this book, both types of data are solicited. For measuring outcomes, hard data are preferred since they are more readily accepted by administrators, board members, and taxpayers and can be elicited under conditions to which students are accustomed. For measuring process, soft data are sought since their collection does not necessitate disrupting the behavior that is the subject of observation.

However, it must be emphasized that evaluators should make every effort to minimize disruption and contrivance when collecting hard data and every effort to minimize subjectivity when collecting soft data. In the latter instance, using reliability observations (that is, additional observations to check on the accuracy of the primary ones) is mandated.

Using Evaluation Data to Influence Decision Making

The collection and analysis of evaluation data is not an end in itself. These data must be used in the decision-making process. Some practical suggestions as to how this can be accomplished will be offered. Below are six "action" rules to try to follow if the results of an evaluation are to influence the subsequent course of events.

Rule 1. Avoid involvement in an evaluation without some assurance of its results being used. It is fair and reasonable to discuss this matter of using the evaluation results to influence the district's educational program with the school board and superintendent before beginning the work. If you are an outsider, it can be built into the contract. If you are an employee of the board, you still can seek reasonable assurances. Even though these assurances are no guarantee of change, they do sensitize the board and administration to the importance of using evaluation results and make them aware of its centrality to your involvement. Without the likelihood of future use, evaluation becomes a mere exercise.

Rule 2. Maximize the involvement throughout of different groups where possible. We are speaking now of administrators, board members, teachers, students, parents, and, where relevant, a funding agency. The results of an evaluation are most likely to be "swept under a rug" when no one knows of its existence. Wide involvement creates interest and concern and brings the obstructions to change out into the open before change would need to occur.

Where it can be done without influencing the evaluation outcomes, the evaluator should discuss the evaluation with as many of the groups mentioned above as possible, particularly before its start. This also may serve to introduce many of the groups to the program itself and give people an opportunity to voice their concerns. Unless serious concerns are dealt with at the outset, the results are likely to have little or no effect on the educational program since change is far easier to subvert than to accomplish.

Involvement and interest may be stimulated through either public meetings or small, more private conferences. Often the latter are more productive. Be receptive to comments and suggestions and be willing to incorporate any that may be suitable into the evaluation plan.

Rule 3. Build decision choices into the evaluation plan. Evaluators usually are called on to prepare an evaluation plan or proposal before beginning the evaluation. This plan focuses on methodology, procedures, and instrumentation. If the program has outside funding, the funding agency may require such a plan in written form.

The results of an evaluation are more likely to be used if the evaluator lays out the various outcome possibilities in the evaluation plan and links each to a particular course of action. Both the district administration and funding agent will see that the evaluator is action-oriented and that decisions can be made to follow from evaluation results.

Considerations for action should go beyond the obvious ones of continuing the program or discontinuing it. Decisions about the possibility of extending the program or improving its level of implementation also should be considered.

Rule 4. Be sensitive to the relevant, internal dynamics of the district (and to the role of the funding agent). Although evaluation is not (or should not be) a political process, change is. Change will never result from data alone; groups and individuals transform data into action or allow data to be so transformed. As an evaluator, you *must* be aware of the political realities of a district if you hope to see your results blossom into action. To gain this awareness if you are an outsider, you must spend enough time in the district to gain some understanding of its internal dynamics. If you are an insider, you probably should follow the obverse of this rule: Insulate yourself from the district's politics so as not to become enmeshed in it. Do not begin this process, in any event, until you have drawn up the evaluation plan, and try to keep the evaluation per se from being influenced by district politics.

When a project is supported by outside funds, the funding agent becomes an additional factor to consider. Often, the funding agency with its power to fund can be a powerful change agent, if properly involved. By being sensitive to the funding agency's role in terms of expectations and influence, you may be able to enlist its active support for action based on the results of the evaluation. All too often, however, the funding agency removes itself and its influence when the funding period ends.

Rule 5. Make strong, operational recommendations for action in the final report. The final evaluation report may be the single most major source of influence the evaluator has. In addition to containing an introductory chapter giving the background and purpose of the evaluation, a methodology chapter, and a somewhat technically oriented results chapter, the report should conclude with a short chapter entitled "Summary, Conclusions, and Recommendations." Usually it is this last chapter that gets reproduced and circulated; often it is the only part that is read.

This chapter should begin with a numbered *summary of the findings* of the evaluation. These findings should come directly out of the results chapter and take a form such as:

1. Students in project classrooms were absent significantly fewer days than students in control classrooms.

The list of findings, hopefully kept to a maximum of ten or twelve, should be followed by a numbered list of *conclusions,* rarely more than five or six, that synthesize the findings into more easily assimilated and applied statements. Below is an example:

1. <u>The project has made school a more positive and more desirable experience for students.</u>

Each conclusion should be followed by a brief paragraph of explanation and support so that readers who do not read the rest of the report will understand it. Each conclusion should be underlined to make it stand out.

The finale of the report is the *recommendations.* Offer about five to ten action-oriented recommendations, each underlined and followed by a paragraph of elaboration. Make sure the recommendations relate to and are based on the findings and conclusions of the evaluation report and not made up from other experience and knowledge you have had. An example follows.

1. Now that the project has successfully increased students' liking for school, emphasis should be placed on improving academic outcomes. In-service training should focus on developing curriculum materials toward this end.

The recommendations should grow out of the findings and imaginatively seek to extend on or improve the results. You might say the goal is to "consolidate the gains and cut the losses." Preparing recommendations is one of the more creative aspects of evaluation; but be cautioned that the recommendations must be: (1) defensible in terms of the evaluation results; (2) politically sensitive so that they make sense in the district context; and (3) guidelines for action. Whereas conclusions are passive, recommendations should be active. They may be your best chance to influence change.

Rule 6. Present the results along with recommendations to the administrators, the board, and the public. Recommendations are more likely to be carried out if they are communicated clearly to the people who can influence school events. Evaluators often are given the opportunity to communicate their results to the board of education. Since the board may not be clearly aware of the program you evaluated, particularly if it was supported by outside funds, this presentation will be an important determinant of future events.

Remember that board members and the public (who will be present if it is a public meeting) are not evaluation experts; it is important that your presentation be geared at a nontechnical level. To facilitate understanding, you should prepare overhead transparencies of tables and figures (particularly the latter) showing each result. As you describe each finding, the accompanying transparency will make your point easier to follow. Also, prepare transparencies listing your conclusions and recommendations, for audience members who are more visually oriented.

You also should be prepared to answer questions clearly and directly and to avoid becoming defensive when detractors challenge your results. Public meetings often are difficult; they demand considerable patience because some board and community members adamantly take a predetermined position. However, a clear presentation of findings and recommendations will be likely to influence the majority of audience members who arrive with an open mind.

Evaluation Pitfalls and How to Avoid Them

Setting Expectations and Schedules

Evaluation is a process in which an opportunity occurs only once; after the time for implementing a procedure or collecting some data passes, that occasion will not recur. Therefore, mistakes are hard to cover. Most mistakes are a function of either expectations or schedules. There are expectations on the parts of central administrators, building administrators, project staff, teachers, evaluation assistants, and anyone else who gets involved. After the evaluation is over or before a particular measurement, a building principal may say that he or she did not expect you to care whether the classes were randomly assigned or whether the same teacher taught both classes, or whether students were allowed to go home after completing the test, or whether teachers were observed in a particular order.

As important as it is to communicate schedules accurately, it is even more important to communicate expectations. Since you cannot anticipate every problem that will arise and therefore plan for it or eliminate it by scheduling, you must make school personnel aware of your expectations—the general way that you want the evaluation to proceed.

Below are some specific suggestions for avoiding this pitfall:

Lay out a detailed schedule in your evaluation plan. Prepare a set of tasks to be completed, such as for testing or observing, and assign each task a specific date. This schedule will make it possible to know when every event is to happen. Remember, any activity that is to be carried out in the evaluation should appear on that schedule!

Prepare lists of responsibilities for everyone who is to be involved in the evaluation. Make out a list of the tasks or activities that you are to do and lists for each of your assistants. Make out such a list for the project director, project staff, building principal(s), and anyone else who will be involved.

Prepare an observation plan. If classroom observations are to be made, lay out in advance a detailed plan for which teacher is to be observed when and by whom. This plan will help insure that observations are conducted as planned.

Conduct briefings for all involved persons. Preparing plans, schedules, and lists of responsibilities and circulating them does not insure that they will be read and understood, or even taken seriously. It therefore is necessary to conduct a face-to-face session called a "briefing." At this time, go over the plan and schedule, list responsibilities, explain them, re-explain them if necessary, indicate why they are important, defend them, and answer questions about them. The questions asked will often suggest potential areas of misunderstanding, conflict, or lack of cooperation. Use the briefing to try to overcome problems before they arise.

Do not restrict all briefings to the outset of the evaluation. Conduct them as necessary as the evaluation proceeds.

Keep tabs. Do not assume that your plans will be carried out or your schedule properly implemented. Provide reminders by phone and/or note before each event, and check up by phone afterward to make sure the event has occurred as planned. In some evaluations, all tasks are done by the evaluator, so this suggestion becomes gratuitous; but in larger scale evaluations, as in large districts, other personnel, such as principals, are called on to carry out tasks on their own (to administer tests and/or to observe teachers) or to supervise tasks. If these tasks are not of long-standing habit or if they represent a change in the regular way of doing things, it is of critical importance to keep tabs so that problems can be caught as they arise.

Establishing Conditions and Testing

Two principal categories of activity in an evaluation are establishing project and control classrooms and carrying out testing. In fact, in many evaluations these are the only activities that occur. They therefore merit special consideration.

Project teachers should carry out the project orientation; presumably they know what it is and have been taught how to do it, whereas control teachers represent a cross-section of all teachers. Otherwise, the two groups should be equivalent. Some pitfalls that can occur here are: (1) the person selecting either the control or project teachers or both systematically attempts to pick the "worst" teachers for the former and the "best" for the latter; (2) teachers for the two groups are drawn from different schools that have vastly different student populations; (3) everyone is afraid to be in the control group and so some are forced into it.

Ideally, teacher choosing is done by the evaluator on a random basis. In fact, it rarely occurs this way. Even though it is usually done by the district, it is best not left to them. The best an evaluator can usually settle for is to: (1) explain to the project director the principles to try to follow in teacher selection; and (2) after selection has been made, check on the characteristics of the teachers in the two groups, both quantitatively and qualitatively, to determine their equivalence or lack of it.

Most problems that occur in an evaluation are in conjunction with testing and are based on either conditions or timing. When the testing done is part of the district's regular testing program, it is likely to run reasonably smoothly. However, when it is special testing—unique to the evaluation—such as attitude testing, be prepared to encounter problems. Consider these suggestions:

1. Conduct briefings to explain all test administrations to teachers and principals who will be the test administrators.
2. Be sure teachers are aware of certain particulars such as whether students

are to sign their names on their test papers, what student information is to be obtained, how much time is to be taken, and how test papers and answer sheets are to be returned.

3. Use whatever techniques you can to get teachers and students to take the testing seriously. One procedure is to ask them to write their names on the paper before they take the test (so that they take it seriously), and then afterward to cross their name out or erase it.

4. Avoid using the classroom teacher to administer attitude-toward-school instruments, where logistically possible. These instruments measure students' liking for the teacher, and the teacher's presence as a test administrator may inhibit student response. It also tends to present a threatening and uncomfortable situation for the teachers themselves. If you can, use assistants or other school personnel to administer this type of test.

5. Try to keep the testing situation as natural as possible. Remember, students are used to taking tests and often take testing in stride, particularly if their teachers do.

Working With Teachers

It probably is fair to say that the single group whose involvement is most critical to the success of an evaluation is teachers. Their cooperation is not only desirable but also necessary to the process of instructional program evaluation. An example of what can go wrong in this sphere is an actual occurrence in a district-wide evaluation. When the teachers saw the test instruments for the first time, two days before their planned administration, they notified their association in alarm. They were particularly concerned with the tests measuring students' attitudes toward self and toward school, which they felt were designed to show teachers in a poor light. As mentioned, evaluation does not occur in a vacuum but in a real, political climate. In this district, a strong conflict existed between administration and teachers over the program that was being evaluated. This conflict formed the backdrop for a controversy in the form of a dispute over these tests brought by the teachers' association to the state commissioner of education. The evaluator and the teachers' association finally settled the matter out of court after six weeks of negotiations. In the final analysis, the evaluation was "saved" by changing the wording on about a dozen items on one scale and removing from another scale another twenty items that were not particularly pertinent to the undertaking.

After that experience, the evaluation proceeded smoothly only because the evaluator cleared all subsequent procedures involving teachers with the association and obtained its endorsement before informing teachers. The moral of the story is *do not take teachers for granted.* Often they must be won over and reassured. This is best accomplished by:

1. Involving them in the design of evaluation procedures insofar as possible, or at least seeking their advice
2. Obtaining the endorsement, cooperation, and assistance of the local teachers' association
3. Briefing participating teachers and teacher representatives on all procedures (and rationales) in which their participation is required
4. Designing into the evaluation procedures protections for the rights of teachers to privacy, confidentiality, and anonymity
5. Monitoring teacher participation as the evaluation proceeds and being willing, in order to allay their fears or meet their needs, to institute reasonable changes that will not alter the basic design of the evaluation
6. Presenting the results of the evaluation and the recommendations to participating teachers and teacher representatives in order to obtain their continued involvement and understanding.

This point cannot be overemphasized. In designing and carrying out an evaluation, do not overlook or disregard the needs and concerns of teachers, or the end result is likely to be much less than desired.

Test Items and Observation Scales

Many evaluators have been foiled by the test items or observation scales they choose to use. If they are borrowed, insuring high reliability and perhaps validity, they may be inappropriate as measures of the program's objectives. If they are constructed for the evaluation, they may lack reliability.

In one evaluation, teachers were asked to help construct the observation scales based on their perceptions of the program's objectives. They found this task to be too threatening even though the evaluator insisted that all teachers, particularly those who were teaching younger children, could not be expected to meet all of the program's objectives. Nevertheless, they wanted to build a contingency or "escape clause" into each statement so they would be likely to meet it. In the final analysis, it became the job of the evaluator to operationalize the program's goals, based on discussions with teachers.

In this same evaluation, on the first round of observations, most teachers obtained high scores. This displeased the project director, who had hoped to use the data as a basis for forcing change in teaching behavior. Moreover, in one school a teacher who was generally afforded low esteem by his colleagues obtained higher scores than a teacher who was highly esteemed, and the word got out. This result made the teachers even more displeased with the observation scale and its implementation.

The problem was solved by firing the observer and bringing in two more observers from the project staff—former teachers themselves. Ironically, on the final observation, their results mirrored those of the poor assistant who had been fired for poor judgment.

How are problems such as these to be avoided? Consider the following suggestions:

1. *Do not rely on too few measuring instruments.* This is akin to saying "Don't put all your eggs in one basket." If some instruments do not work out, others may.
2. *If you can, give teachers a chance to relate to your measures* (or the specific objectives they are intended to measure) and become accustomed to them. Sometimes teachers cannot be shown the actual tests or scales, or they would teach to them in the narrowest sense, but they can always be shown the specific objectives against which the program will be judged.
3. *Give teachers a chance to relate to your observers.* Do not just pop them into the classroom as total strangers; but do not tell your observers which teachers are project teachers and which are controls.
4. *Use the project director as an intermediary and test case.* Let the project director help you win over teachers and principals to your tests and methods.
5. *Use a combination of borrowed instruments and homemade ones* in order to try to maximize the advantages and minimize the disadvantages of each.
6. *Make sure to collect reliability data and present its results.* Do not simply assume that your measures and measurers are reliable. In particular, try to test out your measures and train your measurers in advance.
7. *Do not be afraid to alter things as you go along if you have to.* Your job is to do the evaluation, not to be the "keeper of the faith." Evaluation methodology and devices are not so precise as to be unalterable. If you have enough measures and one is not working or is causing undue controversy (as in the example of the dispute launched by the teachers' association), then eliminate or modify it. Withdrawing as a matter of principle will accomplish little. Knowing where and how to compromise may accomplish much.

Statistics and Conclusions

The last area of concern involves the statistics you use to analyze your data and the conclusions you draw. A major pitfall is not to use statistics at all. Statistics are just tools that allow you to assign probabilities to outcomes based on samples or test cases. They are a help, not a hindrance. A second pitfall is a tendency to overgeneralize or to reach conclusions that are not warranted by the data. Do not make your conclusions before you complete the evaluation.

A group of evaluators studied a large-scale guidance program that they themselves had designed. (It is not a good practice to evaluate your own creations; impartiality becomes hard to maintain.) They reported the test results, which uniformly showed no differences between treatment and control groups. Then, based on a more subjective estimation, they concluded that the program was effective. When asked how they could reach a conclusion so at variance with the test results, one evaluator responded by saying that the state of the art of testing made test results an unlikely source of support. Needless to say, this same remark would never have been made had the test results supported their conclusion.

A few suggestions can be offered:

1. *Do not avoid statistics; seek help if necessary.* You can usually find a statistical consultant on a college campus.
2. *If there are considerable data, analyze them by computer.* Computers are more accurate and efficient data analyzers than people are. Evaluators are responsible for the accuracy of their statistical tests. Locate the nearest computer center (a college campus is a good source) and hire a consultant to assist you if you lack the necessary skills or are out of practice. Computer technology changes at a rapid rate, so you may find that your once appropriate skills are now outdated.
3. Remember that *correlations* (and other ex post facto approaches) *do not necessarily indicate causation.*

   Because two sets of data or variables are related statistically does not mean that one caused the other, or vice versa. There might be a third, unmeasured, variable that has caused them both. That more classroom hours and academic performance are correlated may only indicate that in this particular instance those classroom hours were filled with effective teaching. Ineffective teaching would not yield the same result.
4. *Draw only conclusions justified by the data* and do not prejudge the issue. Let the data be your guide. If they reflect a *lack* of program success, say so. If your job depends on the result, then you should not be doing the evaluation in the first place.
5. *Do not let the project director, local superintendent, or funding agent write the final evaluation report.* That is your job. Do not undertake the evaluation unless this is clearly understood. It is more than a job. Your reputation and your integrity are at stake. Let your professional ethics and judgment, not your employers, be your guide.

Clearly there are potential pitfalls in any evaluation undertaking. There is much at stake for many people, and many people must be involved in it. An evaluation is done within a system that has its own complex procedures, and those of the evaluation are usually considered to be an imposition. Educators often do not want to be bothered with pretests and observers, with attitude scales and control groups. And no one else may really care about the evaluation but you. Faced with this, try to follow as many of the suggestions offered in this chapter as you can. Beyond that you will have to resolve problems as best you can while collecting your own anecdotes. Once, the building principal in a control school decided to impound all the data from his school and wrote a memo to that effect. Fortunately, the data were at that moment safely locked in the trunk of his evaluator's car! A disaster was narrowly averted. But, keep at it. Luckily, we learn from our mistakes.

References

Aleamoni, L. M. (1981). Student ratings of instruction. In J. Millman, ed., *Handbook of teacher evaluation.* Beverly Hills, Calif.: Sage Publications.

Aleamoni, L. M., and Hexner, P. Z. (1980). A review of the research on student evaluation and a report on the effect of different sets of instructions on student course and instructor evaluation. *Instructional Science, 9,* 67–84.

Anderson, L. W. (1981). *Assessing affective characteristics in the schools.* Boston: Allyn and Bacon.

Bloom, B. S. (1956). *Taxonomy of educational objectives. Handbook I: Cognitive domain.* New York: David McKay.

Bogdan, R. C., and Biklen, S. K. (1982). *Qualitative research for education.* Boston: Allyn & Bacon.

Bond, G. L., and Dykstra, R. (1967). Coordinating Center for First-Grade Reading Instruction Programs. Minneapolis, Minn.: University of Minnesota (Contract No. OE-5-10-264).

Borich, G. D., and Madden, S. K. (1977). *Evaluating classroom instruction: A source book of instruments.* Reading, Mass.: Addison-Wesley.

Buros, O. K., ed. (1979). *The eighth mental measurements yearbook.* Lincoln, Neb.: University of Nebraska Press.

Cochran, D. W., and Tuckman, B. W. (1976). A comparison of regular and open classroom process. *Journal of Curriculum Studies, 8,* 61–70.

Cohen, J. (1977). *Statistical power analysis for the behavioral sciences.* Rev. ed. New York: Academic Press.

Cook, T. D., and Campbell, D. T. (1979). *Quasi-experimentation: Design and analysis issues for field settings.* Chicago: Rand McNally.

Cronbach, L. J. (1971). Test validation. In R. L. Thorndike, ed., *Educational measurement.* 2d ed. Washington, D.C.: American Council on Education, 443–507.

———. (1975). Beyond the two disciplines of scientific psychology. *American Psychologist, 30,* 116–27.

Cronbach, L. J., and Gleser, G. C. (1965). *Psychological tests and personal decisions.* 2d ed. Urbana: University of Illinois Press.

Cronbach, L. J., and Snow, R. E. (1978). *Aptitudes and instructional methods.* New York: Irvington.

Domino, G. (1968). Differential prediction of academic achievement in conforming and independent settings. *Journal of Educational Psychology, 59,* 256–60.

Domino, G. (1971). Interactive effects of achievement orientation and teaching style on academic achievement. *Journal of Educational Psychology, 62,* 427–31.

Edwards, J. E., Norton, S., Taylor, S., Weiss, M., and Dusseldorp, R. (1975). How effective is CAI? A review of the research. *Educational Leadership,* November, 147–53.

Elliott, J. M., and Tuckman, B. W. (1976). Differentiated outcomes resulting from individualized instruction at a two-year college. *Community College Research Quarterly, 1,* 1–12.

Fear, F. A. (1978). *The evaluation interview.* N.Y.: McGraw-Hill.

Fry, E. (1964). Judging readability of books. *Teacher Education, 5,* 34–39.

Gagné, R. M. (1971). Instruction based on research in learning. *Engineering Education,* March, 520 ff.

———. (1973). Domains of learning. *Interchange, 3,* 3–13.

Glaser, R. (1972). Individuals and learning: The new aptitudes. *Educational Researcher, 1* (6), 5–13.

Glass, G. V. (1977). Integrating findings: The meta-analysis of research. In L. S. Shulman, ed., *Review of research in education.* Vol. 5. Itasen, Ill.: F. E. Peacock, 351–79.

Gough, H. G. (1957). *Manual for the California Psychological Inventory.* Palo Alto, Calif.: Consulting Psychologists Press.

Guba, E. G., and Lincoln, Y. S. (1981). *Effective evaluation.* San Francisco: Jossey-Bass.

Hopkins, K. D., and Bracht, G. H. (1971). The stability and change of language and non-language IQ scores. Final Report, Project No. O–H–024. Washington, D.C.: Office of Education, Bureau of Research, U.S. Department of Health, Education & Welfare.

Hunt, D. E. (1971). *Matching models in education.* Toronto: Ontario Institute for Studies in Education.

———. (1975). Person-environment interaction: A challenge found wanting before it was tried. *Review of Educational Research, 45,* 209–30.

Indik, B. (1966). *The motivation to work.* New Brunswick, N.J.: Rutgers University, Institute of Management and Labor Relations.

Johnson, O. G., ed. (1977). *Tests and measurements in child development: Handbook II.* San Francisco: Jossey-Bass.

Lewin, K., Lippitt, R., and White, R. K. (1939). Patterns of aggressive behavior in experimentally created "social climates." *Journal of Social Psychology, 10,* 271–99.

Lohnes, P. R. (1973). Evaluating the schooling of intelligence. *Educational Researcher, 2* (2), 6–11.

Mager, R. F. (1962). *Preparing instructional objectives.* Belmont, Calif.: Fearon Publishers.

Millman, J. (1981). Student achievement as a measure of teacher competence. In J. Millman, ed., *Handbook of teacher evaluation.* Beverly Hills, Calif.: Sage Publications.

Nie, N. H., Hull, C. H., Jenkins, J. G., Steinbrenner, K., and Bent, D. H. (1975). *Statistical package for the social sciences* 2d ed. New York: McGraw-Hill.

Northern, E. F. (1980). The trend toward competency testing of teachers. *Phi Delta Kappan, 61,* 359.

Osgood, C. E.; Suci, G. J.; and Tannenbaum, P. M. (1957). *The measurement of meaning.* Urbana: University of Illinois Press.

Piaget, J. (1952). *The origins of intelligence in children.* New York: International Universities Press.

Porter, A. C., and Chibucos, T. R. (1974). Selecting analytic strategies. In G. D. Borich, ed., *Evaluating educational programs.* Englewood Cliffs, N.J.: Educational Technology Publications, 415–64.

Simon, A., and Boyer, E. C. (1967). *Mirrors for behavior: An anthology of classroom observation instruments.* 6 vols. Philadelphia: Research for Better Schools.

Smith, D. D. (1968). An evaluation of the effectiveness of television instruction at Midwestern University. *Journal of Educational Research, 62,* 18–24.

Stake, R. E. (1975). *Evaluating the arts in education: A responsive approach.* Columbus, Ohio: Merrill.

Stallings, J. A. (1976). How instructional processes relate to child outcomes in a national study of Follow Through. *Journal of Teacher Education, 27,* 43–47.

Taba, H., and Elzey, F. F. (1974). Teaching strategies and thought processes. In R. T. Hyman, ed., *Teaching: Vantage points for study.* 2d ed. Philadelphia: Lippincott, 483–500.

Thompson, S. B. (1980). Do individualized mastery and traditional instructional systems yield different course effects in college calculus? *American Educational Research Journal, 17,* 361–75.

Traub, R., Weiss, J., Fisher, C., and Musella, D. (1972). Closure on openness: Describing and quantifying open education. *Interchange, 3* (2–3), 69–84.

Tuckman, B. W. (1975). *Measuring educational outcomes (Fundamentals of testing).* New York: Harcourt Brace Jovanovich.

———. (1976). New instrument: The Tuckman Teacher Feedback Form. *Journal of Educational Measurement, 13,* 233–37.

———. (1978). *Conducting educational research.* 2d ed. New York: Harcourt Brace Jovanovich.

Tuckman, B. W., and Orefice, D. S. (1973). Personality structure, instructional outcomes, and preferences. *Interchange, 4,* 43–48.

Tuckman, B. W., and Waheed, M. A. (1981). Evaluating an individualized science program for community college students. *Journal of Research in Science Teaching, 18,* 489–95.

Tuckman, B. W., and Yates, D. S. (1980). Evaluating the student feedback strategy for changing teacher style. *Journal of Educational Research, 74,* 74–77.

Tyler, R. W. (1951). The functions of measurement in improving instruction. In E. F. Lindquist, ed. *Educational measurement.* Washington, D.C.: American Council on Education, 47–67.

U. S. Department of Health, Education and Welfare. (1975). *A practical guide to measuring project impact on student achievement.* Washington, D.C.: U.S. Government Printing Office (No. 017–089–01460–2).

Veldman, D., and Brophy, J. (1974). Measuring teacher effects on pupil achievement. *Journal of Educational Psychology, 66,* 319–24.

Ward, W. D., and Barcher, P. R. (1975). Reading achievement and creativity as related to open classroom experience. *Journal of Educational Psychology, 67,* 683–91.

Ware, J. E., and Williams, R. G. (1977). Discriminate analysis of student ratings as a means of identifying lecturers who differ in enthusiasm or information giving. *Educational and Psychological Measurement, 37,* 627–39.

Wilson, S. (1977). The use of ethnographic techniques in educational research. *Review of Educational Research, 47,* 245–66.

Winer, B. J. (1971). *Statistical principles in experimental design.* 2d ed. New York: McGraw-Hill.

Wolf, R. M. (1981). Selecting appropriate statistical methods. In R. A. Berk, ed., *Educational evaluation methodology: The state of the art.* Baltimore: Johns Hopkins Press, 110–23.

Case Studies

Formative Evaluation

PROJECT: OPEN CLASSROOM—FORMATIVE EVALUATION REPORT

Bruce W. Tuckman

Introduction

The evaluation described in this report was *formative;* that is, it monitored goal attainment within the project on an ongoing basis and fed these data back into the project in order to make possible the refinement of project inputs and processes so that they might more closely approximate predesignated goals. In essence, a formative evaluation is like a target on a rifle range. After some rounds have been fired, the marksman examines the target to determine his accuracy. Based on his examination, he makes the necessary adjustments in his behavior so that his next rounds will be more accurate. The diagram on page 224 illustrates this approach.

The subsequent sections will provide some degree of detail about the specific formative evaluations undertaken. However, the emergent quality of the evaluation must be emphasized. This does not represent the avoidance of evaluation responsibility. It does represent a willingness toward and tolerance for the nuances within the project goals and their subtle interrelationships. It also represents an attempt to design an evaluation consistent with the open classroom approach.

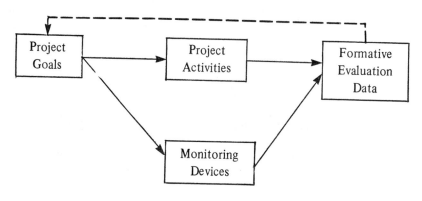

Goals

The following goals were set for project classrooms for the project's second year:

1. 80% of the children will be working on their own ability level in reading and math on an individualized basis
2. 50% of the children will be motivated to work on their own child-interest-centered level in reading, math, language arts, social studies, and art
3. 50% of the children will be displaying responsible values-centered behavior
4. 85% of the children will be able to maintain gains from goals set from the first year
5. 75% of the children, given the option, will involve themselves in interdisciplinary learning experiences that will enable them to manipulate ideas in the cognitive and affective sense and transfer them in the verbal and non-verbal sense.

It must be kept in mind that three levels of the project were operating simultaneously. Grades K–3 in School A were in the most advanced position in project experience, grades 4–5 in School A in the least advanced position (it was their first year), and grades K–5 in School B were intermediate in position. For this reason, all five goals were not expected to be achieved to the same degree in all grade levels at both schools.

Based on these five goals, five goal areas for purposes of evaluation were identified and developed in detail. Each goal area is described below.

Self-Discipline

One major goal of the open classroom approach is to enable children to internalize some degree of responsibility for their own learning. Because of the inherent difficulty in monitoring this kind of behavior, no attempt was made to examine it in the first year. However, in the second year this most important behavior was examined in the following ways:

1. Intensive observations were made in classrooms in the three project stages (School A grades 4–5, newest initiates into the project; School B grades K–5, the intermediate stage; School A grades K–3, the curriculum development stage) to identify instances in which self-discipline was manifested and instances in which it was absent. For documentation, an interview and rating were used by observers to convert observations into data. Such observations were examined longitudinally (by comparing classrooms of children to themselves over the course of the year) and cross-sectionally (by comparing different classes both within the project to one another). On a periodic basis, these observations were fed back to project staff and teachers and the effect of this feedback assessed.

Teacher-Student Interaction Patterns

Consistent with the goal of helping students develop self-discipline is a form of teacher-student interaction characterized by individualization and warmth and acceptance. Again, by using observation schedules, the pattern of teacher-student evaluation was monitored. However, consistent with formative evaluation, these data were collected periodically throughout the school year and fed back to teachers via project staff. Thus, for evaluative purposes, changes in teacher-student interaction patterns were examined over time, and classrooms within the three project stages were compared and contrasted at different times.

Curricular Approach

Because the open classroom approach is committed to curriculums that are consistent with the emphasis on individualization, learning by discovery, and student activity based on student interest, the curricular approach experienced by students in open classrooms should be different from that in traditional classrooms. To determine whether this was in fact the case, curriculum data were collected in the classrooms in the three project stages. These data were observational in nature and were collected by an observer using an observation schedule developed for this purpose.

Achievement of Criterion Behaviors

Since the people who finance public education are unwilling to accept the success of an educational program unless it reflects itself in the area of achievement, achievement data were collected and examined. Criterion behaviors were prespecified in math and language arts as a basis for evaluating achievement. In the absence of comparative or normative data, criterion-referenced achievement testing was mandated.

Strategy

It must be reemphasized that the evaluation system used was both innovative and consistent with the philosophy of the project it was used to evaluate. The three most salient characteristics of the evaluation were that it was:

1. Formative: evaluation data were collected throughout the second half of the school year and fed back to teachers and students in order to increase the likelihood of goal attainment; moreover, teachers participated in the design of the criteria
2. Observational: data were largely collected by an observer using a series of observation schedules focusing on the stream of classroom activities and critical incidents therein
3. Colateral (rather than controlled): inferences about cause and effect were based on comparisons between different stages within the project and by comparisons between project classrooms and project goals.

The purpose of the evaluation, therefore, was to increase the probability that the project achieved its goals rather than to demonstrate that the project was a success relative to nonproject classrooms. The evaluation was project-centered and became a methodology that was consistent with the philosophy of the project. Determining the degree of project success was the degree to which formative evaluation data showed that the project was increasingly approaching its goals of: (1) student self-discipline; (2) teacher-student interaction featuring individualization, warmth, and acceptance; (3) curricular approach allowing individual, interest-centered learning activity; and (4) growth in achievement relative to prespecified criteria.

Measurement

Measurement was undertaken in the four areas of: (1) student self-discipline; (2) teacher-student interaction patterns, which included a) openness of classroom management and b) openness of teacher style; (3) curriculum approach; and (4) achievement of criterion behaviors.

Observer Scales

Self-Discipline of Students. Fifteen scales (appearing at the end of this report) served to measure Student Self-Discipline. These scales reflected: (1) the ability of students to work and proceed on their own initiative without constant teacher supervision (i.e., *task restraint*); (2) the use of classroom resources and self-direction aids to learning (i.e., *task urging*); (3) cooperation between students and avoidance of nonconstructive behavior (i.e., *social restraint*); and (4) inter-student facilitation and help (i.e., *social urging*).

Both teachers and project staff were asked to contribute to the list of self-discipline behaviors and to comment on the list as it was developed. The resulting list is the product of feedback and considerable revision. Other sources of information on the open classroom (e.g., Walberg and Thomas 1974; Bussis and Chittenden 1970) were examined closely to help identify criterion behaviors in this area.

The data that provided the basis for completing the fifteen student self-discipline items were collected using the Student Question List and Student Answer Form. Upon entering the classroom, the observer was instructed to select four children appearing to be involved in highly diverse activities. (This instruction was intended to make it possible to sample the widest range of behavior in the classroom.) The six questions asked were aimed at the four areas of student self-discipline stated above (as well as providing information related to judgments in other parts of the total rating instrument). Answers to the questions were entered in the Student Answer Form. Based on answers so entered and observations made within the forty-five-minute observation period, the observer(s) completed the judgments required by the fifteen items.

The fifteen criterion behaviors measured by the fifteen items were available to all teachers and staff well before the first observation on the Observation Guide in order that the evaluation could be formative. Teachers and project staff both participated in developing the Observation Guide.

Teacher-Student Interaction. This aspect of classroom activity was divided into two areas: verbal interaction and classroom management. Verbal interaction dealt with the content and style of teacher behavior; classroom management dealt with how the teacher controlled or influenced the flow of events in the classroom. In addition to the student interview and recording forms, two other instruments contributed to these judgments: the Teacher Interview Form and the Tuckman Teacher Feedback Form (TTFF). These instruments provided data for completing the scales on Teacher-Student Interaction. (See the end of this report.)

Of the instruments, only the TTFF was not unique to this evaluation. It has been used on previous occasions and its reliability and validity have been documented by Tuckman (1974). It provides data for judging the creativity, dynamism, organized demeanor, and warmth and acceptance of a teacher based on a forty-five-minute observation.

Items measuring teacher-student interaction also were based on reference sources mentioned above. Items dealt with such areas as teacher monitoring, directing, student grouping, movement, activity choice, and others.

Curriculum. Curriculum was subdivided into process and content. Process dealt with the independence that the curriculum provided the student from the teacher; content dealt with the relevance, interdisciplinary nature, and atypicalness of curricular experiences. Information on which these judgments were based was drawn from the teacher and student interviews plus observation and examination of curriculum materials. (See the end of this report.)

Teachers were given the Observation Guide before any observations were made so that they would know about the desired behaviors in the curriculum, teacher-student interaction, and self-discipline areas.

Criterion-Referenced Achievement

Rather than using conventional norm-referenced achievement tests to measure achievement, the strategy of criterion-referenced testing of math achievement and of reading and language arts achievement was adopted. Since it was possible to state objectives in math and language arts for the project in measurable terms, using criterion-referenced testing based on these objectives seemed more appropriate than the more general, standardized testing.

Math Achievement. At the primary level, basically grades 1–3, fifty-eight math competencies were identified. These competencies cover the general areas of sets, numerals, addition, subtraction, simple fractions, multiplication, and counting. At the intermediate level, basically grades 4–5, seventy math competencies were identified. These competencies cover the general areas of fractions, decimals, division, measurement, time, place value, and geometry.

The math competencies were identified by the project's math specialist and were discussed with and communicated to all teachers before any testing or instruction. Math competencies were measured by a math test originally developed for use with the Individually Prescribed Instruction (IPI) program but adapted for use in this project. All students were tested in such a way that they were allowed to continue until they could no longer demonstrate mastery.

Reading and Language Arts Achievement. Measurement of reading and language arts achievement was accomplished in word development, comprehension, and study skills by initially developing a list of competencies to be mastered. This list of competencies was divided into five levels: a readiness level and levels 1–4, covering the range of grade levels 1 to 5. Once the skills list was developed, published reading and language arts tests were culled and items selected from each to measure the competencies. In other words, a number of published reading tests were combined in such a way to result in a criterion-referenced reading test, built around a list of competencies.

A large portion of the school year was spent in "putting together" the test instrument. As a result, pretesting was not possible. However, every teacher was given the reading and language arts competency list early in the school year to guide his or her instruction.

The test instrument was administered on a posttest-only basis in May to all classes in both schools. Teachers were instructed to use the levels at which children's upper limit of success could be determined. For this report, every third test, randomly chosen, was scored and the results included. For subsequent application, all tests will be scored.

Procedures

The first complete observation was made in January and February after having a few sessions with the teachers and gaining their ideas and reactions to the criterion behaviors (an Observation Guide listing the behavioral goals was distributed to teachers; teachers never saw the actual measuring instruments that were based on the Observation Guide). The observer visited the classroom of each teacher in the two schools, grades 1–5, except those teachers who had announced their intention to leave at the end of the school year. In all, seventeen classrooms were visited in School A and twelve in School B.

All observations were made by one observer who spent approximately forty-five minutes in each classroom. She was an employee of the project, had no other contact with the district, and served only in this capacity. During the time in each classroom, four students and the teacher were interviewed, the TTFF and Student Record Form completed, and the scales for Self-Discipline, Teacher-Student Interaction, and Curriculum thereby completed for each. The results of each teacher's observation were written on the Observation Guide and given to that teacher for feedback.

In May, two members of the program staff—persons who had a wide working knowledge of teachers in the two schools—each observed all twenty-nine teachers for a second full observational cycle, using the same instruments and procedures as those used in the first. Each teacher was observed independently by each observer, providing a pair of observations on the second cycle rather than a single observation as on the first cycle.

Criterion-referenced achievement testing in math was done for all students in grades 1–5 of the two project schools on a pretest-posttest basis. The appropriate form (or forms: primary or intermediate or both) was administered in October and again in May to determine gains made from instruction. All teachers had a copy of the competencies in reading and language arts, although the test to measure these was not constructed until the spring. Posttesting on the instrument ultimately put together was done in May.

Results

It must be emphasized that the purpose of the formative evaluation was not to compare project schools to other schools and hence evaluate project schools on a relative basis. The strategy, rather, was to evaluate teacher behavior and student behavior and performance relative to a set of criteria. For this reason, means will be presented where appropriate and evaluated not on a statistical basis relative to other means but on an absolute basis relative to the ultimate or ideal level of such means.

Observation Variables

> *Self-Discipline–Task:* Items 1–9 reflecting continuation and initiation of work without excessive reliance on teacher. (Maximum score = 81.)
>
> *Self-Discipline–Social:* Items 10–15 reflecting cooperative, work-centered interaction. (Maximum score = 54.)
>
> *Openness of Verbal Interaction:* Items 16–21 reflecting structuring and clarifying rather than directing. (Maximum score = 54.)
>
> *Flexibility of Classroom Management:* Items 26–38 reflecting variety and opportunity for self-direction within a structured environment. (Maximum score = 117.)
>
> *Flexibility of Curriculum Process:* Items 39–46 reflecting the opportunity for individualized learning experiences within a systematic framework. (Maximum score = 72.)
>
> *Relevance of Curriculum Content:* Items 47–49 reflecting practicality and overlap in curriculum content. (Maximum score = 27.)
>
> *Creativity in Teaching Style:* Degree of creativity, originality, iconoclasm, imagination, lack of inhibition, experimenting, and adventurousness in teaching, as measured by the TTFF. (Maximum score = 43.)
>
> *Dynamism in Teaching Style:* Degree of aggressiveness, outgoingness, dominance, assertiveness, outspokenness, bubbliness, and extroversion in teaching, as measured by the TTFF. (Maximum score = 43.)
>
> *Organized Demeanor in Teaching Style:* Degree of resourcefulness, control, observantness, purposefulness, organization, system, and conscientiousness in teaching, as measured by the TTFF. (Maximum score = 43.)
>
> *Warmth and Acceptance in Teaching Style:* Degree of patience, gentleness, acceptance, warmth, amiability, fairness, and sociability in teaching, as measured by the TTFF. (Maximum score = 43.)*

---

* Each TTFF score was converted to the 1–9 scale and reported on in items 22–25 of the observation instrument.

Reliability

For the final observation cycle, two project staff members were used as observers, each one observing each teacher. There is little value in comparing the judgments of this pair of observers to those of the initial observer since, in the intervening six months, changes in teacher behavior could be expected based on feedback from the first observation and other project interventions. Differences between pre- and postobservations, therefore, would not necessarily reflect unreliability but would more likely reflect changes in teacher behavior.

For reliability purposes, the judgments of the two staff observers made at the end of the project year were compared. The resulting reliabilities are shown in Table A.1.

It can be clearly seen from Table 1 that the Observation Scales were used with a high degree of reliability by the two posttest judges.

Observation Findings

Due to the difficulty in obtaining data during the initial use of the observation scale in January, and the questionableness of the reliability of these data, this report will present data from the final observation only as a way of reflecting on the end state of the teaching behavior of teachers in the project. The established reliability of these "posttest" data make their interpretation possible. It must be pointed out, however, that data from the first testing were fed back to teachers in a manner consistent with the formative evaluation design.

Mean, maximum possible, and standard deviation scores for all teachers combined are shown in Table A.2. Scores are uniformly high in all areas except two, Teacher creativity and Teacher dynamism. Teachers were found to be ex-

TABLE A.1 Corrected Reliability* Coefficients on the Observation Posttest (N = 31)

Measure	No. of Items	R
Self-discipline (task)	9	.91
Self-discipline (social)	6	.86
Openness of verbal interaction	6	.91
Flexibility of classroom management	13	.93
Flexibility of curriculum process	8	.85
Relevance of curriculum content	3	.80
Teacher creativity	7	.90
Teacher dynamism	7	.78
Teacher organized demeanor	7	.65
Teacher warmth and acceptance	7	.77

*Reliabilities were corrected by Spearman-Brown Formula.

TABLE A.2   Mean, Maximum Possible and Standard Deviation Posttest Scores on the Observation Scales for all Teachers Combined (N = 31)

	Maximum	Mean	Standard Deviation
Self-discipline (task)	81	72.5	5.1
Self-discipline (social)	54	51.4	3.1
Openness of verbal interaction	54	50.4	3.8
Flexibility of classroom management	117	110.9	4.8
Flexibility of curriculum process	72	66.1	5.1
Relevance of curriculum content	27	23.2	2.3
Teacher creativity	43	28.2	7.3
Teacher dynamism	43	27.8	6.5
Teacher organized demeanor	43	36.2	6.0
Teacher warmth and acceptance	43	36.0	5.6

ceptionally high in Self-discipline (task), Self-discipline (social), Openness of verbal interaction, Flexibility of classroom management, Flexibility of curriculum process, Relevance of curriculum content, Teacher organized demeanor, and Teacher warmth and acceptance. Scores within five to ten points of the maximum on all scales except Creativity and Dynamism are far higher than would be expected on the basis of chance.

The magnitude of the scores on the observation scales is further illustrated in Figure A.1. Out of a possible maximum average score of 57.7, all scores fell above 41, with seven scores between 41 and 45, eight scores between 46 and 50, and 16 scores between 51 and 55. Again, point losses were mainly on creativity and dynamism. Figure A.1 shows the distribution of scores for teachers in the three stages of the project. As can be seen, teachers in each stage seem to be doing equally well.

On the basis of the data on the observation scales, it was concluded that the behavior of teachers in Project: Open Classroom was quite open and flexible and hence consistent with the goals of the project, particularly goals 2, 3, and 5 (see page 224).

Math Criterion Achievement Findings

Performance growth in math for the students in Project: Open Classroom is documented in Table A.3, which shows the number of math concepts mastered by 70% or more of the students in each grade level (1–5) of each of the two project schools. Pretest data are shown alongside posttest data. Although the

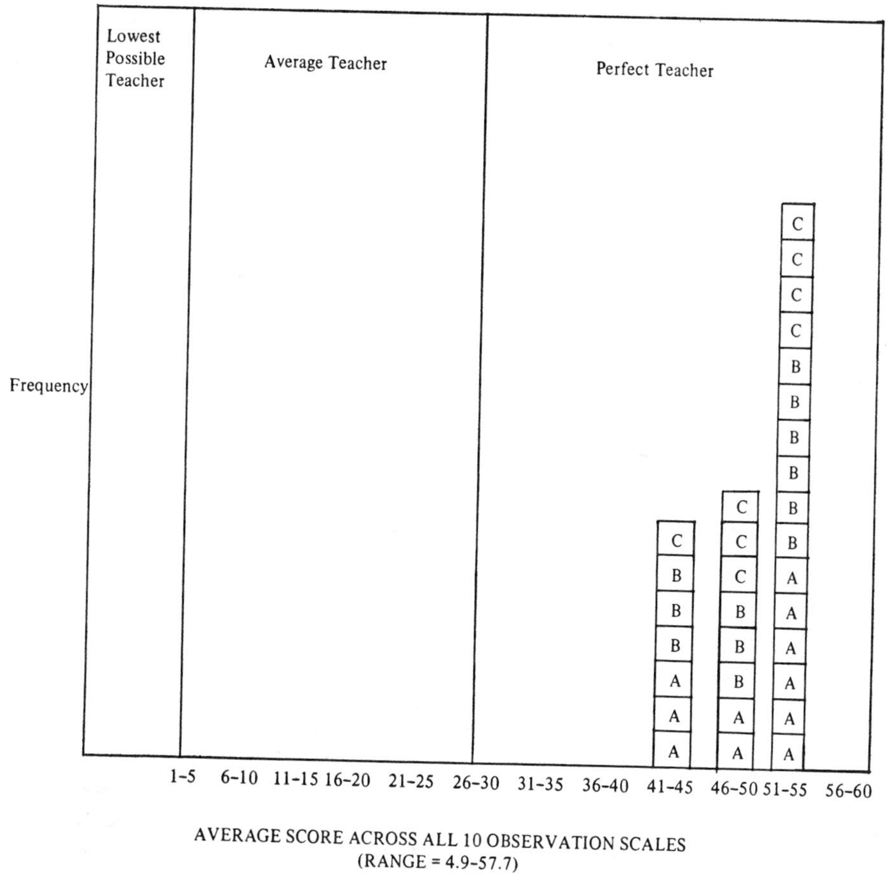

Lowest Possible Teacher	Average Teacher	Perfect Teacher

Frequency

The histogram bars (by score range):

- 41–45: C, B, B, B, A, A, A (bottom to top)
- 46–50: C, C, C, B, B, B, A, A (bottom to top)
- 51–55: C, C, C, C, B, B, B, B, B, B, A, A, A, A (bottom to top)

AVERAGE SCORE ACROSS ALL 10 OBSERVATION SCALES
(RANGE = 4.9–57.7)

Score axis: 1–5 6–10 11–15 16–20 21–25 26–30 31–35 36–40 41–45 46–50 51–55 56–60

A. School A, Grades 1–3
B. School B, Grades 1–5
C. School C, Grades 4–5

FIGURE A.1 *Distribution of the 31 Teachers Across the Total Score Range*

Primary Math Diagnostic Test was designed to go at least half way through the third grade level, it is clear that in both project schools, mastery of primary concepts is virtually complete by the end of the second grade. Overall gains from pretest to posttest were considerable. On the primary test, posttest performance in each of the first two grades is about three times as good as pretest performance, resulting in ultimate mastery of primary math concepts by the end of the second grade.

Gains on the Intermediate Test are not as dramatic as those on the Primary Test; posttest performance averaged a little better than twice pretest performance except in the third and fourth grades at School A. In the third grade at School A, pretest performance was exceptionally low, creating the possibility

TABLE A.3 Evaluation of Criterion Math Achievement: Number of Concepts Mastered by 70% of Students

Primary Test (58)	Pretest	Posttest
School A		
1st grade	12	41
2nd grade	18	49
School B		
1st grade	10	36
2nd grade	16	52

Intermediate Test (70)		
School A		
3rd grade	3	18
4th grade	12	35
5th grade	15	32
School B		
3rd grade	8	20
4th grade	12	22
5th grade	15	32

for the large gains that ensued. In the fourth grade at School A, posttest performance was exceptionally high, so high that these students exceeded fifth graders in both schools. One can only conclude that fourth-grade teachers in School A focused on Intermediate Level Math Criterion behaviors and effectively taught for their mastery. (It must be pointed out that teachers did not have access to the tests other than while administering them, and did not score them. What teachers did have was a list of criterion concepts appearing in the Appendix of the original report which then constituted the goal areas in math for the project.)

Although the performance data in math do not indicate whether such outcomes are unique to and better as a result of the Project: Open Classroom in contrast to other educational approaches, they do indicate that the project is meeting its own educational goal of mastery in math, which is the most useful information to know at this point in terms of keeping the project on target. Although not spelled out in this report, it is possible, from examining the math performance data, to identify the math concepts in which mastery is not occurring on a class-wide or grade-wide basis. Given this information, the teacher and math specialist together can make curricular modifications to better insure mastery on these concepts in the year to come. Another possibility would be to eliminate certain math concepts from the list if they are deemed nonessential in retrospect.

Overall, it must be concluded that the achievement in math in the

Project: Open Classroom schools is on target and satisfactory in relation to criterion expectation.

Reading Criterion Achievement Findings

Performance in Reading (and Language Arts) for the students in Project: Open Classroom is shown in Table A.4, which contains the number of reading con-

TABLE A.4 Evaluation of Criterion Reading Achievement: Number of Concepts Mastered by 70% of Students

Level 1 (25)	Posttest
School A	
1st grade	18
2nd grade	21
School B	
1st grade	17
2nd grade	17
Level 2 (45)	
School A	
2nd grade	33
3rd grade	31
School B	
2nd grade	33
3rd grade	31
Level 3 (73)	
School A	
3rd grade	46
4th grade	52
5th grade	35
School B	
3rd grade	47
4th grade	58
5th grade	35
Level 4 (60)	
School A	
5th grade	34
School B	
5th grade	28

cepts mastered by 70% or more of the students in each grade level (1–5) of each of the two project schools. Since the test was not available for pretest use, no pretest data are available by which to chart growth in reading skills. Thus, posttest data must be evaluated on their own merit.

The number of reading skills mastered at each grade level seems reasonably high on a percentage basis. On the Level 1 test, first and second graders have mastered about 70 percent of the skills, performing roughly equally on this level. On the Level 2 test, second and third graders have mastered about 70 percent of the skills, also performing roughly equally on that level. It is useful to question why students at the higher grade levels have not outperformed those at lower grades on Level 1 and Level 2 tests. Of course, the older students also perform on a higher level than younger students, reflecting their age and increased training. One would have expected, though, for students to have successfully completed all items on the lower level tests. Those items failed by the older students should be carefully examined and seriously considered for revision, replacement, or movement to a higher level.

On the Level 3 test, third graders have successfully completed more than 60 percent of the tasks, whereas fourth graders have successfully completed about 75 percent of the tasks. Quite surprisingly, on the Level 3 test, fifth graders have successfully completed fewer than 50 percent of the tasks, less than either their third-grade or fourth-grade counterparts. Fifth graders do, however, save some face by successfully completing about half of the tasks on the Level 4 test.

Why do the fifth graders perform less successfully than either third or fourth graders on the Level 3 test? It may be that certain tasks are improperly sequenced, but more likely it may be due to the decreasing emphasis on reading as children progress through these grade levels and the consequent forgetting that takes place. Moreover, third- and fourth-grade teachers were expected to concentrate on Level 3 reading skills, whereas fifth-grade teachers probably expected that skills at this level had been mastered and thus concentrated on Level 4. Since this is the first year criterion behaviors have been used, it is not totally surprising to find the best performance on a level test to have occurred for students for which that test was most clearly geared to their grade level. It also must be added that fifth-grade performance was quite variable from class to class, suggesting differential class composition or differential teaching.

Apart from difficulties in the sequencing of test items, and the fact that tests for all students could not be scored in time for this report, it was concluded that reading achievement on criterion tasks was substantial and impressive for project students and that, as for math, the diagnostic value of the testing procedure was considerable.

Conclusions

Observation Findings

The first conclusion was that teachers in Project: Open Classroom in both participating schools at all five grade levels observed were behaving largely in an open manner in managing their classrooms. There was dramatic evidence that Project: Open Classroom teachers' behavior was characterized by the following components:

1. Allowing and encouraging their students to manifest self-discipline in their pursuit of learning task activities and in social interaction
2. Interacting with their students in an open manner and managing the classroom with a high degree of flexibility and tolerance for student initiative
3. Building and adopting curricular experiences and materials that are flexible, student involving, and relevant
4. Manifesting a teaching style characterized by warmth and acceptance toward students and by organized demeanor

The only areas in which teacher behavior left room for major improvement were in the creativity and dynamism of teacher style. It could be argued that dynamism as a teaching style is somewhat inconsistent with the open classroom philosophy, in which case only creativity is an area of teacher behavior meriting improvement.

Thus, it was concluded that teachers' behavior as observed was open, flexible, student-involving, and highly consistent with and contributory to the second, third, and fifth project goals.

Observation Methodology

The observation phase of this evaluation was fraught with problems and difficulties. The teachers challenged the value and appropriateness of the behavior goals listed in the observation guide, and both the teachers and the project director challenged the veridicality of the observations. In fact, in all observation cycles, in each case by a different observer or observers, exceptionally high ratings were obtained by virtually all teachers on virtually all scales. Given these findings, one can conclude that:

1. Nearly all project teachers were models of open-classroom perfection, even by the middle of the year (which in the case of some teachers was their first year in the project); or
2. The observers (the one observer who did the first cycle, and the two staff members who did the final observations) were biased or inept; or

3. The observation methodology and instrumentation is inappropriate as used here.

In fact, it probably was a little of all three. Clearly, many of the project teachers were exemplars of the open classroom approach, although uniformly high ratings minimize the feedback value of the ratings. True also is that some bias is difficult to avoid in such ratings and that all aspects of the observation procedure were neither precise enough nor on target enough for their purposes. Clearly, some improvement is possible in next year's approach.

Achievement Findings

It is difficult to evaluate a criterion-referenced approach for the assessment of achievement the first time around. With each use and reuse, a greater backlog of data is built up for comparative purposes. However, based on this first year of use it must be concluded without equivocation that giving teachers a specific list of concepts to be mastered is a highly effective way to insure that such mastery takes place. Rather than concluding that students are performing at some mysterious plateau called "grade level," the achievement approach allowed the project to specify exactly which concepts a student had mastered and those which he or she had yet to master. Substantial mastery gains occurred during the course of the school year, suggesting that the project had not only changed teacher behavior but also continued to produce positive results in student performance on meaningful criteria, consistent with the project's first and fourth goals.

Recommendations

1. Reexamine and revise the observation scales to be more consistent with project goals and philosophy, using the data reported here as a basis for revision.
2. Use more than one or two observers at a time and afford them opportunity for practice before they start. Such observers may be partly drawn from the ranks of the project teachers as well in order to overcome any question of observer insensitivity.
3. Impress on the observers the importance of being critical, since the purposes of formative evaluation are to detect areas for needed improvement and to provide feedback. Making everyone look good serves no helpful purpose.
4. Undertake intervention aimed at helping project teachers become more creative in teaching style. Encourage teachers to be active experimenters with different instructional materials and strategies.
5. Provide each teacher with the results of the criterion achievement tests for his/her class so that he or she can see those concepts on which mastery has not been achieved and make appropriate instructional adjustments for next year.

References

Bussis, A. M., and Chittenden, E. A. (1970). *Analysis of an approach to open education.* Princeton, N.J.: Educational Testing Service.

Tuckman, B. W. (1974). Teaching: The application of psychological constructs. In R. T. Hyman, ed., *Teaching: Vantage points for study.* 2d ed. Philadelphia: Lippincott.

Walberg, H. J., and Thomas, S. C. (1974). Defining open education. *Journal of Research & Development in Education, 8,* 4–13.

Case Study #1
Project: Open Classroom

SELF-DISCIPLINE
Bruce W. Tuckman

Student(s):

Moved to new task without teacher
   intervention   1 2 3 4 5 6 7 8 9

Worked on a task without the teacher's
   presence   1 2 3 4 5 6 7 8 9

Engaged in task behavior without the
   teacher's prompting or maintaining it   1 2 3 4 5 6 7 8 9

Carried a task beyond its given
   requirements   1 2 3 4 5 6 7 8 9

Made accurate evaluation of the quality
   and completeness of his/her work   1 2 3 4 5 6 7 8 9

Used classmate(s) as a source of
   information about doing or correcting
   his/her work   1 2 3 4 5 6 7 8 9

Used interest center as integral part of
   work activity   1 2 3 4 5 6 7 8 9

Organized his/her work schedule such that
   teacher's task requirements are met   1 2 3 4 5 6 7 8 9

Initiated teacher information-giving
   behavior as resource for on-going activity   1 2 3 4 5 6 7 8 9

Did not treat others violently   1 2 3 4 5 6 7 8 9

Did not attempt to interfere with
   another's activity   1 2 3 4 5 6 7 8 9

Did not compete for the teacher's
   attention and affection   1 2 3 4 5 6 7 8 9

Maintained work areas   1 2 3 4 5 6 7 8 9

FIGURE A.2   *The Measure of Student Self-Discipline Used in Case Study #1*

"Behaved" for an adult other than the
teacher   1 2 3 4 5 6 7 8 9

When asked by peer, contributed effort or
material to another's activity   1 2 3 4 5 6 7 8 9

Case Study #1
Project: Open Classroom

TEACHER-STUDENT INTERACTION
Bruce W. Tuckman

Teacher directs	1 2 3 4 5 6 7 8 9	Teacher uses structuring and suggesting
Teacher reacts with personal criticism	1 2 3 4 5 6 7 8 9	Teacher reacts with performance feed-back
Teacher reacts on a comparative basis	1 2 3 4 5 6 7 8 9	Teacher reacts on an individual basis
Teacher imposes values	1 2 3 4 5 6 7 8 9	Teacher espouses value clarification
Teacher espouses private, subjective values	1 2 3 4 5 6 7 8 9	Teacher espouses cooperative values
Teacher continually offers unsolicited remarks	1 2 3 4 5 6 7 8 9	Other than when engaged in group or individual instruction or when giving feedback, teacher makes few unsolicited remarks
Teacher is cold and critical	1 2 3 4 5 6 7 8 9	Teacher is warm and accepting
Teacher is conventional and noncreative	1 2 3 4 5 6 7 8 9	Teacher is original and creative
Teacher is passive	1 2 3 4 5 6 7 8 9	Teacher is forceful and energetic
Teacher is disorganized and preoccupied	1 2 3 4 5 6 7 8 9	Teacher is organized and alert

FIGURE A.3   *The Measure of Teacher-Student Interaction Used in Case Study #1*

Teacher maximizes barriers between self and students	1 2 3 4 5 6 7 8 9	Teacher minimizes barriers between self and students
Teacher encourages students to revere her/him	1 2 3 4 5 6 7 8 9	Teacher discourages students from revering him/her
One activity at a time is pursued by all students	1 2 3 4 5 6 7 8 9	A variety of activities occurs simultaneously
Teacher does not monitor student progress	1 2 3 4 5 6 7 8 9	Teacher uses a system for monitoring student progress
Teacher does not encourage students to select their own activities	1 2 3 4 5 6 7 8 9	Teacher encourages students to select activities within context
Teacher does not prespecify goals	1 2 3 4 5 6 7 8 9	Teacher prespecifies goals
Teacher does not encourage students to organize their own work schedules	1 2 3 4 5 6 7 8 9	Teacher encourages students to organize their own work schedule in ways that are consistent with goals
Teacher limits activities to those that have been predesignated	1 2 3 4 5 6 7 8 9	Teacher does not limit activities to those that have been predesignated
Teacher does not provide vehicles whereby students can evaluate themselves	1 2 3 4 5 6 7 8 9	Teacher provides vehicles whereby students can evaluate themselves
Teacher habitually uses one mode of imparting information	1 2 3 4 5 6 7 8 9	Teacher makes use of a variety of means for imparting information

Students work on activities in a single class unit	1 2 3 4 5 6 7 8 9	A variety of student groupings occur simultaneously
Space is used in an inflexible and single-purpose manner	1 2 3 4 5 6 7 8 9	Space is used in a flexible and multi-purpose manner
Physical movement, talking, and grouping by students are not allowed	1 2 3 4 5 6 7 8 9	Physical movement, talking, and grouping by students are allowed and encouraged

Case Study #1
Project: Open Classroom

CURRICULUM
Bruce W. Tuckman

Curricular experiences depend on the overt teacher	1 2 3 4 5 6 7 8 9	Curricular experiences exist independently of overt teacher
Curricular experiences proceed randomly and without inner coherence	1 2 3 4 5 6 7 8 9	Curricular experiences have a sequence and structure
Curriculum does not allow the inclusion of unplanned experiences	1 2 3 4 5 6 7 8 9	Curriculum allows for unplanned but relevant experiences to be included
Teacher materials are not used	1 2 3 4 5 6 7 8 9	Teacher materials are introduced into the classroom on an emergent basis
None of the materials used in the classroom is provided or generated by students	1 2 3 4 5 6 7 8 9	Some materials used in the classroom are provided or generated by students
Curricular experiences only allow the student to move one step at a time	1 2 3 4 5 6 7 8 9	Curricular experiences allow the student to move more than one step at a time
Curricular experiences dictate the student's rate of of movement	1 2 3 4 5 6 7 8 9	Curricular experiences allow the student to proceed at his or her own rate

FIGURE A.4   *The Measure of Curriculum Implementation Used in Case Study #1*

Curricular experiences provide for no alternative courses of action	1 2 3 4 5 6 7 8 9	Curricular experiences provide for alternative courses of action
Each student project involves only one discipline	1 2 3 4 5 6 7 8 9	Students pursue practical problems that require interdisciplinary skills
No curricular experiences relate directly to the child's life	1 2 3 4 5 6 7 8 9	Curricular experiences are included that relate directly to the child's life
Only typical or common classroom activities occur	1 2 3 4 5 6 7 8 9	Some curricular activities occur that are not typical or common for classroom use

CASE STUDY *2*

Summative Evaluation*

**EVALUATING AN INDIVIDUALIZED SCIENCE PROGRAM FOR
COMMUNITY COLLEGE STUDENTS**

Bruce W. Tuckman and Mohammed A. Waheed

Abstract

Two classes of community college students having less than the usual minimal preparation required for admission were taught half of a basic science course using individualized instruction and half using traditional instruction. The course was divided into chemistry and physics segments and random halves of each class received the individualized treatment in one segment and the traditional treatment in the other. The individualized treatment was found to yield superior achievement gains and more positive attitudes toward science than the traditional treatment while both resulted in equivalent student satisfaction. No differences

* Reproduced from the *Journal of Research in Science Teaching*, 1981, *18*, 489–495, by permission of the authors and publisher.

between segments were obtained. Of the four treatment-segment combinations, individualized physics appeared to yield the greatest achievement. Individualized instruction was concluded to be effective.

Introduction

The purpose of this study was to investigate whether or not a self-paced, individualized instruction course in basic chemistry and physics would result in (1) a greater level of mastery among academically underprepared students learning Basic Science, (2) more satisfaction with instruction and (3) a more positive attitude toward Basic Science than a program of more traditional, whole class instruction.

Some work has been done on the evaluation of individualized instruction in science. Kahle (1976) found that when students studied a science unit with one of four instructional modes—timed individualized, self-paced individualized, traditional with guides, and traditional with visual aids, the self-paced individualized group performed better than the other groups. In 14 research studies conducted by Taveggia (1976) during 1967–1974, it was found that students achieved higher scores in individualized instruction classes compared to lecture classes. Silberman and Parker (1974) compared students' attitude toward chemistry. They reported that the students in the individualized instruction program had significantly more positive attitudes toward the subject than students in the traditional lecture program. Fulton (1971) found that in addition to a better attitude, students in an individualized setting displayed eagerness in understanding the subject matter. Johnson et al. (1975) reported that compared to a traditional lecture class, students in the individualized class had a lower course withdrawal rate. Anderson and Artman (1972) reported that a self-paced individualized instruction physics course ultimately helped all students achieve the specified level of mastery and retain competence over an extended period of time, accompanied by more positive attitudes toward the course.

Some of these studies were conducted at the community college level, some at the senior college level and some at the high school level. Some few were focused on underprepared students while the others were not. The current study contributes to the literature by focusing on the effectiveness of *individualized science* instruction at the *community college* level for *underprepared* students, a unique combination of circumstances, and by examining three criteria of effectiveness: *achievement, satisfaction,* and change in *attitudes toward science* rather than a single one.

Hypotheses

Based on the results of the studies cited above, the following hypotheses were tested: (a) Students experiencing individualized instruction would demonstrate a greater level of academic achievement than students who experience traditional instruction. (b) Students would be more satisfied with individualized instruction than with traditional instruction. (c) Students who experience individualized instruction would exhibit a more positive attitude toward science than students who experience traditional lecture instruction.

Methods

Subjects

Forty students in two sections of the Basic Science course at Bristol Community College participated in the study. The students were of lower to middle socio-economic level and were enrolled in a special program for educationally disadvantaged students. The two class sections were assigned by the Registrar of the College. Because of the design used (see below), the functional N of the study, however, was 80.

Independent Variables

Individualized instruction: unitized instructional modules were completed by students at their own pace. Behavioral objectives were followed by self-instructional learning activities and then by a self-assessment test. Students achieving 70% success went on to a post-assessment test which, if passed by a 70% score or better, marked completion of the unit. Failure on either test led to a cycle of additional learning activities followed by retesting until success on both tests was achieved.

Traditional instruction: students listened to lectures and were encouraged to participate in classroom activities by asking relevant questions. The subject matter covered in this condition was similar in content to that in individualized instruction.

Moderator Variable

The moderator variable for this study was the subject matter taught, which was in two segments: chemistry and physics. The chemistry segment was offered in the first half of the semester and the physics segment in the second half.

Dependent Variables

The dependent variables in this study were student achievement and attitudinal assessments. Student achievement was measured by performance on pretests and posttests, scored on an interval basis with grades varying from 0 to

100. The achievement tests used for both groups were of the objective type, consisting of multiple choice, fill-in-the-blanks, and true/false questions. The attitudinal assessments were conducted by administering the Remmers Attitude Scale and the Satisfaction Scale (Tuckman, 1978).

Due to a lack of standard tests in basic chemistry and physics, the achievement tests were constructed by the authors. Test *validity* was insured by applying appropriateness criteria (Tuckman, 1975), that is by "mapping" test questions to the subjects covered which were as follows: Chemistry—definition, structure, periodic table, bonding, writing formulas, balancing equations; Physics—scientific notation, metric system, motion, energy, light, sound, electricity.

To ascertain the *reliability* of the achievement pretest and posttests, Kuder Richardson Formula 21 was used. The obtained reliability values were as follows: (1) pretest = 0.75, (2) chemistry posttest = 0.90, (3) physics posttest = 0.96.

Procedures and Design

In the first half of the semester, one class (Section A) was presented with individualized instruction in chemistry, the experimental condition (cell 1.1). The other class (Section B) was presented with traditional lecture instruction in chemistry, the control condition (cell 2.1). At mid-term, the two sections rotated for instruction in the second segment of the course—physics. Section A now experienced traditional instruction, the control condition (cell 2.2) and Section B individualized instruction, the experimental condition (cell 1.2). Each group thus received the treatment previously given to the other, making it a "flip-flop" pattern of study.

At the beginning of the first segment, students in the two groups were pretested in both chemistry and physics. A *t* test was conducted to determine the equivalency of the two groups. After the completion of instruction in chemistry, the students were given an achievement posttest. The students in each group were also given the Remmers Attitude Scale Test and Satisfaction Scale to measure their attitude toward the subject and their satisfaction with each instructional approach respectively (Tuckman, 1978). Then, for instruction in physics, the experimental group became the control group and vice-versa. At the end of the semester, the achievement posttest scores for physics were obtained for the two sections. Attitudes toward the subject and satisfaction with the instructional mode were remeasured.

Data Analysis

All test scores of students under study were converted to standardized gain scores (posttest minus pretest standard *T* scores) in order to be able to analyze chemistry and physics results simultaneously. Using these standardized figures, mean gain scores and source of variation among group (SS group) were calculated for each of the four cells in the design. Finally, t-tests were used for the analyses as follows: (1) main effect of treatment (cells 1.1 + 1.2 vs. cells 2.1 + 2.2) = test of hypotheses; (2) main effect of segment (cells 1.1 + 2.1 vs. cells 1.2 + 2.2) = determination of differences in difficulty and likeability of subject matter; (3) interaction (cells 1.1 + 2.2 vs. cells 1.2 + 2.1) = to see whether the treatment worked better with one subject matter than with the other.

The denominator for the t test in calculating each of the three effects was the estimated population variance (sum of squares of the first group minus sum of squares of the second group divided by $n_1 + n_2 - 2$) multiplied by $1/n_1 + 1/n_2$. For each of the main effects $n_1 = n_2 = 40$. For the interaction, $n_1 = n_2 = 20$.

Differences in ability between groups were controlled for by using subjects as their own control, but since this overlapped with the conditions by segments interaction, there was a confounding of between-section differences and the interaction effect. However, in testing the main effect of treatment, with which the study was concerned, between-section differences were controlled for by the design since all students experienced both conditions.

Results

At the beginning of the first segment, students in the two sections were given a pretest to measure their reading ability, comprehension, and previous knowledge of science. A two-tailed t test at the 0.05 level of significance was conducted to determine the equivalency of the two sections. The resulting $t = 0.46$ ($df = 38$) failed to attain significance and supported the conclusions that the sections were equivalent.

Effect of Treatment

The main gain scores and t value of difference for the treatment effect on (a) achievement, (b) satisfaction and (c) attitude toward science appear in Table A.5. In *achievement,* the combined experimental conditions yielded a mean gain of 9.19 in comparison to a mean loss of 7.88 for the combined control conditions, the difference resulting in $t = 8.10$, significant at the .001 level. On *satisfaction,* the means were 1.80 and 1.95 for experimental conditions and control conditions respectively (a lower score indicated greater satisfaction), resulting in a nonsignificant t value of 1.25. On *attitude toward science,* experimental conditions yielded a mean of 8.36 which was significantly greater than the mean of 7.72 for control conditions ($t = 2.88$).

TABLE A.5 Mean Scores and *t*-Test Results for Treatments ($df = 78$) Segments ($df = 78$) and Sections (interaction $df = 38$) on the Three Dependent Variables

TREATMENT:	Individualized (Experimental)	Traditional (Control)		
Variable	$\bar{X}$	$\bar{X}$	*sd*	*t*
Achievement	9.19	−7.88	9.42	8.10**
Satisfaction	1.80	1.95	0.52	1.25
Attitudes Toward Science	8.36	7.72	1.00	2.88*

SEGMENT:	Chemistry	Physics		
Variable	$\bar{X}$	$\bar{X}$	*sd*	*t*
Achievement	1.15	0.16	9.42	0.47
Satisfaction	1.88	1.87	0.52	0.06
Attitudes Toward Science	7.97	8.11	1.00	0.63

INTERACTION:	Section A	Section B		
Variable	$\bar{X}$	$\bar{X}$	*sd*	*t*
Achievement	−4.70	7.32	11.48	3.31*
Satisfaction	3.68	3.82	0.83	0.53
Attitudes Toward Science	16.34	15.82	1.61	1.02

Note that a minus mean signifies a loss.
* $p < 0.05$.
** $p < 0.001$.

Effect of Segment

On none of the three measures was the effect of segment significant (see Table 2). For chemistry and physics segments respectively, means were 1.15 and 0.16 for achievement gain ($t = 0.47$), 1.88 and 1.87 for satisfaction ($t = 0.06$) and 7.97 and 8.11 for attitude toward science ($t = 0.63$).

Interaction Effect

To test the interaction of instruction treatment (individualized versus traditional) and segment (chemistry versus physics), scores for students in cells 1.1 and 2.2 (Section A) and in cells 1.2 and 2.1 (Section B) were pooled. In *achievement,* Section A students (individualized chemistry/traditional physics) had a mean loss of 4.70 while Section B students (traditional chemistry/individualized physics) had a mean gain of 7.32 yielding a significant *t* value (3.31). A cell comparison (see Figure A.5) indicated that individualized instruction worked

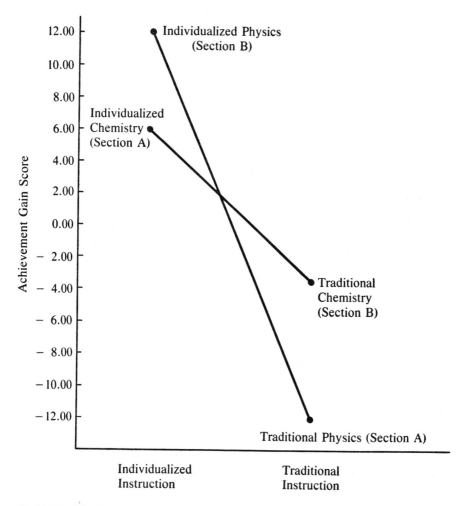

FIGURE A.5 *Interaction between chemistry-physics segments and individualized-traditional treatment on achievement posttest scores.*

best in the physics segment. The interaction effect in neither satisfaction ($t = 0.53$) nor attitude toward science ($t = 1.02$) was significant.

Discussion

The findings of this study summarized as follows, present strong evidence of the effectiveness of individualized instruction in teaching Basic Science to underprepared community college students: (1) experimental conditions produced significantly greater achievement gains and significantly more positive attitudes toward science than control conditions, although the two yielded equal satisfaction; (2) achievement gains, satisfaction and attitudes toward science were equivalent for chemistry and physics segments; (3) of the four cells, achievement gains were greatest for the combination of individualized instruction and physics, although neither satisfaction nor attitudes toward science varied by cell.

The findings of this study led to the following conclusions: (1) individualized instruction is a highly effective method for improving student achievement in science; (2) while students may not prefer individualized instruction in science, it does improve their attitude toward science. Since the individualized approach involved small increments in learning, underprepared students, with their history of marginal academic performance, may have found it easier to master a small section or unit at a given time, pass the test, and move on to the next section in place of studying the whole course at once. Moreover, as instruction in this setting was individually based, it was easier to detect the strengths and weaknesses of the students and provide them with positive reinforcement and encouragement. This method of instruction also discounted the difference in students' educational preparations and allowed for an independent rate of learning.

From a methodological perspective, the study illustrated how instructional effects can be compared with a small number of classes (2) using subjects as their own controls. However, the design is limited by the fact that since every student did not experience all four of the condition/segment combinations, it is not possible to separate out student effects as one can in an analysis of variance repeated measure design. This limits any firm conclusions regarding the "interaction" of conditions and segments since the combinations lack control for student effects. This same limitation is minimal in the interpretation of main effects so that the design works well for the evaluation of instructional conditions.

References

Anderson, O. T., and R. A. Artman. (1972). A self paced independent study, introductory physics sequence: Description and evaluation. *American Journal of Physics, 40,* 1737–42.

Fulton, H. F. (1971). A comparative study of student attitudes toward science and the ability of the teacher to make material understandable in individualized and group approaches in BSCS biology. *School Science of Mathematics, 71,* 198–202.

Johnson, W. G., et al. (1975). A traditional lecture versus a PSI course in personality: Some comparisons. *Teaching of Psychology, 2,* 156–58.

Kahle, J. B. (1976). An analysis of an alternative instructional model for urban disadvantaged high school students. *Science Education, 60,* 237–43.

Silberman, R., and B. Parker. (1974). Student attitudes and the Keller Plan. *Journal of Chemical Education, 51,* 393–95.

Taveggia, T. C. (1976). Personalized instruction: A summary of comparative research, 1967–74. *American Journal of Physics, 44,* 1028–33.

Tuckman, B. W. (1975). *Measuring educational outcomes: Fundamentals of testing.* N.Y.: Harcourt Brace Jovanovich.

Tuckman, B. W. (1978). *Conducting educational research,* 2d ed. N.Y.: Harcourt Brace Jovanovich.

Ex Post Facto Evaluation

AN EVALUATION OF INDIVIDUALLY GUIDED EDUCATION IN A SCHOOL DISTRICT

Bruce W. Tuckman and Alberto P. S. Montare

Introduction

This document represents the final report of an evaluation study that was undertaken to use already existing achievement and intelligence test data in an attempt to provide answers to the following three general questions:

1. What has been the effect of the Individually Guided Education Program (IGE) on achievement scores in an entire District?
2. Do any differences in achievement test scores exist between the three elementary schools of the District?
3. Are pupils in the District achieving at levels commensurate with their intelligence test scores?

After some consideration, it was decided that Question 3 would be answered in three different ways:

1. As an adjunct to Question 1
2. As an adjunct to Question 2
3. As an independent analysis based on coefficients of correlation.

The data that constituted the basis on which the questions were answered consisted of the achievement test scores of the pupils in Grades 2, 3, 4, 5, and 6 in the three elementary schools and in the one Middle School in a School District for the years 1971, 1972, 1973, 1974, and 1975. The data base also included the results of group intelligence testing at the fourth and sixth grades, which was conducted in the same schools and during the same years as the achievement testing.

The achievement test administered in the fall of the year since 1972 was the Metropolitan Achievement Test, which contains twelve different subtests that are scored separately. These subtests are:

1. Word Knowledge
2. Word Analysis
3. Reading Comprehension
4. Total Reading
5. Language
6. Spelling
7. Mathematics Computation
8. Mathematical Concepts
9. Mathematical Problem-Solving
10. Total Mathematics
11. Science
12. Social Studies

(Note, however, that all twelve scores are not provided by all the levels of the test used.)

The thirteenth score that was used in the analysis was the verbal intelligence test score from the Lorge-Thorndike Intelligence Test. Therefore, a total of thirteen scores (twelve achievement and one IQ test score) were used to answer the three major questions of this evaluation study.

It is very important for the reader to realize that psychometricians emphasize that the particular score attained by any given child or any given test is the total resultant of many complex and interacting processes. Personality, motivation, mood swings, health, social class orientation, race, and sex, are but a few factors that may influence a given child at any given test session. For this reason, it has long been recognized that the test results of any group never can be *proven* to have been caused by any *one* factor. Although *proof* is not possible, when analyzing the results of test scores *before* and *after* the introduction of an educational program, one can reasonably assume that: all other factors being held equal, the results *after* the program are most likely, and most reasonably, to be attributed to the effects of the educational program.

Finally, one definition of a test states that: a *test* is a sample of behavior and a *test score* represents a measure of relative standing. The measure used in this analysis is the "national percentile score," which directly allows one to compare all twelve achievement and the one IQ score in terms of relative standing in the national population. Thus, any test score that is at, say, the sixty-third percentile can be directly interpreted as a statement of relative standing—this score is such that 63% of the national population scores *below* this score.

The IGE Program

Individually Guided Education (IGE) is a comprehensive system of education and instruction designed to provide higher educational achievements by providing for differences among students in rate of learning, learning style, and other characteristics. Organizationally, IGE utilizes a multi-unit structure in which the staff are assigned to instructional teams, hierarchical instructional roles are established within each instructional team (unit leader, unit teacher, intern teacher, instructional aide, and clerical aide), and students are multi-aged grouped within a team for instructional purposes. More specifically, instructional objectives to be mastered are established, students are preassessed to determine strengths and weaknesses in relation to these objectives, instructional strategies and materials are used to correct the weaknesses, and a post-assessment procedure is used to determine the success of the instructional strategies.

Originally developed by the Wisconsin Research and Development Center for Cognitive Learning at the University of Wisconsin-Madison, during the years 1965 to 1971 the IGE system has spread to thousands of elementary schools throughout the nation as a practical alternative to the age-graded, self-contained school.

The program was adopted for use in the school district in 1972. It should be noted that the evaluators have at no time advocated either a positive or a negative position as to the merits of the IGE system within elementary schools.

Effects of IGE on Achievement

In order to test the overall effects on the achievement and intelligence test scores of the IGE program within the district since its inception in 1972 (Question 1), the total sample of scores was divided into a preprogram group and a postprogram group. Since the program effects were not reflected in the data until the 1973 testing, the preprogram scores were those of 1971 and 1972 and the postprogram scores were those of 1973, 1974, and 1975.

In order to provide a test score that could be directly comparable across all thirteen variables, all scores used in the present analysis were the national percentile scores for each of the 3,145 separate scores used in the total study. As seen in Table A.6 and in Figure A.6, an overall effect of the IGE program has been that nine out of the total twelve achievement areas have increased in mean performance levels when the preprogram scores are compared to the postprogram scores (*before* and *after* the start of the IGE program).

However, when this overall trend towards increased achievement performance scores is evaluated by performing a separate analysis of variance for each of the twelve achievement areas, only two statistically significant increases occurred: in Total Reading (the increase from a mean of 66.1 to a mean of 68.1 being significant at the 5% level of confidence) and in the Language Test (on which the increase from 66.3 to 68.8 also was significant at the 5% level of confidence).

An examination of the overall pattern of increases and decreases shown in Figure A.6 shows that IGE may be more effective in the verbal areas than in the nonverbal areas. Word Knowledge, Word Analysis, Reading, Total Reading, Language, and Spelling all increased from before to after the start of the program, whereas two of the Mathematics scores decreased slightly and two increased slightly.

An unexpected and even startling finding was that the greatest mean increase of all thirteen scores from *before* to *after* the start of the IGE program occurred in the intelligence test scores data. The mean IQ score increase from 70.7 to 74.8 was statistically significant at the 1% level of confidence. Since the composition of the community has not changed much over the course of this evaluation, the most reasonable conclusion from this finding is that the IGE program has facilitated a significant growth in intellectual performance within the children of the district.

Thus, assuming that all other factors are operating in a random fashion and are not systematically affecting the data, it is possible at this point to conclude that:

- There is an overall trend towards increased scores (nine of twelve areas increased) associated with the IGE program.
- The effects of IGE seem to be more pronounced in the verbal than in the nonverbal areas.
- The IGE program is associated with statistically significant increases in the Total Reading and Language scores.
- The IGE program is associated with statistically significant increases in intellectual performance.

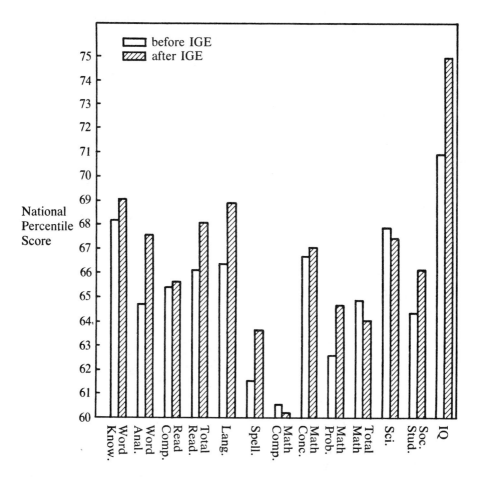

Test Area (Metropolitan Achievement Test and Lorge-Thorndike IQ Test)

FIGURE A.6   *Achievement and IQ Before and After IGE Program*

A final procedure that was applied to the two significant increases in Total Reading and in Language scores was an attempt to check on whether the observed significant differences in these two areas might more properly be attributed to differences in initial levels of intellectual functioning as revealed by the IQ scores. Analysis of covariance procedures revealed that the Total Reading scores remained significantly different from each other even when initial IQ differences were taken into account by the ANCOVA procedure. However, the results of the Language tests became nonsignificantly different from each other, indicating that when the ANCOVA procedure takes into account initial IQ differences, the observed amount of increase in Language scores is less than the

TABLE A.6 A Summary of Major Findings

	Word Know.	Word Anal.	Read. Comp.	Tot. Read.	Lang.	Spell.	Math Comp.	Math Conc.	Math Prob.	Tot. Math	Sci.	Soc. Stud.	IQ
Task #1: IGE Effects													
District Mean: Pre-IGE	68.1	64.7	65.1	66.1	66.3	61.4	60.5	66.5	62.5	64.9	67.9	64.2	70.7
District Mean: Post-IGE	69.0	67.5	65.6	68.1	68.8	63.6	60.0	67.0	64.4	63.9	67.3	66.1	74.8
Diff.	+0.9	+2.8	+0.5	+2.0	+2.5	+2.2	–0.5	+0.5	+1.3	–1.0	–0.3	+1.9	+4.1
ANOVA Sign.	N.S.	N.S.	N.S.	$p<.05$	$p<.05$	N.S.	N.S.	N.S.	N.S.	N.S.	N.S.	N.S.	$p<.01$
ANCOVA Sign.	–	–	–	$p<.023$	N.S.	–	–	–	–	–	–	–	–
Task #2: School Diff's													
School 1 Mean	66.1	66.6	62.3	64.5	63.4	61.0	56.8	62.7	61.8	62.3	64.4	62.4	69.8
School 2 Mean	69.0	67.8	63.3	66.2	66.2	63.5	52.8	62.8	59.8	59.3	67.7	62.6	73.0
School 3 Mean	70.2	65.7	67.6	69.1	72.5	64.5	66.3	71.0	65.9	66.8	70.5	75.6	74.8
ANOVA Sign.	**	N.S.	**	**	**	N.S.	**	**	**	**	*	**	N.S.
ANCOVA Sign.	N.S.	–	N.S.	N.S.	$p<.025$	–	**	**	*	**			
Middle School Mean	69.3	–	68.7	69.5	68.1	62.8	63.0	70.3	66.4	68.6	67.7	63.6	73.3

Task #3: Ach. at Potential?

	Word Know.	Word Anal.	Read. Comp.	Tot. Read.	Lang.	Spell.	Math Comp.	Math Conc.	Math Prob.	Tot. Math	Sci.	Soc. Stud.	IQ
District Corr. c̄ IQ	.77	–	.79	.81	.79	.69	.65	.74	.73	.77	.83	.80	
School 1: Corr. c̄ IQ	.78	–	.79	.81	.79	.69	.67	.76	.74	.74	–	–	
School 2: Corr. c̄ IQ	.78	–	.80	.82	.79	.71	.57	.73	.74	.74	–	–	
School 3: Corr. c̄ IQ	.67	–	.79	.80	.74	.69	.69	.76	.76	.80	–	–	
Middle Sch. Corr. c̄ IQ	.81	–	.80	.83	.81	.69	.68	.74	.70	.77	.83	.80	
Correlation: Pre-IGE	.78	–	.79	.81	.79	.69	.63	.75	.70	.78	.80	.76	
Correlation: Post-IGE	.76	–	.79	.81	.79	.69	.67	.75	.75	.77	.84	.82	
Overall District Mean	68.7	66.7	65.5	67.3	67.8	63.0	60.1	66.8	63.6	64.3	67.7	65.6	72.9

* = p < .05
** = p < .01

amount that would have been expected on the basis of initial differences in intellectual functioning.

Effects of IGE on Growth in Achievement

A second way of looking at the data was used in order to study changes over time and to attempt to control for the effects of possibly "brighter" versus "less bright" classes on the results. Rather than using IQ as a measure of student capability, as was done in the analysis of covariance procedure, this approach employed the mean score for any one class on any one variable in any one given year as a pretest for the mean score obtained by that same class the following year. Since all scores were expressed in terms of national percentiles, scores from two succeeding years could be considered together, even though students had advanced from one grade level to the next during that period.

This type of analysis requires that at least one year's data be available in order to assess the data for the present year. Since data for the 1971 testing was incomplete, the analysis using this method was begun using 1972 as the pretest year for 1973, using 1973 as the pretest year for 1974, and using 1974 as the pretest year for 1975; thus, since the program began in 1972 (at the same time as the 1972 testing), all three data points (1972–73, 1973–74, and 1974–75) represent the effects of the program. Since more students would progressively experience the effects of the program for more years as time passed, it was expected that program success would be reflected in a steady increase in the size of the gain scores from year to year. Also, the use of pretest scores would insure that the results plotted as gain scores would reflect the quality of the program and not the levels of capability of the students.

Results were analyzed by grade level in order to see the levels at which changes were or were not made. For each grade level, changes in Total Reading and Total Mathematics were examined. In addition, the changes in Language and in Spelling also were examined at the fifth and sixth grade levels.

The results are shown in Table A.7 and in Figure A.7. As the results show, in all but fifth grade, the reading scores steadily increased in all year-to-year comparisons. This finding affirms the previous finding that Total Reading scores were significantly increased by the IGE program.

In Total Mathematics, the overall result is that an improvement occurs across all grade levels from 1972 to 1974, but that in all grades but third, there is a decrease in this measure of achievement in the 1974–75 data point.

The pattern for Spelling is clearly a decreasing one at all grade levels where it is measured and across all of the years used in the present study.

Language scores increase in fourth grade and first increase then decrease in fifth grade. This again points to the earlier finding that Language increases in a significant manner in the ANOVA but not in the ANCOVA procedure.

TABLE A.7 Changes in Percentile Test Scores for Successive Years

Total Mathematics

*Grade Level Tested**

Years	3rd	4th	5th	6th
72–73	−7.1	−2.9	−1.9	+4.0
73–74	+2.5	+1.2	+5.7	+9.7
74–75	−2.3	+5.1	+2.4	+0.6

Total Reading

Grade Level Tested

Years	3rd	4th	5th	6th
72–73	−2.7	−7.9	+3.5	+0.4
73–74	−0.6	−3.9	+6.8	+4.8
74–75	0	−0.4	+10.6	−0.5

Language

Grade Level Tested

Years	3rd	4th	5th	6th
72–73			+2.2	−3.2
73–74			+5.5	+1.3
74–75			+7.1	−7.4

Spelling

Grade Level Tested

Years	3rd	4th	5th	6th
72–73		+2.6	+3.1	+2.4
73–74		+0.6	+1.7	+2.5
74–75		+0.4	+2.7	−6.5

* Since the test was given at the start of the year, the 3rd-grade testing reflects gains made during the 2nd grade, the 4th-grade testing reflects 3rd-grade gains, the 5th-grade testing 4th-grade gains, and the 6th reflects 5th-grade gains.

Thus, the results of using the change-scores parallel the results obtained by the combined use of ANOVA and ANCOVA procedures for the Language performance scores of the present study.

Looking at the results by grade level, it appears that the experiences of

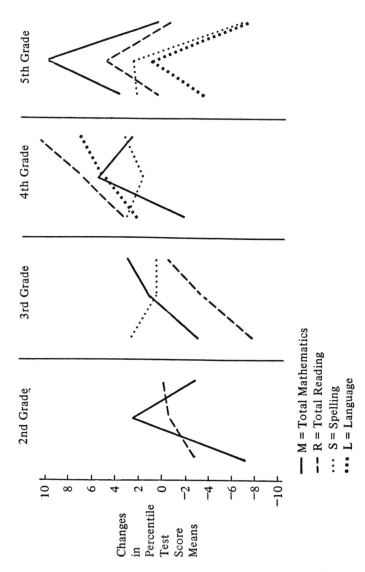

FIGURE A.7 Progressive Changes in Test Scores Over Time

grades three and four are most successful whereas those of grades two and five are relatively less successful. It should be noted, however, that grade five experiences are assessed at the beginning of middle school rather than in the familiar surroundings of the elementary school, and this situational factor may play some role in the decreased scores. It also should be noted that program impact may not be strongly felt as early as second grade; the most important effects of the program may be cumulative.

An Examination of School Differences

The second major question to be answered involved the evaluation of any possible differences between the three elementary schools in the District. This analysis was performed by first doing thirteen ANOVA procedures, one on each of the thirteen variables, to evaluate differences in performance levels between the three schools. Each ANOVA was followed by a Scheffé Test of differences among the means to reveal where the major differences actually exist in terms of the three schools. Results appear in Table A.6.

The overall finding is that in ten of the thirteen instances, School 3 performed in a manner superior to the other two schools that proved to be statistically significant. Differences in Word Analysis, Spelling, and IQ were not significantly different among the three schools.

The ANCOVA procedures led to a very interesting set of conclusions regarding the differences between the three schools when seen in terms of differences in intelligence scores. When initial IQ differences between the three schools are accounted for in the ANCOVA procedures, three out of the four originally significant differences in the verbal area are no longer present. This means that the significant difference in Word Knowledge between the three schools is *not* a significant difference when the initial IQ differences are accounted for. In other words, since the *actual* differences are not greater than the differences predicted to exist on the basis of IQ, the originally significant differences in Word Knowledge are more likely due to IQ differences than to any superiority or inferiority of teaching or instruction. Thus, when one uses IQ scores as the basis for predicting how well the schools should be doing in Word Knowledge, there are no significant differences in the level of achievement in this area between the three schools.

In the same manner, original significant differences revealed by the ANOVA procedures in Reading and in Total Reading also disappear when IQ level is taken into account.

However, the same result did not occur in the Language achievement levels on which the original difference showing School 3 to be superior in this area was statistically significant not only in the ANOVA, but in the ANCOVA as well. Thus, even when one accounts for the IQ levels, the superiority of

School 3 is still present. The most reasonable conclusion, assuming all other factors to be randomly and equally operative, may be that the difference probably is due to teaching and instruction.

A very consistent set of findings was that for all four Math achievement scores, the performance levels of School 3 were significantly superior in both the ANOVA and ANCOVA procedures. Given the data base used, the most reasonable conclusion may be that the math teaching and instruction at School 3 is producing significant achievement superiority within its students beyond the level expected on the basis of their higher IQ scores alone.

The overall conclusions on this question, then, can be divided into two areas:

> *Verbal:* When IQ differences are taken into account, the original superiority of School 3 in three out of four verbal areas disappears. Thus, only in the Language achievement scores does School 3 remain statistically superior after accounting for IQ differences.
>
> *Nonverbal:* In mathematics, School 3 appears to remain statistically superior both with and without taking IQ scores into account. Thus, an inference that can be made may be that the IGE program is not providing sufficient mathematics instruction at the other two schools.

Results show that the same conclusion that was just drawn regarding mathematics also applies to social studies.

Relation Between Student IQ and Achievement

In addition to asking about the extent to which students are achieving at levels commensurate with their potentials as given by their IQ scores in each of the preceding two sections, the question also may be answered directly.

The procedure used to answer this question directly is the correlational analysis based on the Pearson Product-Moment Correlation Coefficient. Simply put, this procedure gives an indication of the degree of association between any two variables.

An analysis of the correlations shown in Table A.6 reveals that the correlations are positive and very high. The overall conclusions, then, from these correlations are that:

1. For the entire district, the brightest students are achieving at the highest levels and the slowest students are achieving at the lowest levels.
2. No really important differences in correlation with IQ exist between the three elementary schools.
3. There is *no* difference in the degree to which IQ and the twelve achievement scores correlate *before* or *after* the start of the IGE program.

The highest correlations occur with the Science and Social Studies scores when given at the middle school. Thus, when the students from the three elementary schools merge into the middle school, their achievement scores in Science and Social Studies are highly associated with their IQ scores—the *brighter* the student, the higher the scores, and the *slower* the student, the *lower* the scores.

The next highest group of correlations occurs in the four verbal areas of Word Knowledge, Reading, Total Reading, and Language. These correlations are high and positive and lead to the conclusion that in terms of verbal achievement scores students are indeed performing very near the levels expected on the basis of IQ scores.

Spelling stands out! The relatively low correlation ($r = +.69$) indicates that spelling scores are not as strongly associated with IQ scores as are the other verbal measures. This may mean, among other things, that teachers do not stress Spelling as much as the other verbal areas.

The mathematics correlations with IQ are slightly lower in all cases than those of the verbal area (except for the Spelling scores just mentioned). Combining these relatively low correlations between the Math areas and IQ with the original finding that there were *no* significant differences *before* and *after* the start of the IGE program, one must conclude that perhaps students are not performing in Math areas at the levels indicated by their IQ scores because, somehow, IGE does not provide the same *degree of emphasis* on mathematics that it does on verbal and general language skills.

Remember, this is a relative statement of *riches!* The *average* child in this community is still doing better than 60%, 67%, 64%, and 64%, respectively, on the four Math achievement areas than the entire national population!

The *average* child is also doing better than 69%, 68%, 66%, 68%, 69%, and 64%, respectively, on the *first* six verbally loaded achievement tests than the entire national population.

And finally, the *average* child scores higher than 75% of the entire national population in general intelligence!

Conclusions

The purpose of this evaluation was to determine whether an individually guided education program operating for three years in the community's three elementary schools had a positive effect on student achievement. Intelligence was examined both as a factor influencing achievement and as a learning outcome in its own right.

Results showed that IGE had produced continuous improvement in reading but little enhancement in mathematics. Performance in language, like reading, was improved, but spelling, like mathematics, was not. Interestingly, but unpredictably, intelligence scores rose considerably during the IGE test period. Analyses of covariance suggest that these IQ gains were *not* the cause of the reading and language gains, but like them, resulted from the IGE program.

Most impressive in their successes with IGE district-wide were the third and fourth grades, with the second grade and fifth grade results being mixed. Most impressive among the three schools was School 3, where strong reading and language gains could not be accounted for on the basis of IQ and so were presumably a function of IGE implementation.

Finally, characteristically high correlations between IQ and achievement scores were obtained both before and after the program. It would appear that with or without IGE, students in the district were performing up to their potential (if IQ tests are accepted as a measure of this) and that IGE raised this potential as well as the achievement that goes with it. More likely, though, is the interpretation that IGE is improving verbal performance, which is reflected not only on the verbal portions of the achievement test but also on the all verbal "IQ" tests. It is suggested that the failure of the schools to affect improvement in math be closely examined and that IGE materials and techniques be supplemented in this area.

Qualitative Evaluation

EVALUATION OF THE INSTRUCTIONAL PROGRAM FOR PREPARING SCHOOL COUNSELORS AT ALPHA COLLEGE

Introduction

Alpha College is an urban college that prepares instructional service and administrative personnel for certification as a prerequisite to working in the elementary and secondary schools of the state. One such program is designed to prepare students for state certification as school counselors. The purpose of this evaluation was to determine whether the School Counselor Training Program offered by Alpha College met the eight criteria or standards set forth by the National Association of State Directors of Teacher Education and Certification (NASDTEC) in the 1979 revision of their Manual (pp. 96–97). These eight standards, which pertain to advanced programs for preparing school counselors, are listed below.

Standard I The program shall assure understanding of the philosophy, organization, and professional activities related to the practice of school counseling.

Standard II The program shall assure that the prospective school counselor has knowledge of referral agencies and other services outside the school setting.

Standard III The program shall provide an understanding of the individual, including the dynamics of human behavior.

Standard IV The program shall include study of educational philosophies and school curriculum patterns.

Standard V The program shall assure understanding of family relationship, societal forces and cultural changes with particular reference to sex-equity and socioeconomic, ethnic, and racial groups.

Standard VI The program shall provide for competence in the following areas:

a. interpretation of aptitude, interest, and educational assessment
b. individual and group counseling
c. group processes
d. assisting student in developing career planning decision-making skills (vocational and educational)
e. assisting student in developing personal and social decision-making skills
f. placement and follow-up
g. planning, implementation, administration, and evaluation of counseling programs
h. performance, interpretation, and utilization of educational research

Standard VII The program shall provide supervised laboratory and practicum experiences in a school setting to give the prospective school counselor the opportunity to work effectively with pupils, teachers, parents, and the community, and

a. practice guidance and counseling methods and techniques
b. observe how the duties of a school counselor are discharged
c. perform the duties of a school counselor

Standard VIII A K–12 program shall include separate and distinct counseling experiences at both elementary and secondary levels.

Methodology

The steps listed below constituted the methodology of this evaluation. Each was carried out by the evaluator in the sequence presented.

First, Alpha College submitted to the evaluator its self-analysis of the School Counselor program. In this document the college listed each of the eight standards, indicated that it thought each was met, and cited the evidence on which this self-judgment was based.

Second, the evaluator studied this document in detail as well as the college-catalog description of the program.

Third, the evaluator made a one-day site visit to the campus of Alpha College. During the visit, the evaluator met with and interviewed (a) the coordinator of the program, (b) the only other full-time faculty member who taught in the program, and (c) three students currently enrolled in the program. During the site visit the evaluator also examined (a) the folders and transcripts of six current students in and three graduated students of the program, (b) course outlines of all specialized program courses, and (c) curriculum labs and libraries containing relevant reference materials. The interviews and examination of documents and facilities focused on the following topics and areas:

- enrollment
- admissions requirements
- program objectives and competencies
- program resources: library, laboratory, curriculum materials, audiovisual materials, equipment
- teaching staff
- supervision of laboratory experiences
- correspondence of observed data and self-analysis
- correspondence of program as written and as actually operated
- availability and content of course outlines

Each area was cast in the form of a question and evidence to answer each was listed in the final report as "Results."

Fourth, the evaluator considered each of the eight standards in the light of the evidence and then did the following (in writing):

- judged whether each standard was met or unmet
- indicated the basis by which each of the above judgments was made

Fifth, the evaluator then listed the strengths of the program as well as a number of recommendations for program improvement.

Results

1. What is the student enrollment? 67
2. Does the college require students to complete all certification prerequisites (i.e., teaching certificates in another field, years of teaching or occupational or clinical experiences) prior to admission into programs requiring such prerequisites?

√ Yes   No

There are, however, students who desire an M.A. and do not want certification, such as those who are employed in drug rehabilitation, pre-trial intervention, etc.

3. Are stated objectives of the program, and the competencies expected of its graduates appropriately job related and consistent with college and departmental philosophy?

√ Yes   No

The objectives and competencies are appropriately job related (entry level counselor); constant attention is given to instruction and training that take into account realities of the job situation.

4. What is the adequacy of:
   a. Library resources for this program?
      There is an identified need for current periodicals and books relating to student personnel services (SPS).
   b. Laboratory resources for this program?
      Physical facilities are, overall, very good. The new counseling lab with one-way glass and videotape capability is particularly good in light of departmental emphasis on experiential training.
   c. Curriculum materials available through a curriculum materials laboratory or center?
      The curriculum materials center for SPS is meager; the department desires to build a library of current literature within the physical confines of the department that would be readily accessible to students.
   d. Audiovisual materials, equipment, and supporting services?
      New videotaping equipment has been ordered and most has been received by the department. The system will be installed shortly and will be considered a very crucial instrument for counselor training.

5. What is the adequacy of the staff, in number, and in graduate preparation for teaching assignments, and, where relevant, in public school experience?

There was some concern that there is only one full-time associate professor who has a guidance background in the SPS program; there is also one adjunct who is a guidance person. While acknowledging the qualifications and recognized competence of the other teachers, some consideration may be given to either another full-time person or, at least, another adjunct who has a guidance background. Students report, however, that they feel they profit from teachers with diverse backgrounds.

6. To what extent does this department participate in planning and supervising the professional laboratory experiences program?

The department fully plans, supervises, and implements the laboratory experience program. Much attention is given to this.

7. Is the program in the college catalog the same as indicated in the self-analysis and observed through your review?

√ Yes   No

The only exception is the course Group Process and Procedures: Group Counseling, which is not listed as a required course. The department has made it a required course.

8. Does the latest approved program file copy agree with the actual program offered?

√ Yes   No

Is the revision of the approved program recommended?

Yes   √ No

The present program conforms.

9. Are current syllabi or course outlines for each course included in this program area available?

Yes   √ No

10. Student Transcripts: Does an examination of transcripts demonstrate that students have followed the program outlined in the self-analysis and the approved program on file in the Bureau of Teacher Education and Academic Credentials?

Yes. The folders of six current students and three graduated students were examined.

Conclusions

Standard I   √ is met   is NOT met

Consideration should be given to defining "persons of integrity" and adding an effective dimension to the admissions process.

Standard II   √ is met   is NOT met

Specific coverage is provided in courses Basic Principles of Guidance, Interviewing and Counseling, and on an ongoing basis throughout training.

Standard III   √ is met   is NOT met

Certification requires at least one year of teaching experience and many candidates have more than one year of experience.

Standard IV   √ is met   is NOT met

Coursework as well as other strategies assist candidates in understanding the dynamics of human behavior

Standard V   √ is met   is NOT met

Electives, practicum placement, and assigned reports contribute to meeting this objective.

Standard VI   √ is met   is NOT met

Student population itself is from a range of cultures; great attention is given to cultural differences—particularly in counselor training.

Standard VII   √ is met   is NOT met

Coursework seeks to provide required competencies.

Standard VIII   √ is met   is NOT met

Very strong area.

To what extent does this program meet the NASDTEC Standards?

Completely	*Substantially*	*Insufficiently*
Meets all NASDTEC and State Standards. May include minor recommendations for the program. Receives full five-year approval and is included in the NASDTEC Reciprocity System.	Meets all NASDTEC and State Standards substantially. Includes minor recommendation. Receives full five-year approval and is included in the NASDTEC Reciprocity System.	Fails to meet at least one NASDTEC or State Standards and major recommendations or a recommendation to discontinue the program are made. Receives conditional two-year approval pending a revisit or termination. Is included in the NASDTEC Reciprocity System for only the next two years.

Recommendations

A. The three major strengths of the program are as follows:
1. Great emphasis on quality counselor training for the entry level.
2. A faculty, very responsive and very available to students.
3. Departmental mission to work with an urban population.

B. Recommendations for program improvement in order of need are as follows:

1. Candidate training in counseling should permeate all segments of the program. Counseling components can be added to such courses as Interpretation and Use of Tests in Guidance, Ed and Voc Guidance, and Pre-College Guidance and Counseling. Example: a tape of a career counseling session could be presented in class.
2. The department should continue to develop pragmatic approaches to counseling an urban population with problems in the area of drugs, sex, family living, crisis intervention, and the like.
3. A continuing "Current Problems" course should be added.
4. A follow up of graduates should be made to assist in program evaluation.

Glossary

Acceptability (of objectives) All objectives represent what teachers at a particular grade level or block of grade levels are trying to accomplish, as understood and accepted by themselves, administrators and parents, and teachers at adjacent grade levels or blocks of grade levels.

Achievement test A test that measures the extent to which a person has acquired specific knowledge or skills as the result of instruction.

Affective domain Those activities, tasks, and processes that involve "feeling" in the form of attending, responding (holding attitudes), or valuing.

Analysis of variance A statistical procedure for determining whether mean score differences between two or more groups are greater than would be expected on a chance basis.

Appropriateness The extent to which test items fit or match the objectives that they are intended to measure. **Appropriateness** is maximized when all test items match objectives and all objectives have test items that match them.

Aptitude-treatment interaction The degree to which the outcomes of instruction reflect on or are caused by the combination or simultaneous influence of the learning capabilities of the students being taught and the instructional program or approach being used to teach them.

Attitudes and values   Outcomes that reflect students' feelings and subjective reactions to themselves, others, and specific experiences. **Attitudes and values** usually are measured by attitude scales.

Audit   A quantitative determination of a set of prescribed outcomes in terms of both actual levels achieved, comparison or criterion levels, and their differences.

Behavior sampling   Selection, observation, and recording of the acts or actions of randomly chosen students during selected observation periods. The purpose of **behavior sampling** is to be able to draw conclusions about the acts or actions of all students without the necessity of observing all students.

Certainty   The likelihood that the outcomes obtained in evaluating a program are indeed a function of the program being evaluated and not of other variables or causes operating at the same time as the program. The degree to which program outcomes can validly be said to have caused program inputs.

Cognitive domain   Those activities, tasks, and processes that involve "thinking" in the form of knowing, understanding, analyzing, synthesizing, applying, or evaluating.

Comparison group (*see* **Control group**).

Comparison score   (*see* **Criterion score**).

Completeness (of objectives)   All objectives match instructional events and for all instructional events there are objectives.

Control group   Group that does *not* experience the program to be evaluated and to whose outcomes the program or **treatment group**'s outcomes are compared (also called the **comparison group**) in a **summative evaluation.**

Control variable   Any factor that is controlled by the evaluator to cancel out or neutralize its effect on the evaluation outcomes that are being studied (e.g., student intelligence or prior achievement).

Covariate   Measure of a stable student characteristic that tends to relate to or predict program performance outcomes as well as or better than the presence or absence of the program experience. Such a measure must be controlled or otherwise taken into account in program evaluation.

Criterion group   Group of persons who already have attained the outcomes to which the program to be evaluated is aimed and who provide a basis for the **summative evaluation** of program outcomes. (*See also* **Control group.**)

Criterion-referencing   Comparing individual test results to an absolute standard in order to report individual outcomes in terms of percent of items or objectives gotten right.

Criterion score   The desired or desirable level of an outcome measure determined on the basis of preset standards, prior outcomes, or the outcomes required for some ensuing activity. (Also called a **comparison score.**)

Cross-sectional design   A retrospective examination of the outcomes of a number of entering classes at the same grade level, both before and after the program onset (i.e., holding grade level constant and comparing across classes) to determine the effect of the program. This is one of the ex post facto designs.

Degree of proficiency The extent to which, after experiencing relevant instruction, a student is able to carry out a skill or exhibit a knowledge as specified in an instructional objective. Where a prespecified cutoff score is used for evaluation, this is referred to as mastery or nonmastery.

Design A procedure used in conducting an evaluation that provides for comparison data or benchmarks relative to which program outcomes can be interpreted.

Differentiated outcome hypothesis The expectation that different programs, when successful, will yield different outcomes peculiar to those programs; that is, that those outcomes a program will maximize are consistent with the unique features of that program.

Difficulty The frequency with which individual test items are answered correctly by test takers as determined by a procedure called **item analysis.**

Discriminability The extent to which individual test items are more likely to be answered correctly by students who do well on the total test and answered incorrectly by students who do poorly on the total test. It is determined by a procedure called **item analysis.**

Efficiency (of a program) The degree to which students experiencing a program make significant gains on the outcome measures of that program relative to the program's costs.

Environment effects The degree to which the outcomes of instruction reflect on or are caused by the organization or use of the classroom independent of the instructional program in use.

Evaluation, instructional program A procedure and design used to determine whether, and to what extent, the measured outcomes for a given set of instructional inputs match the intended or prespecified outcomes.

Ex post facto design A examination of outcomes "after the fact" by comparing a group to itself over time or to other groups that have operated in the past.

Formative evaluation An examination of the outcomes of a group experiencing a program relative to the objectives of the program.

General achievement Outcomes that reflect the abilities of students to know and understand information not necessarily taught in school. These outcomes are typically measured by intelligence, aptitude, and mental ability tests.

Generality The likelihood that the outcomes obtained in evaluating a program would recur if the program were to be operated at another time or place. The degree to which program outcomes validly can be said to be replicable.

Growth curve A graph depicting changes in test scores for a group over years of schooling. This can be compared to curves for national samples in an **ex post facto evaluation.**

Higher cognitive processes The manipulation or creation of information or solutions through the processes of analysis, synthesis, application, and evaluation.

Input The elements and characteristics of the program that are to be evaluated.

Input/Process Survey A determination of the nature and characteristics of currently operating inputs in the form of processes, which are then compared to desired levels. A procedure used to assess the *level of implementation* of program inputs.

Instructional program effects The degree to which the outcomes of instruction reflect on or are caused by the instructional program itself and not by other variables.

Intact group Group existing prior to the evaluation, such as a classroom group, for which student assignment has been made by someone other than the evaluator.

Interpretability The extent to which a test provides a teacher with meaningful and useful evaluative information about the students who took it and the instructional experiences that preceded it. It is based largely on the determination of the degree of proficiency of students based on scores on the test.

Item analysis A procedure for determining the performance characteristics of individual test items in terms of: (1) their ability to discriminate between good and poor performers on the total test and (2) the frequency of students who get them right. (*See also* **Discriminability** and **Difficulty**).

Knowledge/Comprehension Acquired facts and information that are available for recall and an understanding of the meaning of those facts and that information.

Learning-related behavior Outcomes that represent students' actions and activities in a classroom or other instructional setting. These outcomes are usually measured by observation scales.

Level of comparison The size or nature of the unit on which the program to be evaluated is being tried and to which it is being compared (e.g., classroom, grade level, class, building, district).

Level of implementation The degree to which how the program operates in the classroom or school matches how its designers intend for it to operate (i.e., the extent to which teachers' behavior in classroom and instructional management and use of inputs fits the specifications of behavior called for by the program).

Longitudinal design A examination of outcomes of a single group over a period of time (one of the ex post facto designs). If performance improves beyond that "normally expected," then the program is a success.

Mastery (*see* **Degree of proficiency**).

Matrix sampling Randomly dividing up the students in a class or grade level into groups and giving each group a portion of the testing program. This is an alternative to giving a large-scale testing program to all students when the purpose of the testing is program evaluation rather than individual student evaluation.

Mental ability (or **intelligence**) **test** A test to measure the extent of a person's capabilities in verbal, quantitative, and figural comprehension.

Normative approach The use of data drawn from a national sample (via a test's **norms table**) to compare to outcome scores obtained by a program group in an ex post facto evaluation. (*See also* **Norm-referencing**.)

Norm-referencing Comparing individual test results to group results in order to report individual outcomes in terms of relative standing in the group (e.g., percent of test takers who got lower scores).

Norms table A chart or listing of scores on a published, **norm-referenced test** for a large national sample of students to which the scores on that same test obtained by local, individual students or groups may be compared. (*See also* **Normative approach.**)

Objectives A set of desired outcomes, stated in measurable terms, that those students experiencing a program are expected to achieve if the program is effective.

Outcome (or output) The performance of students in a program on measures of the objectives of that program.

Outcome audit (*see* **Audit**).

Percentile The percent of test takers in a national sample whose scores were exceeded by a given score.

Performance criterion Standard used for evaluating or judging the **degree of proficiency** or **mastery** of an objective on the basis of scores on a test. The test score that constitutes the requirement for **mastery** and the basis by which it is chosen.

Process How the program operates in the classroom or school; that is, the classroom behavior of teachers and students involved in the program.

p-value The proportion of students who have taken a test who have gotten an item or cluster of items correct. The **p-value** can be used as a **performance criterion** or basis for judging **mastery.**

Quality (of a program) The degree to which students experiencing a program make significant gains on the outcome measures of that program.

Random assignment Dividing students between treatment and control conditions so that all students available have an equal likelihood of being assigned to either group.

Ratification The procedure wherein a group of teachers, administrators, or parents judge the **acceptability** and **completeness** of a set of instructional objectives and choose to approve their use.

Reliability The extent to which a test is consistent over time and over items; that is, whether it yields equivalent scores over testing occasions or over individual items or subparts of the test.

Selection effect (*see* **Student assignment bias** and **Student effects**).

Specific achievement Outcomes that reflect the amount of knowledge and comprehension students have acquired and are able to recall about a given, discrete body of subject-matter facts basically acquired from their school experience. These outcomes are typically measured by **achievement tests.**

Student assignment bias Differences in outcomes between the group experiencing the program and the comparison group that can be accounted for by differences between the two groups of students independent of the program being evaluated (also called a **selection effect**).

Student effects The degree to which the outcomes of instruction reflect on or are caused by the characteristics of the students independent of the instructional program in use. (*See also* **Student assignment bias.**)

Subject matter effects The degree to which the outcomes of instruction reflect on or are unique to particular subject matter being taught independent of the instructional program used to teach it.

Summative evaluation   An examination of the outcomes of a group or groups experiencing the program to be evaluated in comparison to the outcomes of another, similar group from which the program is withheld.

Teacher effects   The degree to which the outcomes of instruction reflect on or are caused by the behavior or personality of the teacher independent of the instructional program in use.

Test item specifications   An operational delineation of the conditions, action, and criteria that the measurement of an objective requires.

Thinking and problem solving   Outcomes that reflect the abilities of students to analyze and synthesize information without benefit of direct recall, that is, in unfamiliar situations. These outcomes require untimed, open-book types of tests to measure.

Transfer of learning   Demonstrating the ability to solve unfamiliar problems using knowledge and skills learned in related situations.

Treatment group   Group that experiences the program to be evaluated (also called the **Program group**).

Usability   The degree to which the requirements of test administration and use are practical and convenient.

Validity   The extent to which a test measures what it is supposed to measure; that is, whether it discriminates between students who have more and less of the characteristic being measured.

Index

Acceptability (of objectives), 5, 142–144, 281
Achievement:
auditing of, 70–74, 92, 94
of criterion behavior, 226, 228–229, 232–237, 238
general, 30, 61–63, 72–74, 92, 248, 251, 252, 254, 283
norms, 181–184
prior, analysis of, 172–176
relation to IQ, 268–269
reliance on, 19–21, 27–28, 59
results, 259–264
specific, 31–34, 59–61, 70–72, 186, 285
testing, 59, 61, 71, 146–147, 174, 176, 177–180, 181, 183–184, 248, 249–250, 258, 281
Administrators, and preparation of objectives, 5, 133
Affective domain, 281. *See also* Attitudes and values; Behavior, learning related
Aleamoni, L., 102, 105, 216
Analysis of covariance, 50, 165–166, 261–268
Analysis of data, 250–251

Analysis of variance, 51, 165, 261–268, 281
Analysis, unit of, 43, 188
Anderson, O.T., 248, 255
Appropriateness (of test), 111, 114, 116–118, 158–160, 281
Aptitude X treatment interaction, 36, 281
Attendance, 169
Attitudes and values, 30–34, 65–66, 74–80, 186, 191, 282
Audit Form, 76, 77
auditing of, 73–77
characteristics, 65
considerations, 30–34
description, 65
recommendations, 66
toward school, 249–250, 251–254
toward science, 248, 251, 254
uses, 65–66
Auditing outcomes. *See* Outcomes, auditing and evaluation of

Behavioral objectives. *See* Objectives
Behavior, learning-related, 30–34, 67–68, 78–80, 186, 284

Behavior, learning-related (*continued*)
  Audit Form, 76, 77, 78, 80
  auditing of, 78–79
  characteristics, 67
  considerations, 30–34
  description, 66–67
  recommendations, 68
  uses, 67–68
Behavior sampling, 82, 83, 84, 87, 282
Bloom, B. S., 63, 64, 74, 216
Bogdan, R. C., 189, 216
Bond, G. L., 36, 216
Borich, G. D., 103, 216
Buros, O. K., 216
Bussis, A. M., 227, 239

California Psychological Inventory, 37
Campbell, D. T., 43
Case Study #1, 39, 67, 103, 105, 133,
  223–246
Case Study #2, 33, 155, 165, 247–255
Case Study #3, 44, 48, 49, 61, 63, 72,
  172, 175, 257–270
Case Study #4, 158, 271–277
Case study evaluation, 11, 189–201,
  271–277
Certainty, 41–42, 43, 49, 164, 282
Checklist, The Program Evaluator's, 11,
  185, 186–188
Chi-square test, 169, 170
Cochran, D. W., 88, 91, 216
Cognitive Abilities Test, 73
Cognitive domain, 282. *See also* Knowl-
  edge and comprehension; Think-
  ing and problem solving
Cohen, J., 166, 216
Combined longitudinal-cross-sectional
  design, 46–49, 54
Comparison group, 49, 162, 164–165,
  170, 282
Comparison, level of, 43, 282
Completeness (of objectives), 5, 142–144,
  282
Computers:
  and data analysis, 165
  and testing, 6

Conclusions, 207, 213–214, 237–238,
  269–270
*Conducting Educational Research, Second
  Edition,* 43, 166
Control group, 49, 162, 170, 188, 282
Control variable, 50, 62, 282
Cook, T. D., 166, 216
Correlation, 268–269
Covariate, 282. *See also* Control vari-
  able; Analysis of covariance
Criterion of performance, 22, 144–145,
  150, 285
Criterion group, 162–163, 282
Criterion-referenced:
  achievement, 226, 228, 232–236, 238,
    282
  tests, 7, 60, 61
    checklist for, 110–113
    evaluating the quality of, 109–128
Criterion score, 282
Critical incident technique, 194
Cronbach, L. J., 29, 32, 36, 216
Cross-sectional design, 45–46, 54, 71,
  225, 282
Curriculum, 225, 228, 230, 237

Data:
  collection, 145–149, 165
  hard vs. soft, 205
  reporting of, 207–208
  use, 205–208
Data analysis, 165–166, 169–170, 198,
  213–214. *See also* Analysis of covariance; Analysis of variance;
  Chi-square test; *t*-test
Decision making, 151, 166–167, 184–185,
  188
  use of data to influence, 205–208
Design, 7–8, 39, 41–55, 187, 283
  ex post facto, 43–49, 250, 257–270
  summative, 49–55, 247–256
Deportment. *See* Behavior, learning-
  related
Differentiated outcome hypothesis, 29,
  283
Difficulty (of test items), 121–122, 283

Dimensions of Schooling, 38
Discriminability (of test items), 121–122, 283
Documents, 195
Domino, G., 35, 37, 216

Educational Goal Attainment Tests, 19, 65, 66, 77, 78, 79
Edwards, J. E., 35, 216
Effect size, 166
Effects (of)
  environment, 35, 38–40
  instruction, 34, 36, 42
  students, 35, 36–38, 42
  subject-matter, 35, 38
  teachers, 35, 36, 42
Efficiency, 23, 283
Elliot, J. M., 32, 216
Environment:
  effects of, 35, 38–40, 187, 283
  level of implementation of, 91
  measurement of, 92, 93
Ethnography, 190
Evaluating Classroom Instruction: A Source Book of Instruments, 103
Experimental and Quasi-Experimental Designs, 43
Ex post facto evaluation, 4, 8, 9, 10, 43–49, 55, 171–188, 187, 257–270, 283
  combined longitudinal-cross-sectional, 46–49, 55, 172–176, 264–268
  cross-sectional, 45–46, 55, 172–176, 282
  longitudinal, 44–45, 55, 172–176, 284
  normative approach, 176–184, 183–184, 284
  prior achievement approach, 172–176, 264–266

Fear, F. A., 99, 217
Findings, 207
Flexible Use of Space Scale (FUSS), 91, 92, 93

Formative evaluation, 4, 9, 10, 61, 131–151, 187, 223–246, 283
Fry, E., 118
Fulton, H. F., 248, 255

Gagne, R. M., 29, 217
General ability outcome audit, 92
General achievement: *Audit Form,* 72, 73
  auditing of, 72, 73, 92
  characteristics, 62
  considerations, 30
  description, 61–62, 283
  recommendations, 62–63
  uses, 62
Generality, 41–43, 50, 283
Glaser, R., 29, 217
Glass, G. V., 166, 217
Goal identification, 155–156, 224
Goals, Phi Delta Kappa, 16–19
Gough, H. G., 37, 217
Growth curve, 174, 175–176, 177–181, 266, 283
Guba, E. G., 190, 217

Higher cognitive processes, 283. *See also* Thinking and problem-solving
Hopkins, K. D., 62, 217
Hunt, D. E., 36, 217
Hyman, R., 93

Implementation, level of. *See* Level of implementation
Indik, B., 217
Individualized evaluation, 247–255
Individually Guided Education, evaluation of, 257–270
Input, 13–14, 23–24, 34–40, 283
  effects, 34–40
Input/process outcomes, 192
Input/process survey, 81–95, 151, 166, 187, 283
Instructional:
  activities, 84–86
  Survey Form, 86

Instructional (*continued*)
  effects, 34–36, 42, 187, 284
  materials, 84
    Survey Form, 85
  organization, 85, 86, 87
    Survey Form, 87
Instructional Objectives Exchange, 61, 66
Intact group, 284
Intended outcomes. *See* Objectives
Interpretability (of test results), 112–113,
    123–127, 149–150, 284
Interview schedule, 192
Iowa Tests of Educational Development,
    176, 177–181
Item analysis, 119–122, 284

Johnson, O. G., 161
Johnson, W. G., 248, 255

Kahle, J. B., 248, 255
Knowledge and comprehension, 284
  auditing of, 70–71, 72, 73, 92, 94
  general, 30, 61–63, 72, 73–74, 92
  specific, 30–34, 59–61, 70–72, 186
Kuder Richardson Formula, 21, 250

Level of comparison. *See* Comparison,
    level of
Level of implementation, 34, 40, 81–95,
    191
  determination of, 81–95, 151, 166, 284
Lewin, K., 40, 217
Lohnes, P. R., 29, 218
Longitudinal design, 44–45, 54, 72, 225,
    284
Lorge-Thorndike Intelligence Test, 258

Mager, R. F., 116, 217
Mann-Whitney *U* test, 170
Mastery. *See* Proficiency, degree of
Matrix sampling, 148–149, 284
Maturation bias. *See* Student maturation
    bias

*Measuring Educational Outcomes: Funda-
    mentals of Testing,* 6, 68, 111, 140
Mental ability testing, 62, 73, 258, 284
Mental Measurements Yearbook, 161
Millman, J., 102, 117
Minnesota Teacher Attitude Inventory,
    100
*Mirrors for Behavior: An Anthology of
    Classroom Observation Instru-
    ments,* 103

National Educational Development Tests,
    182, 183–184
Naturalistic evaluation, 190
Norm-referencing, 7, 60, 61, 127, 284
Norms:
  group, 181
  tables, use of, 181–184, 284
Northern, E. F., 100, 217

Objectives, 4–6, 68–69, 103–104, 111,
    114, 285
  mastery of, 123–127
  measurement of, 158–161
  preparation of, 133–145, 156–158, 167
  ratification of, 142–144, 186, 285
  test of proficiency in identifying and
    preparing, 116–118
Open classrooms, evaluation of, 223–
    246
Osgood, C. E., 100, 217
Outcomes, 4–7, 27–34, 59–80, 158, 186,
    285
  auditing and evaluation of, 69–80, 282
  differentiated, 29
  predetermination of, 204–205
  specification and measurement of,
    68–79
Output, 13–14, 16–23, 285. *See also* Out-
    comes

Pearson product-moment correlational
    coefficient, 268
Percentile score, 181, 259, 285

Piaget, J., 64–217
Pitfalls, in evaluation, 208–215
Porter, A. C., 165, 218
Practical Guide to Measuring Project Impact on Student Achievement, A, 181
Preparing Instructional Objectives, 116
Problem solving. *See* Thinking and problem solving
Process, 13–14, 23, 34, 40, 285
   level of implementation, 34, 40, 81–95
Proficiency, degree of, 119, 123–127, 150, 283. *See also* Standard of performance
Program Evaluator's Checklist, 11, 185, 186–187
p value, 145, 146–147, 285

Qualitative evaluation, 11, 189–201, 271–277
Quality (of a program), 13–26, 285
Quasi-Experimentation: Design and Analysis Issues for Field Settings, 166

Random assignment, 285
Readability, 118
Recommendations, 207–208, 238
Regents examinations, 20
Reliability, 250, 285
   rater, 87, 231
   test, 112, 118–123
Remmers Attitude Scale, 250
Report of results, 207–208
Report preparation, 200
Responsive evaluation, 190

Sampling, 163–164
   behavior, 82, 83, 85, 87, 88, 282
   matrix, 148–149, 284
Satisfaction, 248, 251, 254
Satisfaction Scale, 250
Scheduling, 208–210
Scheffe test, 267

Selection bias. *See* Student assignment bias
Self-discipline, 67, 225, 227, 231–232, 237
Semantic differential, 100, 101
Significant gain score, 144–145, 182
Silberman, R., 248, 255
Simon, A., 103, 218
Smith, D. D., 38, 218
Specific achievement:
   Audit form, 70, 71
   auditing of, 70–72
   characteristics, 60
   considerations, 30–34
   description, 59, 285
   recommendations, 61
   uses, 60–61
SRA Achievement Series, 176, 172–180
Stake, R. E., 190, 218
Stallings, J. A., 38, 218
Standard (or criterion) of performance, 22, 144–145, 150, 285
Standard score, 176, 182, 183
Stanford Achievement Test, 146–147
Statistical Package for the Social Sciences, 165
Student, 43
   assignment bias, 50, 163–164, 176, 285
   effects, 35, 36–38, 42, 188, 285
   exit requirements, 203–204
   factors, 91–92, 187
      auditing of, 94
   maturation bias, 174–176
   ratings by, 101–102, 105–107
Student Instructional Report, 106
Study skills:
   Behavior Output Audit Form, 80
Subject matter:
   effects of, 35, 38, 285
   level of implementation of, 88
   Survey Form, 88
Summative evaluation, 4, 8, 10, 49–55, 60, 153–170, 187, 247–255, 286
   between classrooms, 50–51, 164
   between districts, 53–55, 164
   between schools, 51–53, 164
   illustration of, 167–170

Taba, H., 74, 75, 218
Taveggia, T. C., 248, 255
Teacher:
  appraisal interview, 99
  evaluation, 98, 100, 204
  involvement, 205–206
  objectives, 103–104
  observations, 100–101, 103–105
Teacher-student interaction, 225, 227,
    231, 237
Teacher Observation Form, 77
Teaching style:
  assessment of, 97–107
  dimensions of, 97–107
  effects of, 35, 36, 42, 102–103, 187,
    188, 286
  level of implementation of, 88–91
  measurement of, 89, 90
Tests:
  achievement. *See* Achievement, testing
  attitude. *See* Attitudes and values, to-
    ward careers, school, self
  locating of, 160–161
  mental ability. *See* Mental ability test-
    ing
  use of, 210–211, 212–213
Test item specifications, 141, 160, 286
*Tests and Measurements in Child Devel-
    opment: Handbook II,* 161
Thinking and problem solving, 30–34,
    63–64, 74, 286
  Audit Form, 72, 73, 75
  auditing of, 73–74
  characteristics, 63–64

considerations, 30–34
description, 63
recommendations, 64
uses, 70
Transfer of learning, 63, 286
Traub, R., 38, 218
Treatment group, 286
t-test, 51, 170
Tuckman, B. W., 6, 37, 43, 60, 68, 74, 80,
    88, 90, 106, 110, 111, 115, 140,
    166, 218, 223, 227, 239, 250
*Tuckman Teacher Feedback Form
    (TTFF),* 89, 90, 91
Tyler, R. W., 29, 218

U. S. Department of Health, Education
    and Welfare, 181, 218
Usability (of tests), 113, 127–128, 286

Validity (of tests), 111–112, 114–119, 250,
    286
Values. *See* Attitudes and values
Veldman, D., 36, 218
Visitation schedule, 197
Volunteerism, 53, 168

Walberg, H. J., 227, 239
Ward, W. D., 38, 218
Ware, J. E., 102, 219
Wilson, S., 190, 219
Winer, B. J., 166, 219
Wolf, R. M., 165, 166, 219